et Ned Snell (the author of this book) in Bermuda, this past winter, where both of us were speaking at a ﬀerence on the Internet (and might I note that if you have to talk about the Internet, Bermuda is one of the ﾠst places to do so). In Bermuda, Ned and I and a couple other folks got together for dinner and drinks, and were talking about what was up with our respective books and what we were doing next. Ned mentioned t although he had published a number of successful books about Microsoft Windows and the Internet, at moment he had no new books on his plate.

ﾠll," said I, thoughtfully, "there's this series of books Sams and I have been talking about...."

this book you hold in your hands, dear reader, is the first book in that series, which became known as "Laura ﾠay's Web Workshop." (They tell me if this series is successful, there will be a complete line of Laura Lemay ﾠucts from Sams: mugs, t-shirts, action figures....)

ﾠdea for this series sprang from the success of the "Teach Yourself Web Publishing with HTML" books and ﾠ my philosophy that books about technical subjects do not have to be boring and difficult to read—or ﾠe, dumbed down to the point of inanity. ("This is a computer. Now click the button marked Start.") When ﾠ technical books (and, being the nerd that I am, I read a lot of them), I prefer the books that treat me like ﾠan being who wants to learn something. I prefer the books with a very straightforward, practical, hands-ﾠproach, with lots and lots of useful examples, friendly, conversational writing, and a good sense of humor.

ﾠ what this series is all about—books with clear writing, lots and lots of hands-on, practical examples, ﾠ that are fun to read while still being educational. Books that make you interested in the topic and make ﾠant to do more with it. And, since this is the Web Workshop, the series will cover all aspects of the World ﾠVeb, from the tools such as HTML editors and site-building tools to Web page design ideas and techniques ﾠanced server administration, and on and on.

ﾠbrings me back to this book. Netscape Gold is a particularly good book to start this series with, because ﾠpe Gold is a particularly good way to get started with HTML. Of all the dozens of HTML editors I've seen, ﾠpe Gold is one of the better ones, allowing you access to a good number of HTML features and providing ﾠYSIWYG control over various aspects of a Web page, without having to know a lot about HTML itself. ﾠtause it's integrated with the enormously popular Netscape Navigator browser, linking between pages ﾠting an idea of how a new page integrates with the rest of a site is faster and easier than with other ﾠditors.

ﾠ't want to spoil the book. Whether you're an experienced HTML Web page designer or a rank beginner ﾠuldn't know an HTML from an ICBM, I think you'll find this book useful, and more importantly, fun. ﾠ ﾠE

ﾠra Lemay
ﾠes Editor
ﾠ\y@lne.com
ﾠ://www.lne.com/lemay/

LAURA LEMAY'S
WEB WORKSHOP

NETSCAPE
NAVIGATOR™ GOLD 3
DELUXE EDITION

LAURA LEMAY'S
WEB WORKSHOP

NETSCAPE
NAVIGATOR™ GOLD 3
DELUXE EDITION

Laura Lemay
Series Editor

Ned Snell

201 West 103rd Street
Indianapolis, Indiana 46290

President, Sams Publishing: Richard K. Swadley

Publishing Manager: Mark Taber

Managing Editor: Cindy Morrow

Marketing Manager: John Pierce

Assistant Marketing Manager: Kristina Perry

Acquisitions Editor
Mark Taber

Development Editor
Fran Hatton

Software Development Specialist
Bob Correll

Production Editor
Mary Inderstrodt

Copy Editor
Bart Reed

Technical Reviewers
Jim Anderson
Vincent W. Mayfield

Editorial Coordinator
Bill Whitmer

Technical Edit Coordinator
Lynette Quinn

Formatter
Frank Sinclair

Editorial Assistants
Carol Ackerman
Andi Richter
Rhonda Tinch-Mize

Cover Designer
Alyssa Yesh

Book Designer
Alyssa Yesh

Copy Writer
Peter Fuller

Production Team Supervisor
Brad Chinn

Production
Mary Ann Abramson, Stephen Adams, Carol Bowers, Charlotte Clapp, Bruce Clingaman, Mike Dietsch, Jason Hand, Mike Henry, Daniel Harris, Clint Lahnen, Paula Lowell, Casey Price, Laura Robbins, Bobbi Satterfield, SA Springer, Mark Walchle, Jeff Yesh

Dedication

To Nancy, José, and John

and

to Altagracia, Sam, and Sammy

for all their help and support.

Overview

Contents

Acknowledgments

Books like this require nothing much—just body, mind, and spirit.

By typing the silly thing with my own two hands, I provided the body myself. The mind of this book was provided by the good people at Sams.net who still had theirs long after mine had split—most importantly Mark Taber, Fran Hatton, and Mary Inderstrodt. The spirit had help from Wes Tatters, a fine author whose writing forms the basis of the JavaScript chapter, among others.

But the true guiding spirit of this book, and of this series, is Laura Lemay. Her groundbreaking books about Web authoring, and her uncanny ability to illuminate the shadowy regions of HTML with clarity and with humor, have set the standard to which this book aspires.

About the Author

Ned Snell is an award-winning computer journalist and author. Ten years ago, after a brief career as a teacher, Snell entered the software industry as a documentation and training specialist for several of the world's largest software companies. He then moved into the computer trade magazine business, where he served as staff writer and eventually as editor for several national publications.

In 1991, he became a freelancer so he could pursue his dual professions: computer journalist and actor. Since then, he has written for international publications such as *Datamation* and *Software* magazine, and has also developed documentation and training materials for diabetes management software. At the same time, he has acted in regional professional theaters, commercials, and industrial films. Snell is the author of the Sams titles *Souping Up Windows, Curious About the Internet, Navigating the Internet with Windows 95* (now in a Deluxe Edition with CD), and *Navigating the Microsoft Network*. He lives with his wife—Nancy Gonzalez, a writer and translator—and their two sons in Florida, 'cause it's warm there.

Introduction

This strange, amorphous thing we call *programming* keeps deconstructing itself, and then reconstructing itself. And the reason Web authoring is such a weird, funky subject is that it rests on the cusp of the latest deconstruction. Shall I explain? Don't mind if I do ….

I took my first job in the software industry in the mid '80s, in a company that had achieved its success through something called a *fourth-generation programming language,* or *4GL*. A 4GL, so it was said, was a programming language so simple to learn and use that even nonprogrammers could easily write their own little routines for generating reports from corporate databases. Of course, that whole idea presumed that nonprogrammers really *wanted* to write their own little programs which, as it turned out, they didn't; the great 4GLs of the '80s were used primarily by programmers to save time over using older programming languages (yes, *3*GLs), which were themselves once proposed as tools for nonprogrammers before everyone came to their senses. And the beat goes on.

As each new advance or application in programming emerges, somebody promotes it as the tool that will turn anybody into Bill Gates at 19. Inevitably, the new tool winds up in the programmer's toolbox, not the everyday user's, for three reasons:

1. All advances in programming methodology are made by programmers, and programmers—though good people, by and large—have never ever ever ever ever ever (ever!) fully understood how difficult the logical rules of structured programming—even in simple languages—seem to a nonprogrammer.

2. Despite their often complex appearance, most modern programming languages really are simple enough for anybody to learn. But to learn one, a fledgling programmer must have a strong incentive to overcome his or her intimidation. And historically, the potential rewards of learning a little programming have been insufficient to provide that incentive. (Who *needs* a report from the company database, anyway? Better not to know.)

3. Within a half-hour of the emergence of a simpler programming method, some half-crazed genius on the west coast comes up with an exciting way to expand the new method's capabilities—and in doing so, raises the bar, makes the easy method complicated, and reverts it to the programmer's domain.

Now, for the first time, we have a task that overcomes reason number 2. Lots of ex-nonprogrammers want so dearly to write Web pages that they're willing to accept the challenge of Web authoring, the latest in the long line of programming for everybody entries.

Of course, Web authoring, pen-and-paperish as it sounds, is programming. We don't call it that, because we know that many people who don't want to be programmers do want to be Web authors. People always think they can transmute a thing by renaming it—programming is to authoring as weapon is to anti-personnel device, or as Unrecoverable Application Error is to General Protection Fault, or as Bernie Schwartz is to Tony Curtis.

The basis of nearly all Web pages is program code written in a language called Hypertext Markup Language (HTML). The plain truth is that HTML is a pretty simple language when the goal is a pretty simple Web page. (Complex pages call for more complex code, but that's only fair, isn't it?) Still, even simple little HTML hasn't proved good enough for the masses. It seemed too much like programming.

Enter graphical HTML editors, which offered a what-you-see-is-what-you-get (WYSIWYG) authoring environment. Users of these editors could compose and format the page onscreen as it would look through a browser on the Web. The editor automatically translated the user's formatting into HTML, behind the scenes. Suddenly, Web authoring wasn't programming; it was word processing.

Great idea—with just two minor flaws. First, the WYSIWYG editors were best at simple things, which were pretty simple in HTML in the first place. For complex tasks, the editors offered little advantage over straight HTML coding, and often, the editor even got in the way, limiting the user's capabilities to the easy stuff. But more important, graphical editors have traditionally applied a one-size-fits-all approach. As you'll discover in Chapter 1, "Planning Your Page," and rediscover throughout this book, there's a wide range in the HTML features browsers do or don't support. Trying to be democratic about things, most graphical editors have aimed their feature set at the lowest common denominator, or just a notch above.

Enter Netscape Navigator Gold. Although it's packaged as one program, it's really two: a full-featured Web browser (henceforth known in this book as the Browser) plus a WYSIWYG page editor (henceforth the Editor). The Browser—itself just a copy of the non-Gold version of Navigator with an added Edit button—and the Editor are linked somewhat loosely together by toolbar buttons that let you jump between the hemispheres of the Gold authoring planet.

Thanks to its dual-personality and its synergy with Netscape Navigator, Gold is an ideal authoring environment for those who want to make the most of the bells and whistles supported by the Netscape line of browsers. Instead of trying to be all editors to all people, Gold wants to be the page-maker for the Netscape world (which makes up more than 80 percent of the Web). And for good-looking, Netscape-oriented Web pages, Gold is indeed a quick and easy way to crank out a solid HTML program.

But just at the moment when WYSIWYG editing has dipped the skill curve nice and low, JavaScript is raising it up again. A recent wrinkle, JavaScript, allows authors to add special functions to their pages. It's powerful, but it's programming; there's no way around it. Netscape promotes JavaScript as a language for novices, and in fact, a motivated novice can learn it. Still, JavaScript introduces a level of difficulty into Web page creation that had been absent since HTML programming became *authoring.* Whether JavaScript becomes the novice's friend or the latest 4GL remains to be seen. (You can decide for yourself when you hit Chapter 13!)

But to the extent that this churning, spinning world of Web authoring has been made comprehensible, advancements in editing did not make it so; Laura Lemay did. In a series of best-selling books, Lemay has invented and refined a superior methodology for teaching Web authoring. The goal of the book you're holding is to apply Lemay's proven methods to the most effective general-purpose authoring tool for the Netscape environment: Navigator Gold.

I hope you find the combination illuminating—and fun.

Who Should Read this Book

This book has been carefully designed to reach anyone who's already a Web surfer, but might or might not already be a Web author. Authoring newcomers will find here everything they need to know, while intermediate and experienced authors will learn how to do what they already do (plus more, perhaps) in the Navigator Gold way.

The book assumes that you

- ❏ Are generally familiar with the Web from a surfer's (not necessarily an author's) perspective.
- ❏ Know what Web pages, links, and URLs are.
- ❏ Use Windows 95, and know enough to get around in it and stay out of trouble. You'll do best if you know how to drag and drop, and how to right-click items to open their context menus. (These two Windows 95 features are put to good use in Gold.)
- ❏ Have installed Netscape Navigator Gold (if not, see Appendix A, "Installing and Updating Netscape Navigator Gold.") Ideally, you should browse the Web with it a bit, just to get the feel of it, before moving on to authoring.

NOTE: This book is about Web authoring, not about Web surfing or about using the Browser component of Netscape Navigator Gold (except as it pertains to authoring tasks).

If you want to know more about browsing, may I suggest the following Sams.net titles:

> *Netscape Unleashed* (by Dick Oliver)
>
> *Navigating the Internet with Windows 95, Deluxe Edition* (by me)
>
> *The World Wide Web Unleashed* (by John December and Neil Randall)

After picking up the browser skills you want, be sure to return here to become a Web author.

How to Read this Book

The first 14 chapters in this book (Parts I, II, and III) are arranged in general order of ambition and/or difficulty. That's for two reasons:

❏ So beginners can start with Chapter 1 and then build their skills and confidence by moving through the chapters in order. By Chapter 2, readers will already have built a complete page in the Page Wizard. By the end of Chapter 6, they will be able to compose a complete Web page with links and graphics. Subsequent chapters provide subsequent skills, but the reader can stop as soon as he or she has a page that pleases.

❏ So experienced authors can bypass the stuff they know and get right to what they want to learn. For example, few experienced authors will have much interest in the basics of Web page structure (Chapter 1) or in the Netscape Page Wizard (Chapter 2). Pros may therefore choose to skip Part I altogether and begin by exploring the Editor in Chapter 3.

However, the chapters don't particularly depend upon those that precede them. If you want to jump ahead, or jump around, you'll find that the chapters are more or less self-contained. Where a chapter mentions a concept from another chapter, a cross reference appears in the margin to tell you where to look for more information, if you choose to.

Margin notes tell you more about the current topic, as well as give you cross-references to places in the book that you can find further information about a specific subject.

The following examples show how this book's tips, sidebars, notes, and cautions help guide you through information you will need to know. CD-ROM icons are placed next to text that shows what you can find on the CD-ROM that comes with this book.

TIP: Tips offer important (or at least interesting) hints and suggestions related to the topic at hand.

General Sidebar

Sidebars give you general information about a topic related to the discussion at hand.

NOTE: Notes provide you with interesting, added information about the subject at hand.

CAUTION: Cautions prompt you with gentle warnings, to help you stay out of trouble.

 CD-ROM notes alert you to programs and files on the CD-ROM at the back of this book that help with the topic at hand.

The final part of this book—Chapters 15, 16, and 17—provides information that's valuable to all Web authors, at all skill levels: how to publish your pages on the Web, how to test them and keep them up-to-date, and how to continue your education and development as a Web author.

Finally, just remember that Browser (with a capitol B) means the browser side of Navigator Gold, and Editor (with a capitol E) means the editing side of Gold, the Netscape Editor.

Enjoy, and good luck.

I

Fast-Track to a Home Page

CHAPTER

ONE

Planning Your Page

When Francis Ford Coppola makes a movie, he tosses the script out the window and improvises. When Steven Spielberg makes a movie, he makes a rigid plan before shooting begins and sticks to it. He decides exactly what he's going to do before he does anything. Both directors have made good and bad movies, so I suppose either approach can work. But Coppola's way takes much longer and courts disaster. (See *One From the Heart*.) More importantly, Coppola gets away with habits that would destroy other artists because he is, as they say, *a genius*. And, of course, neither approach can work unless the director knows something, before shooting begins, about how movies get made.

I can't know whether you're a genius. I'm not one. So assuming that neither of us is a genius, we must approach our task like Spielberg. Before we begin page-production, we need to acquire that rudimentary understanding of how Web pages are born, and we need to do some planning about what we want our page to be. Could we improvise? Sure—especially with the easy-to-use authoring tools in Navigator Gold (henceforth, "Gold"). But improvising at this stage might produce a less effective page, take much longer, put us millions of dollars over budget and weeks behind schedule, antagonize the critics….

In this chapter, you'll get a quick tour of what Web pages are made of and a rundown on the important issues to consider when conceiving your own Web documents.

Anatomy of a Web Page

There are other optional parts, but a complete Web page nearly always includes all the following elements. It's important to know what these parts are, because the principle task in Web authoring is deciding what content to use for each standard part, and a principle challenge is dealing with the different ways each browser treats the different parts (more on that later).

NOTE: The real title of a Web page does not appear within the page itself, but as the title of the window. However, most pages have another *title* of sorts, or rather, text or a graphic on the screen doing the job we typically associate with a title in books or magazines—sitting boldly and proudly near the top of the page to give it a name. This title you see in the layout of the page itself is typically made out of a heading or graphic, and is not the true title of the page, but one for show. It might be identical to the real title that appears as the window title, or it might be completely different.

❏ A *title*, which graphical browsers (such as most for Windows, Macintosh, and X Window) typically display in the title bar of the window in which the page appears. Although the title does not appear on the page itself, it is an important element, as you'll learn in Chapter 3, "Using the Netscape Editor."

❏ A *heading*, which browsers typically display in large, bold or otherwise emphasized type. A Web page can have many headings, and headings can be *nested* up to six levels deep; that is, there can be subheadings, and sub-subheadings, and so on.

❏ *Normal text*, which makes up the basic, general-purpose text of the page. Traditionally, Web authors refer to lines or blocks of normal text as *paragraphs.* But in the parlance of the Netscape Editor, *any* discrete block of words on the page is called a paragraph—whether it's a heading, normal text, or something else is determined by *properties* assigned to that paragraph. (See Chapter 3, "Using the Netscape Editor.")

❏ A *signature*, typically displayed at the bottom of the page. A signature usually identifies the page's author and often includes the author's (or

Webmaster's) e-mail address so visitors can send comments or questions about the page. The e-mail address is sometimes formatted as a mailto link, so visitors can click it to open their e-mail program with a message preaddressed to the author.

Figure 1.1
The basic parts of a Web page.

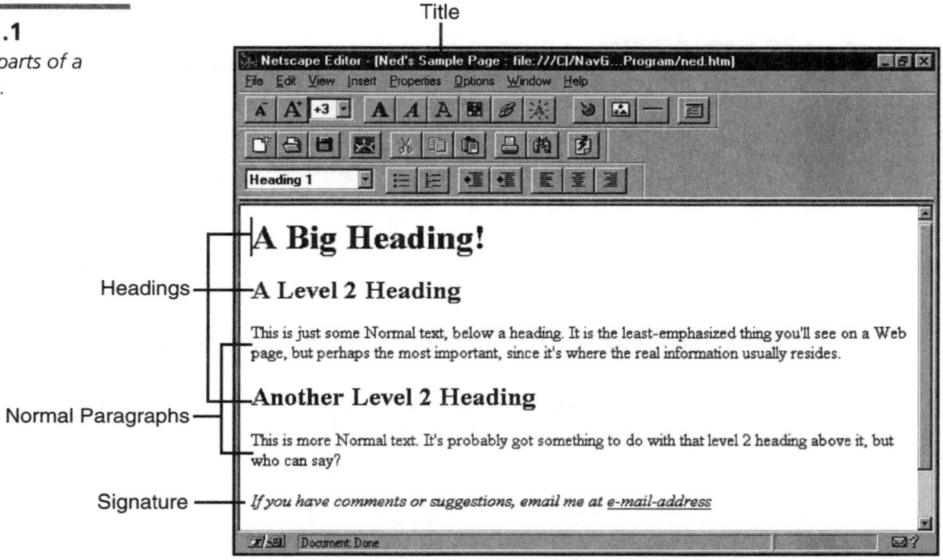
Title
Netscape Editor - [Ned's Sample Page : file:///C|/NavG...Program/ned.htm]
File Edit View Insert Properties Options Window Help
Heading 1
Headings
Normal Paragraphs
Signature
A Big Heading!
A Level 2 Heading
This is just some Normal text, below a heading. It is the least-emphasized thing you'll see on a Web page, but perhaps the most important, since it's where the real information usually resides.
Another Level 2 Heading
This is more Normal text. It's probably got something to do with that level 2 heading above it, but who can say?
If you have comments or suggestions, email me at e-mail-address
Document: Done

- Horizontal *rules* that dress up the page and separate logical sections.
- *Inline* images—pictures that are incorporated into the layout of the page to jazz it up or make it more informative
- *Links* to many different things: other Web pages, multimedia files (external images, animation, sound, video), document files, e-mail addresses, and files or programs on other types of servers (such as Telnet, FTP, and Gopher).
- *Image maps*—inline images in which different areas of the image have different links beneath them
- *Lists*—bulleted (like this one), numbered, and otherwise.
- *Forms*—areas wherein visitors can fill in the blanks to respond to an online questionnaire, order goods and services, and more.

In this book, you'll learn how to create all of these Web page elements, and a few more. (See the section titled "Extensions: Love 'Em, Hate 'Em," later in this chapter.)

Figure 1.2.

A Web page dressed up with optional elements.

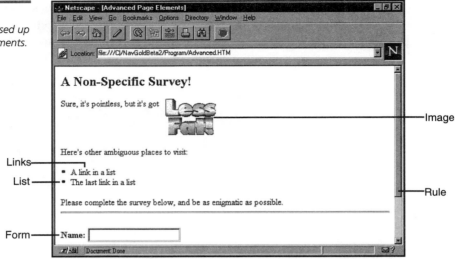

How a Web Page Works

A Web page, as you probably know, is essentially a text file written in a simple language called HTML (Hypertext Markup Language). When you author a Web page, no matter how you go about it—running a page generator like the Netscape Page Wizard, using a WYSIWYG editor like the Netscape Editor, or just typing it into a text file—what you end up with is an HTML file that can be published on a Web server.

An HTML file contains all of the text that appears on the page, plus codes, called *tags,* which label each chunk of text as a particular element of the page. For example, HTML tags identify one line of text as the page's title, blocks of text as paragraphs, certain lines or words as links, and so on.

Other HTML tags designate the filenames of inline images to be incorporated into the page by the browser when the page is displayed. Another type of HTML code, called *attribute*, controls the effects of tags with which they are associated. In addition to identifying the elements of the page, HTML tags and their attributes control, to a varying extent, the formatting of the page—but more about that a little later.

NOTE: The point of the Netscape Editor is to insulate you from having to work directly with HTML code, or even see it. Instead, you work in a WYSIWYG (what you see is what you get) environment, arranging and formatting text and graphics on screen as they would appear when seen through the Netscape browser and similar browsers. As you do this, Navigator Gold creates the HTML document for you, behind the scenes.

Nevertheless, there are reasons to become familiar with HTML. For the purposes of Part I of this book, it's important only to know that, when using the Page Wizard (see Chapter 2, "Making the Page Wizard Do the Work"), you're really creating HTML code. But in later chapters, you'll discover powerful features you can deploy in your Web page for which the Page Wizard and the Editor supply no tools. To exploit those features, you'll have to pull the curtain and work with HTML directly—which isn't difficult, as you'll discover as soon as you take the plunge.

Figure 1.3.
An HTML source file seen in its naked state, not interpreted by a browser.

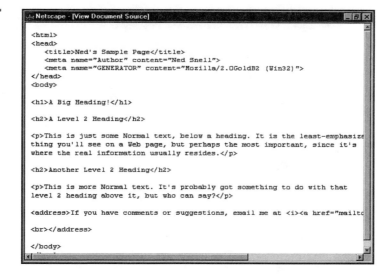

```
Netscape - [View Document Source]

<html>
<head>
    <title>Ned's Sample Page</title>
    <meta name="Author" content="Ned Snell">
    <meta name="GENERATOR" content="Mozilla/2.0GoldB2 (Win32)">
</head>
<body>

<h1>A Big Heading!</h1>

<h2>A Level 2 Heading</h2>

<p>This is just some Normal text, below a heading. It is the least-emphasize
thing you'll see on a Web page, but perhaps the most important, since it's
where the real information usually resides.</p>

<h2>Another Level 2 Heading</h2>

<p>This is more Normal text. It's probably got something to do with that
level 2 heading above it, but who can say?</p>

<address>If you have comments or suggestions, email me at <i><a href="mailto

<br></address>

</body>
```

A Web browser is a program that knows how to do at least two things:

❏ Retrieve HTML documents from remote Web servers (using a communications protocol called HTTP, about which you need know nothing right now).

❏ Interpret the HTML tags in the document in order to display a heading as a heading, treat a link like a link, and so on.

What's important to remember is that the HTML tags do not offer you the kind of control over the precise formatting of a page that you would have in a word processor. Except when extensions are used (see the section titled "Extensions—Love 'Em, Hate 'Em," later in this chapter), HTML mostly just identifies what's what. Each browser decides differently how to format those elements on screen.

You can download the browsers shown in Figures 1.5 and 1.6 and display your pages in them to see how your work appears in non-Netscape browsers. URLs for getting these browsers appear in Chapter 17.

At this writing, Netscape Navigator comprises 80 to 90 percent (according to various estimates) of the browser market, so to most people, your Web page will look roughly the same as it does to you. To the remaining 10 to 20 percent, your page will always show the same text content and general organization, but its graphical content and other aesthetics might vary dramatically browser to browser. In fact, in some cases, pictures and any other graphical niceties might not show up at all.

To illustrate this browser-to-browser variation, Figures 1.4 through 1.6 show the same Web page seen through three different Windows browsers: Netscape Navigator Gold 2.0 on top, Cello (a freeware browser from Cornell University) in the middle, DosLynx below. Observe how the formatting differs in each.

Figure 1.4.
A page seen through Navigator Gold 2.0.

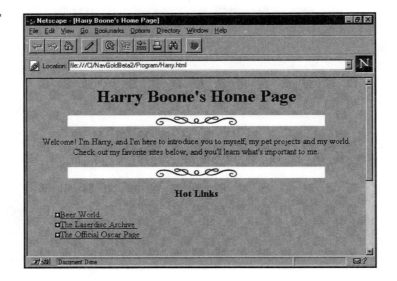

DosLynx, the browser shown in Figure 1.6, is a *text-only* browser for DOS. (You still remember DOS, don't you?) Disappearing rapidly from the Web (but still out there), these browsers cannot display inline graphics and display all text in the same size typeface, though important elements such as headings may be made to stand out with bold type or underlining. Some people use text-only browsers out of choice, although most do so because they lack a SLIP/PPP account or the proper hardware for a graphical browser.

Any place this book discusses a technique that might present problems in non-Netscape browsers, I'll alert you to it and offer suggestions for dealing with the differences.

Because of the lingering presence of text-only browsers (and because some surfers switch off the display of inline graphics when browsing, to speed up their Web sessions), it's important to duplicate in text any important information that's also communicated in a graphic. In particular, links buried in an image map should be duplicated with text elsewhere on the page. You'll learn more about this in Chapter 5, "Linking Everywhere, Anywhere," and in Chapter 12, "Creating Interactive Forms and Image Maps."

Figure 1.5.

The same page as in Figure 1.4, as seen through Cello.

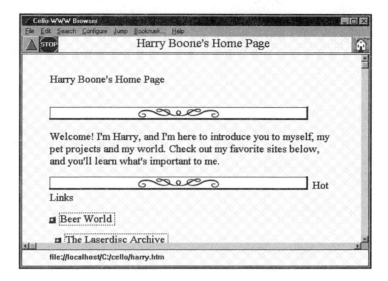

Figure 1.6.

The same page as in Figures 1.4 and 1.5, seen through DosLynx.

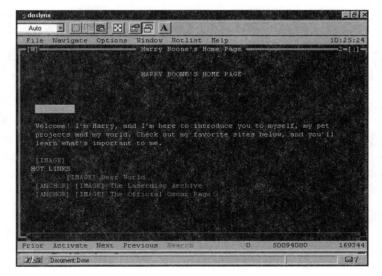

Pictures, Sound, and Other Media

Because an HTML file contains only text, the graphics that you see in Web pages, and the multimedia you can access from them, are not exactly a part of the HTML source file itself. Rather, they're linked to the page in either of two ways:

❏ *Inline images* are graphics files whose filenames and locations are noted in the HTML file itself and identified as images by tags. Inline images are images incorporated into the layout of the page—all of the images you see through Navigator when you access the page.

❏ *External media* are image, sound, or video files whose names and locations appear as links in the HTML file. These files do not appear or play automatically as part of the page. Instead, the page shows links that, when activated, download the file to play or display it.

Whether inline or external, the media files you use in your Web pages challenge the browsers that will be used to view your page. The browser itself must be capable of displaying graphics in order to display inline graphics. External media files can be played by the browser itself or, more commonly, played by helper applications opened by the browser.

When choosing to incorporate media into your page, you'll have to consider carefully the file types you use. The text-only rule of HTML files is what allows users of many different types of computers to access Web pages. Graphics files are less likely to be readable by a wide range of systems, and sound and video files even less so. Even within the confines of PCs and Macs, you'll need to consider whether your media will be supported by a broad spectrum of browsers and/or helper applications.

For more about inline images, see Chapter 6, "Working with Graphics." For more about external media, see Chapter 7, "Embedding Multimedia."

Extensions: Love 'Em! Hate 'Em!

HTML is standardized so that any Web browser can read any Web documents... sort of.

Here's the deal: Nearly all browsers support HTML 2, a generally accepted set of tags that has been around for awhile and is on the verge of being sanctioned as a *bona fide* standard by the committees that oversee Internet standards. Standardization is good, because it provides Web authors with a way to ensure that most browsers will be able to read what they publish. Because most browsers can understand and interpret all of the HTML 2 tags, authors need only stick within the confines of those tags to ensure that their pages are accessible to the biggest possible audience.

The problem with standards, though, is that they evolve slowly. On the Web, only downloads are permitted to be slow; *evolution* is required to be *fast*. Think about it: The first graphical browser emerged three years ago, and now we're talking inline video. The entire birth and maturation of the Web as a graphical, interactive environment has taken place within a single presidential term. Yikes!

HTML 2 includes support for all of the basics—headings, normal text, horizontal rules, lists, links, inline pictures, and so on. But HTML 3, the next generation, has been in the works for some time. It's not finished and it's far from official approval. Still, HTML 3 builds on version 2, adding support for sexy new Web page features like

❏ Centered and right-aligned text

❏ Tables

❏ Math functions

❏ Ways to position text alongside inline images (instead of just above or below images)

❏ Tab support

Hoping to stretch the envelope for both Web authors and surfers, Netscape—and others to follow—has been incorporating preliminary portions of HTML 3 into its browsers for a few years. In addition, Netscape has added new tags of its own for certain kinds of formatting; for example, these Netscape tags can vary font sizes, or the length and thickness of horizontal rules, or the colors used for text.

When used in a Web document, the effects of these *Netscape extensions,* as they're called, can be seen only through Navigator and the few other browsers that support the Netscape extensions. The latest and most radical of the Netscape extensions, Frames, allows you to create a Web page that's broken up into separate panels, each of which has its own URL and behaves like an independent page. (See Figure 1.7 and Chapter 11, "Making Frames.")

Netscape is working closely with the WWW Consortium to get its extensions incorporated into HTML 3, but a carved-in-stone HTML 3 is still a few years away. In the meantime, Web authors have three distinct (but overlapping) sets of HTML tags to use:

❏ HTML 2 tags, which build conservative-looking pages that can be fully read by almost any browser

❏ HTML 3 tags, which support snappier formatting but are understood, to varying degrees, by a handful of browsers (including, though, the most popular browsers)

❏ Netscape extensions, which overlap some of the HTML 3 capabilities and add significant formatting enhancements—all of which can be appreciated only when viewed through Netscape Navigator and a few other browsers

Netscape is no longer the only extension purveyor. Microsoft has created its own extensions, as yet understood only by its Internet Explorer browser, for inline video, scrolling banners and other new features.

The application of preliminary HTML 3 features and of Netscape extensions greatly expand your page formatting options. However, not all browsers support HTML 3 and/or the Netscape extensions.

In general, when an incompatible browser accesses a page that uses these tags, nothing dire happens. The fancy extension-based formatting doesn't show up, but the meat of the page—its text and graphics—remain readable. For example, when a page uses Netscape's extensions to control its font sizes, colors, and rule thickness, an extension-deprived browser simply displays the fonts in its own normal sizes and colors, and the rules in their standard thickness. The content of the page survives the translation; only some of the style gets lost.

Still, authors who want to take advantage of extensions are concerned that some visitors are not seeing the page in its full glory. That's why, more and more, you'll see messages like "Best when viewed through Netscape Navigator 1.1 and Above," or "Enhanced for Internet Explorer," on Web pages. That's the author telling you that he or she has used extensions—and if you want to enjoy all the features of the page, you'd best pick up a compatible browser.

In developing your page, you must consider carefully whether or not to use extensions and HTML 3 features. If you reject them, you're denying your page the benefit of the sexiest new features (which isn't necessarily bad; you can wow people with substance rather than style). If you choose to climb down that slippery slope into extension-ville, you should always check your pages through browsers that don't support extensions, to make sure it remains an effective page for visitors who may be extension-challenged. (See Chapter 3, "Using the Netscape Editor.")

The Netscape Editor includes support for several Netscape extensions, including text centering and alignment, font sizes and custom colors, and backgrounds (all of which are covered in Chapter 4, "Composing, Editing, and Formatting Text "). Other extensions are covered in later chapters of this book.

In Figures 1.7 and 1.8, you'll see a small example of the variation that extensions can cause. Both figures show the exact same Web document (Netscape's home page). But only Navigator (see Figure 1.7) can show the version that uses frames. (For more about frames, see Chapter 11.)

In a few special cases, an extension-enhanced page might not display at all through nonextension-compatible browsers. Such cases are covered in Chapter 11.

In a way, Netscape's JavaScript language is also an extension, because the routines it lets you add to your Web pages (see Chapter 13) work only when viewed through a Java-compatible browser. Today, Netscape's the only one (even though more are coming).

Figure 1.7.

Seen through Netscape Navigator, Netscape's Home Page, which exploits its own Frames feature, among other extensions.

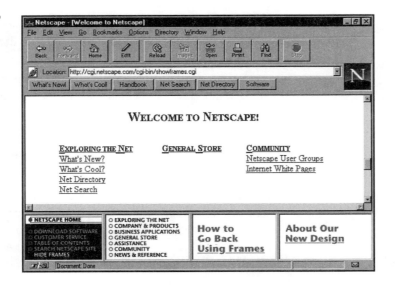

Figure 1.8.
Netscape's home page seen through Internet Explorer, which supports most Netscape extensions, but not frames.

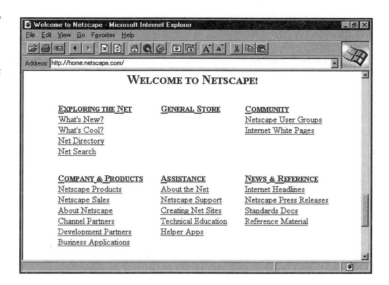

Ways to Organize a Document

Finally, before you dive into creating a Web document, you must give some thought to

- ❏ How can my message be broken down into a organized series of topics?
- ❏ How long a page, or how many pages, will be required to say what I have to say?

Jot down a list of the topics or subtopics your document will cover. How many do you have, and how much material will be required for each topic? After this simple exercise, you'll begin to get a good sense of the size and scope of your document.

Now look at the topics. Do they proceed in a logical order from beginning to end, with each new part depending on knowledge of the parts that came before? Or does the material seem to branch naturally to subtopics (and sub-subtopics)? How might you reorder the topics to make the flow more logical, or group related topics together?

After you've developed and refined the topic breakdown and outline of your message, you might find that you've already composed the headings for your document.

As you work on your breakdown (not *that* kind of breakdown… your topic breakdown), a simple outline begins to emerge. The more you refine that outline before you begin composing your document, the more focused and efficient your authoring will be. More importantly, the resulting Web document will present your message in a way that's clear and easy to follow.

While you're building your outline, consider the logical organization of your presentation and how its material may fit into any of the common organizational structures seen on the Web:

Billboard: A single, simple page, usually describing a person, small business, or simple product. Most personal home pages are this type. They'll often contain links to related (or favorite) resources on the Web, but not to any further pages of the same document. (The Netscape Page Wizard, covered in the next two chapters, builds this type of page.)

One-Page Linear: One Web page, short or long, designed to be read more or less from top to bottom. Rules are often used to divide up such a page into virtual "pages." Readers can scroll through the entire page, but a table of contents and anchors (see Chapter 5) may be used to help readers jump down quickly to any section. This type is best used for fairly short (less than 10 pages' worth) documents wherein all the information flows naturally from a beginning to an end.

Multipage Linear: Same general idea as one-page linear, but broken up into multiple pages that flow logically, one after the other, from beginning to end, like the pages of a story. You can lead the reader through the series by placing a link at the bottom of each page, leading to the next page.

Hierarchical: The classic Web structure. A top page (sometimes confusingly called a *home page*) contains links to other pages, each covering a major subject area. Each of those pages may have multiple links to still more pages, breaking the subject down further and getting into even more specific information. The result is a tree structure, like the one shown in Figure 1.9.

Figure 1.9.
A hierarchical structure.

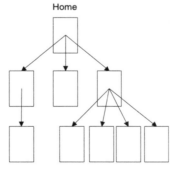

Home

Web: A Web structure (see Figure 1.10) is a hierarchical structure without the hierarchy. It's a multipage document in which any page may have a link leading to any other page. There may be a "top" page, but from there, readers can wander around the webby thing in no particular path. Web structures are loose and free-flowing and are therefore best suited to fun, recreational subjects, or to subjects that defy any kind of sequential or hierarchical breakdown. (Hint: Before you resort to a Web structure, make sure your message really calls for one—you may just be having trouble focusing.)

Figure 1.10.
A Web structure.

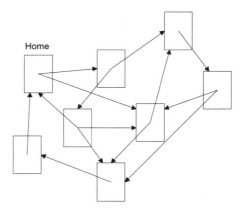

To plan a document with three or more pages, *storyboard* it by roughing out each page on a piece of paper to decide which information belongs on each page. Tape the papers to a wall and draw lines or tape strings to plan links among the pages.

There are other ways to organize information; variations on each of the structures presented here. But one of these structures should resemble the general shape of your message, and thus your document. To put it another way, if you can't yet decide which of these structures is best for the Web page you want to create, you need to play with your message some more and break it down different ways until a structure reveals itself to you.

Workshop Wrap-Up

You could, if you so choose, create your Web page by getting some good coffee (or a Diet Coke, the official caffeinated beverage of the Lemay Method), sitting down and fiddling for awhile with the Page Wizard or the Netscape Editor. In the end, you'll have an HTML file suitable for publishing (if not for reading).

But will it be a file that achieves your goals for wanting a Web page in the first place? If you're looking for cyber-friends, will your page appeal to them? If you're looking for clients or customers, will your page make you look better than your competitors do? If you're offering useful information, are you doing so in a way that visitors to your page will find intuitive and easy to navigate?

Clearly, Web authoring is more than mechanics; it's also aesthetics, ergonomics, social science, and much more. To create a page that hits its mark, you must first ground yourself in the basics of how a Web document works, and what it can and cannot do. That's what you've picked up in this chapter. I didn't attempt to dictate how your document should look, feel, or operate—that has to be your inspiration. But I've tried to feed your thoughts so that you can make informed choices during whatever tasks you choose to take on next.

Next Steps

Now…

- ❏ To create a simple personal homepage almost instantly, see Chapter 2, "Making the Page Wizard Do the Work."
- ❏ To get a sense of the results you can expect from the Page Wizard (plus a little tinkering) and other techniques, see Chapter 8, "Real-Life Examples I."
- ❏ To learn how to build a page from scratch with the Netscape Editor, see Chapter 3, "Using the Netscape Editor."

Q&A

Q: So basically you're telling me I can do all these cool things to my page in Gold, but I should stick with the boring stuff alone since the cool stuff is based on extensions and also some people can't see graphics…? Isn't that, well, ever so slightly a bummer?

A: Bummer—not. In practice, it's really not such a big deal. First of all, remember that the overwhelming majority of the folks browsing the Web can view graphics, and most use Netscape or another browser that understands at least some of the Netscape extensions. So even if you go completely nuts with pictures and extension-based formatting, your page will look great to most people.

And using techniques I'll show you in later chapters, you can accommodate the graphics-impaired or extension-impaired so that your page is as useful to them as to everyone else—just not as pretty. There are a few things—Frames and JavaScript routines especially—that are not as widely supported, but you'll learn how to deal with that when the time comes.

But still, it's important to remember that just because you're writing a page *in* Netscape doesn't mean you're writing it solely *for* Netscape. A smart author makes his or her document informative *and* cool to look at, *and* accessible to all.

Q: Should I use the Page Wizard to create my page, or write it in the Editor?

A: The Page Wizard builds a very simple (but efficiently organized) personal home page. With a little finagling, you can also use the Wizard to create a business announcement or other simple presentation. But if your needs are any more elaborate than that, you're better off getting straight into the Editor.

If you want, you can use the Wizard to build your first page, just to get a feel for things. Then you can use the page you created as raw material in the Editor, and build upon it.

TWO

Making the Page Wizard Do the Work

Netscape's Page Wizard is one of a growing field of fill-in-the-blanks "home page generators" that enable new Web authors to crank out personal home pages in a matter of minutes. Like anything built for speed and simplicity, the Page Wizard forces on the author a lot of compromises when compared with other approaches. It's like a Polaroid camera: You can't do much with it and the results are small, fuzzy, and unprofessional looking, but the gratification is almost instantaneous.

Still, the Page Wizard can't be beat for speed or simplicity, and it offers a great way for new authors to wet their Web feet before moving onto the more demanding (and powerful) authoring techniques described later in this book.

What (and Where) Is the Page Wizard?

The Netscape Page Wizard is like the Wizard of Oz: It's called a Wizard and pretends to be one but it really isn't one. ("Pay no attention to that man behind the curtain!") But in the end (also like Oz), the Page Wizard delivers what you came for. ("Oh the friends I'd be makin' and the cash I'd be rakin' if I only had a home page....")

As a Windows 95 user, you're familiar with Wizards. They're the friendly, automated routines that lead you, step by step, through otherwise complicated tasks, such as installing Windows 95, creating shortcuts, or installing Netscape Navigator Gold. The Page Wizard is not, technically, a Windows 95 Wizard, and it neither looks nor acts like one. It serves the same purpose, though. It leads you through the creation of a basic, custom-built home page.

The Page Wizard is an HTML document stored at

`http://home.netscape.com/assist/net_sites/starter/wizard/index.html`

Because the Page Wizard requires processing by server-based programs, you cannot save the Wizard page and then use it offline. You must use the Wizard while connected to the Internet.

Should I Use the Wizard?

When you fill in the blanks in the Page Wizard, your entries are automatically plugged into the appropriate spots in a Web page *template*. (See Chapter 3, "Using the Netscape Editor.") The template used is a very simple, straightforward home page— no more, no less.

You can use the Page Wizard to quickly cobble together a basic page, and then enhance and expand that page in the Netscape Editor.

Although different entries result in different content, the organization of the page remains the same, regardless of what you type in the Wizard. The Wizard offers you the ability to dress up the look of the page by choosing a background texture, custom colors for text, and stylized bullets and rules (although these formatting choices have drawbacks, as you'll see later in this chapter). But the layout of the text elements on the page remains unchanged, no matter what you do. All pages created with the Wizard look essentially the same (see Figure 2.1); only the content changes.

The template used by the Wizard is designed for a personal home page and is effective in that regard, if a little short and overly simple. By making a few creative choices when filling in the blanks (see Chapter 8, "Real-Life Examples I") and then tweaking the page a bit in the Editor, you can also use the Wizard to create a simple business page.

To see how creative entries in the Wizard forms—plus subsequent editing with the Editor—can expand the range of a Wizard-built page, see Example 2 in Chapter 8.

Whether you should use the Wizard depends on whether the overall organization of the resulting page is reasonably close to what you want to achieve. If you want a dramatically different look for your page or if you plan to build an elaborate Web document made up of multiple linked pages and files, you're probably better off diving right into Chapter 3 to learn how to build your page without the Wizard's help—or its interference.

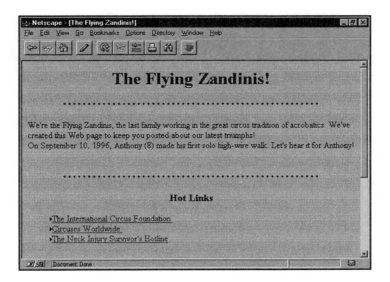

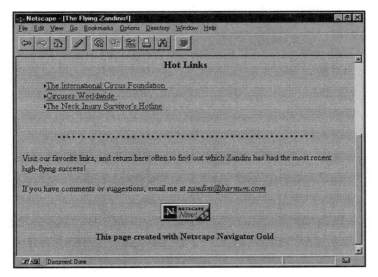

Figure 2.1.
A typical home page (top and bottom) produced by the Netscape Page Wizard.

 # Running the Wizard

Running the Wizard is an online affair. You can't simply download the Wizard page and then use it offline, because the Wizard creates your page by taking entries you make in online forms and running those entries through a script processor that resides on Netscape's server.

Note that you run the Wizard in Navigator Gold's Browser window. You do not need to open the Editor until you save the finished page, as described later in this chapter.

NOTE: The Page Wizard page uses frames (see Figure 2.2) to show different activities in different portions of the page. The procedure for running the Page Wizard assumes you're familiar with frames, which are used heavily throughout Netscape's home page.

If you are unfamiliar with frames or want to know more about using them before proceeding with the Page Wizard, connect to Netscape's home at

`http://home.netscape.com/`

and select About Our New Design.

To learn how to create your own frame-based Web documents, see Chapter 11, "Making Frames."

To Start the Wizard

If you use Windows 95's auto-connect feature, you needn't connect to the Internet before performing step 2. The Browser opens the Connect dialog automatically when you perform step 2.

1. Open the Browser and connect to the Internet.

2. In the Browser, choose **F**ile I **N**ew Document I From **W**izard. This instructs the browser to connect to the Page Wizard page at

   `http://home.netscape.com/home/gold3.0_wizard.html`

   You can also simply point the browser to that URL, though going through the menus is easier.

   A screen appears like the one in Figure 2.2.

Figure 2.2.
The opening screen in the Page Wizard.

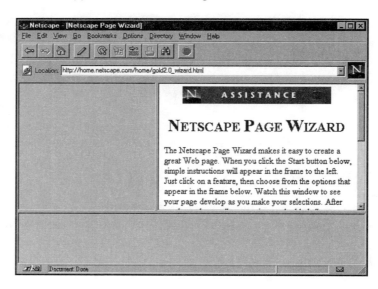

3. In the active frame (upper-right), scroll down past Netscape's cheery intro-ductory copy to display the START button.

4. Click the START button in the upper-right frame. The page appears as shown in Figure 2.3.

Figure 2.3.

The first form in the Page Wizard.

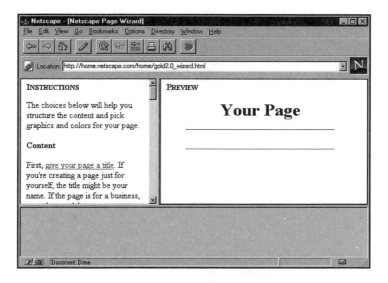

As Figure 2.3 shows, the Wizard page is split into three frames:

❑ The upper-left frame, INSTRUCTIONS, describes each element you will create. Within each description are links that, when clicked, display a form or list of choices in the bottom frame.

❑ The bottom frame, CHOICES, is where you will type text in forms (to create page content) or choose aspects of the look of your page from lists of choices.

❑ The upper-right frame, PREVIEW, shows a preview of your page. As you complete each form or selection in the CHOICES (bottom) frame, the preview is updated to show you the result. (After the first few forms, you'll need to scroll down in the PREVIEW frame to see the area of the page you've just created.)

NOTE: The next several sections of this task describe how to complete all of the forms and make all of the selections required to complete your page. The forms and choices are discussed here in the order in which you encounter them in the INSTRUCTIONS (upper-left) frame.

You don't need to make your entries and choices in order. You may scroll ahead in the INSTRUCTIONS and make later choices and entries before making earlier ones. You may also scroll forward or backward in the IN-STRUCTIONS at any time to revisit earlier entries, and change or delete them if you want to.

Finally, keep in mind that you needn't fill in every blank in the Wizard. If you leave a form empty, the Wizard simply deletes that element of the page and any text used to label it. If you don't bother making a selection under the "Looks" portion of the Wizard, defaults are used.

To Fill in the Content of the Page

In the Content section of the INSTRUCTIONS (upper-left) frame, you choose links that open text-entry forms in the CHOICES (bottom) frame.

1. Scroll the INSTRUCTIONS until you see the link `give your page a title`. (See Figure 2.4.)

2. Click the link. A form appears in the CHOICES frame, as shown in Figure 2.4.

Figure 2.4.

Entering a title.

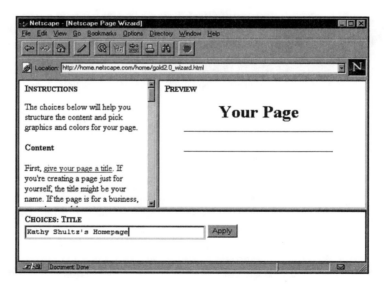

3. Delete the descriptive text that appears in the form and type a title for your page. The Wizard uses this as the document title (refer to Chapter 1, "Planning Your Page") and as a level 1 heading at the top of the page itself.

The on-page title in your page is centered by a Netscape extension. (See Chapter 4.) Viewed in a browser that doesn't support extensions, the title appears left-aligned.

Figure 2.5.
Entering an intro-duction.

4. Click Apply. The new title appears in the PREVIEW frame (upper-right), centered at the top of the page. (See Figure 2.5.)

5. Scroll the INSTRUCTIONS until you see the link `type an introduction`. (See Figure 2.5.)

6. Click the link. A form appears in the CHOICES frame, as shown in Figure 2.5.

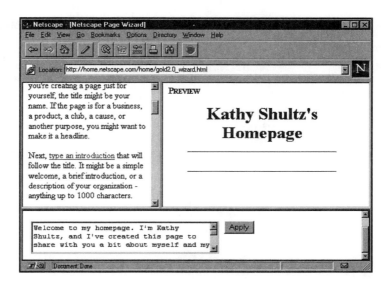

7. Delete the descriptive text that appears in the form and type an introduction of up to 1,000 characters for your page. When typing the intro, you can press Enter to break lines or create a blank line. That way, you can create an introduction that is several paragraphs long (up to 1,000 characters total).

   The Wizard inserts your introduction as a normal paragraph, left-aligned, following the title. (See Figure 2.6.)

8. Click Apply. The new introduction appears in the PREVIEW frame.

9. Scroll the INSTRUCTIONS until you see the link `add some hot links`…. (See Figure 2.6.)

10. Click the link. A form appears in the CHOICES frame, as shown in Figure 2.6.

11. The CHOICES: HOT LINKS form allows you to create a bulleted list of links to other pages or documents. Creating each link in the list takes three steps:

    a. Delete the descriptive text that appears in the Name line of the form and type the text you want to appear in your page as the link source (the text to click to activate the link).

The Wizard inserts a rule above and below the introduction. Later, you'll get a chance to customize the look of that rule.

Figure 2.6.
Entering Hot Links.

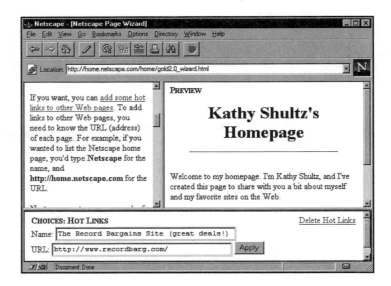

b. Delete the descriptive text that appears in the URL line of the form and type the complete URL to which visitors should be taken if they click the text entered in Name.

c. Click Apply.

The Wizard inserts the Name text as one item in a bulleted list under a centered heading, Hot Links. (See the PREVIEW frame in Figure 2.7.) You may now add to the list by entering another hot link (using steps a, b, and c) or move on. (It makes sense to use at least two hot links or none at all; a bulleted list with only one item looks a little silly.)

The Wizard formats your Hot Links in a bulleted list. Later, you'll get a chance to customize the look of the bullets.

NOTE: If you apply a hot link and decide later you don't want it anymore, scroll the INSTRUCTIONS to the link for hot links (`add some hot links….`) and click the link to reopen the CHOICES: HOT LINKS form. Then click Delete Hot Links. A new CHOICES form opens, as shown in Figure 2.7.

The checkmarks appearing next to each link in the list indicate that the link is to remain in the document. To delete a link, click its checkbox. The link instantly disappears from the list and from the PREVIEW.

Figure 2.7.
Deleting Hot Links.

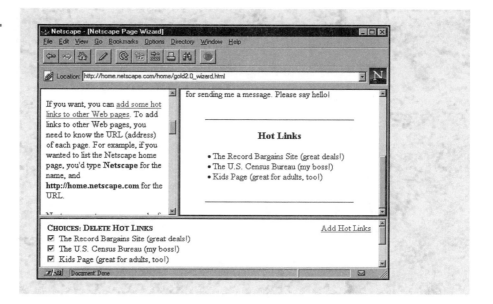

12. Scroll INSTRUCTIONS until you see the link `type a paragraph of text to serve as a conclusion`.

13. Click the link. A CHOICES: CONCLUSION form appears in the CHOICES frame.

14. Delete the descriptive text that appears in the form and type a conclusion of up to 1,000 characters for your page. Just as in the introduction, you can press Enter to break lines or create a blank line.

    The Wizard inserts your conclusion as a normal paragraph, left-aligned, following the Hot Links. (See Figure 2.15, later in this chapter.)

15. Scroll the INSTRUCTIONS until you see the link `add an email link`. (See Figure 2.8.)

16. Click the link. A form appears in the CHOICES frame, as shown in Figure 2.8.

17. CHOICES: EMAIL LINK form allows you to create a signature for the bottom of your page (see Figure 2.15, later in this chapter), including a mailto link that allows visitors to conveniently send you e-mail. Delete the descriptive text that appears in the form and fill in your complete Internet e-mail address.

18. Click Apply.

    The Wizard builds a signature at the bottom of the page. In the signature, your e-mail address appears as a mailto link.

To learn more about mailto links, see Chapter 5.

Figure 2.8.

Entering a signature.

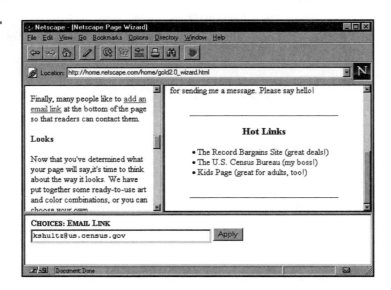

To Choose "Looks" for Your Page

In the Looks portion of the Wizard, you customize the look of your page in four ways:

- ❏ Choose a background color or pattern
- ❏ Choose custom colors for text, links, and visited links
- ❏ Choose customized bullets (for the bulleted list of Hot Links)
- ❏ Choose customized rules (horizontal lines)

Note that you do not have to make any of these selections. If you ignore the Look choices, your page will use no background color or pattern, each browser's default text/link/visited link colors, and ordinary, default bullets and rules.

NOTE: All of the Looks options are based on Netscape extensions. (See Chapter 1.) Choices you make here will appear as you intend them to only when viewed through Netscape Navigator versions 1.2 and above or through other browsers that support Netscape extensions.

In browsers that do not support Netscape extensions:

- ❏ The background pattern (if you have chosen to use one) does not appear.
- ❏ All colors (text, links, or background) default to the browser's standard color scheme, regardless of your color selections.

Also, the customized bullets and rules are not bullets and rules at all, but inline images. A Netscape extension for positioning text next to images (see

Chapter 6, "Working with Graphics") is used to put the *faux*-bullet images where bullets go.

In browsers that can display GIF graphics but aren't compatible with Netscape extensions, the custom rules should still show up (though not properly centered), but the custom bullets will not appear at all or will appear above (rather than next to) each line of the list. In browsers that do not support graphics, the rules and bullets will not appear at all (even as regular bullets and rules). The list items would appear as unadorned lines of text, left-aligned.

If you do not choose custom bullets or rules, however, the Wizard uses real HTML bullets and rules. They're not fancy, but they'll display properly in almost any browser.

1. Scroll the INSTRUCTIONS until you see the link a `preset color combination`. (See Figure 2.9.) This link allows you to choose in one step a complete set of color selections that already work well together, so you needn't select each color (background, text, link, visited link) separately. (If you'd rather choose each color separately, skip to step 4.)

2. Click the link. A row of color choices appears in the bottom frame, as shown in Figure 2.9. Each choice includes a text color, link color, and visited link color, all set against a square of background color. The four colors are all properly color-coordinated.

Figure 2.9.
Choosing a preset color combination.

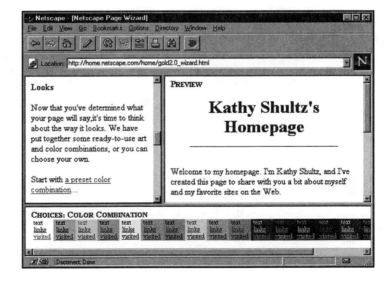

It's usually best not to use a custom color for `visited links`. Web surfers have conditioned responses; they expect a visited link to appear in their browser's default color everywhere.

Figure 2.10.
Choosing colors.

3. Choose a color combination by clicking it. (There is no Apply button.)

4. If you did not choose a preset color combination or if you want to change any of the colors within your selection for preset colors, scroll the INSTRUCTIONS to the list of links beginning with `background color`.

5. Click any item (other than `background pattern`) to display a row of color choices like the one shown for BACKGROUND COLOR in Figure 2.10.

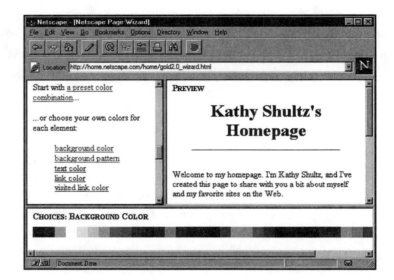

6. Click a color block to choose the color.

NOTE: When choosing colors, try to contrast text, link, and background colors so that links are easy to spot. Also, keep your eye on your background selection, to make sure the text and links will stand out from the background but not clash with it. (If you happen to be color blind, like me, leave the defaults; they know better than we do.)

Choosing a background pattern overrides any selection for background color but does not affect your color choices for text, links, and visited links.

7. To choose a background pattern, click the link for `background pattern`. A row of choices appears in the CHOICES frame, as shown in Figure 2.11.

8. Click the desired background pattern. After a few moments, the results appear in the PREVIEW frame.

Figure 2.11.
Choosing a background pattern.

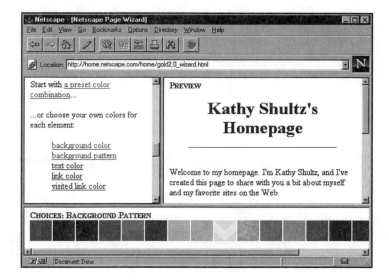

9. Scroll the INSTRUCTIONS to reveal the link for `choose a bullet style`, as shown in Figure 2.12. Your bullet-style selection decorates the bulleted list of Hot Links created earlier.

10. Click the link. A row of custom bullets appears in CHOICES, as shown in Figure 2.12. (The first choice, a solid circle, is not a custom bullet. It's the default choice, a standard HTML bullet.)

Figure 2.12.
Choosing a bullet style.

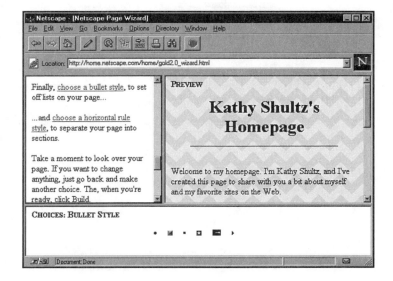

11. Click a bullet style to select it.

12. Scroll the INSTRUCTIONS to reveal the link for `choose a horizontal rule style`, as shown in Figure 2.13. Your rule-style selection affects all the rules the Wizard inserts automatically to divide up the sections of the page.

13. Click the link. A row of custom rules appears in CHOICES, as shown in Figure 2.13. (The first choice, a simple line, is not a custom rule. It's the default choice, a standard HTML rule.)

Figure 2.13.
Choosing a rule style.

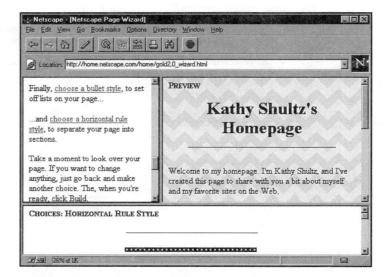

14. Click a rule style to select it.

NOTE: When making bullet and rule selections, keep your eyes on the PREVIEW, and evaluate carefully your previous choices for background texture and text/link colors. Rules and bullets must stand out against the background but not clash with the background, text, and links—or with each other. When in doubt, use the default choices (the leftmost bullet choice, the top rule choice).

To Create the Completed Home Page

1. Scroll up and down through the PREVIEW, and review your choices and entries. Have you said all you want to say? Are you satisfied with your

"Look"? Are your e-mail address and any URLs you've entered complete and accurate (don't forget to double-check capitalization on URLs). Howz yer speling?

2. After checking your entries and making any changes or corrections, scroll to the bottom of the INSTRUCTIONS frame, as shown in Figure 2.14.

Figure 2.14.
Finishing up.

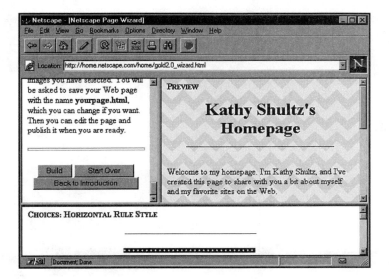

NOTE: The only reason you would ever want to click the Start Over button shown in Figure 2.14 is that you hate not just *some* of your choices and entries, but *all* of them—which is unlikely, unless you have severe self-esteem issues.

Even if you hate what you've done, you can click Build to see the results (full-page, not squeezed in the PREVIEW). Having seen the results, you can then click Navigator's Back button to return to the Wizard and make edits (your entries remain in all fields) and then click Build again. Or you can keep the Wizard-created page, no matter how bad it is, and retool it in the Netscape Editor, as described in Chapters 3 through 7.

If you simply want to change (or delete) portions of your work, scroll back and do so and then click Build. If you really want to wipe out everything you've done and start over, click Start Over.

3. Click Build. The button activates a script that takes your entries and selections, plugs them into a template, and opens the finished page in the Browser, as shown in Figure 2.15.

Figure 2.15.

The finished home page (top and bottom).

CAUTION: You must save the page when finished (as described in the next section), or you'll lose it when you close the Editor. You must save using the Editor as described below, rather than simply choosing **F**ile | Save **A**s in the Browser, because only the Editor will download to your PC the image files for the background pattern, custom bullets, and rules.

Having come this far, you are henceforth authorized to declare yourself a Web author, and may now swing your hand upward in a regal flourish and exclaim, "Tah-dah!" (unless doing so makes you feel silly).

To Save the Completed Home Page

1. Click the Edit button on the toolbar. The Netscape Editor opens (closing the Browser behind it) and immediately displays the dialog shown in Figure 2.16.

Figure 2.16.
Saving the finished page.

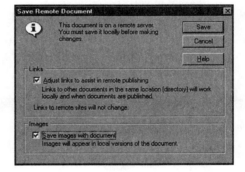

2. The two checkboxes in the dialog shown in Figure 2.16 simply confirm entries in the Editor Preferences. (See Chapter 3, "Using the Netscape Editor," and Chapter 15, "Publishing Web Documents.") Make sure both boxes are checked, and click Save. A message appears like the one shown in Figure 2.17. (To learn more about these checkboxes, see Chapter 15.)

Figure 2.17.
A warning about copyrights.

To prevent the Copyright warning shown in Figure 2.17 from appearing in the future, click the checkbox next to Don't display this message again.

3. The Hint shown in Figure 2.17 simply reminds you that you shouldn't use copyrighted materials you save from the Web; it doesn't know that you're the author of the remote document you're saving. Click OK. A standard Windows 95 Save File dialog appears.

4. The page is given a default filename of YOURPAGE.HTML. You can change this name to anything you like, but make sure the file extension remains .HTM or .HTML. Click OK to save the file.

Your page is complete, and its HTML file, plus image files for any custom bullets or custom rules or a background pattern, are all stored on your PC. You may now publish your document on a Web server (as described in Chapter 15), or edit, refine, and expand your document in the Netscape Editor as described beginning in Chapter 3.

NOTE:
If you're curious, recall from Chapter 1 that what you've just done (indirectly) is create an HTML file. The file is simple text with HTML tags and pointers to image files containing the background pattern and custom bullets/rules (if you chose to use these features).

To see the HTML file itself, in the Editor, click **V**iew | View Document **S**ource. You'll see a file like the one in Figure 2.18. If you examine it carefully, you'll begin to get an excellent sense of how HTML tags work. To learn more about editing an HTML source file, see Chapter 9, "Editing HTML Source Code."

Figure 2.18.
The HTML source code of the finished page (shown earlier in Figure 2.15).

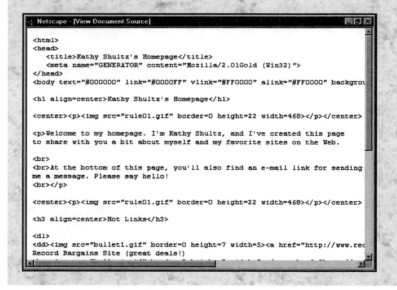

Workshop Wrap-Up

The Page Wizard offers a quick, easy way to build a complete, properly designed Web page. It's ideal for building a first personal home page, and for laying down a basic page you will later enhance and expand with the Editor.

To make the most of the Wizard, you must make carefully considered entries in each form field. You also must consider the effect of all of your choices together. It's not uncommon for new authors to become so enamored of fancy backgrounds and colors that the resulting page looks like Walt Disney threw up. And of course, consider how your page will look in browsers other than Netscape Navigator.

Next Steps

Now…

❏ To publish your new home page, see Chapter 15, "Publishing Web Documents."

❏ To enhance and expand your Wizard-built home page (or create a new page from scratch), see Chapter 3, "Using the Netscape Editor," and Chapter 4, "Composing, Editing, and Formatting Text."

❏ To add new links to your page or to make creative changes to the links you have, see Chapter 5, "Linking Everywhere, Anywhere."

❏ To add pictures to your page, see Chapter 6, "Working with Graphics."

Q&A

Q: Wait a cotton-pickin' minute. The Page Wizard isn't really *in* Navigator Gold—it's just a page on the Web, accessible to anyone (and any browser). So how come Netscape Communications Corp. and this book both treat it like a "feature" of Netscape Gold?

A: True, any browser can access the Page Wizard page. But to actually use the Wizard, the browser must be able to do three things: display frames, save a copy of a remote Web page locally (including all inline graphics), and understand Netscape's extensions (in order to recognize most of the formatting and the background). Right now, the only browser that does all three things is Navigator Gold. Netscape set up the Wizard to exploit Gold's unique capabilities.

When another browser emerges with the same capabilities, it will be able to use the Wizard, as well (if the Wizard is still around). But the pages created by the Wizard in the other browser will still say "Created with Netscape Navigator Gold" at the bottom!

Q: Speaking of that… I see that little Netscape slogan, along with a "Netscape Now!" button, at the bottom of every page I make with the Wizard. What gives?

A: Like any living thing, Netscape wants to procreate. To that end, it pollinates every page created with the Wizard (or with Netscape's templates, as described in Chapter 3) with the Netscape Now! button, which is an inline image and also a link. The link connects to a page at Netscape that allows visitors to conveniently select and download a version of Netscape Navigator for their system.

From a practical standpoint, there's a good reason for that. Visitors to your page who don't use Netscape Navigator (or another browser that understands Netscape's HTML extensions) can't view your page in its full, extension-rich glory.

On the other hand, you might object to allowing your home page to serve as a free billboard for Netscape Communications Corp. (You use Navigator Gold... what *more* do they want from you?) If so, you can easily delete the plug, as described in Chapter 4 (to delete the text "This page was created with Netscape...") and Chapter 6 (to delete the button image and underlying link).

Can't wait? I understand.... The Wizard attracts the impatient :-). Okay, open your new Wizard-built home page in the Netscape Editor, click the Netscape Now! button to highlight it, then press Del. Position the mouse pointer to the left of the text and double-click to highlight it. Click Del again. *Fini.*

II

Web Authoring with the Netscape Editor

THREE

Using the Netscape Editor

The Netscape Editor puts the "Gold" in "Navigator Gold." After all, without the Editor, Netscape is just… Netscape. But with the addition of this powerful, easy-to-use editing window, Netscape becomes a place where building Web pages is just like everyday Windows-style word processing.

When you work in the Editor, your document looks (with some exceptions, described in this chapter) just the way it will look to most visitors on the Web. That's a powerful convenience; without it, Web authors have had to guess about the appearance of the page while fiddling with a page full of HTML code. To check their work, they had to open the file in a browser and then go back to the HTML to make adjustments. With the Gold Editor, it all happens in one window, live and in color.

Perhaps more importantly, the Editor saves time and effort. You'd have to type the content of your page, or copy it from another source, whether you used the Editor or created an HTML file the traditional way. However, typing a set of HTML tags to specify the properties of a single item in an HTML file usually requires at least 10 keystrokes, whereas the same operation in the Editor takes choosing one item from a menu. Editing is made still more convenient by a complete selection of toolbar buttons and by the Editor's support for Windows 95 conventions such as cut and paste, drag and drop, and context menus.

In this chapter, you

- ❏ Learn how to create, save, and open Web pages in the Editor
- ❏ Learn how to make opening the Editor quicker and more convenient
- ❏ Use and customize the Editor's toolbars
- ❏ Enter Document Properties, the important information that's included in every Web page, even though it doesn't show up on the screen
- ❏ Set preferences that specify editors for images and HTML files, a location for templates, and more
- ❏ Pick up and edit document templates to make quick work of good-looking pages

Tasks in this chapter:

- ❏ Opening the Editor
- ❏ Entering Document Properties
- ❏ Configuring General Editor Preferences
- ❏ Opening and Saving a Template

This chapter examines the general operation of the Editor, so you'll know your way around when you approach the specific authoring tasks coming up in later chapters. In fact, you'll use the Editor in all of the remaining chapters, so it's smart to get a firm handle on the basics now, before moving ahead. You'll also discover templates here and see how they can streamline page creation.

Opening the Browser for an Editing Session

Merging a browser with an editor has its drawbacks. In Navigator Gold's case, the problem is that you cannot open the Editor without first opening the Browser. This can subject you to an awkward opening when you want to create or edit a document and aren't immediately interested in going online.

By default, upon opening, the Browser immediately attempts to access the Netscape home page. Also, if you have used Microsoft's Internet Setup Wizard to configure Windows 95 for the Internet, Windows 95's AutoDial feature automatically opens the Internet connection dialog when you open the Browser.

Under these circumstances, to create or edit a document in the Editor, you must

1. Open Navigator Gold.
2. Click the Stop button (to stop Netscape from attempting to access the home page).
3. Wait for the Internet connection dialog to open, and then cancel it.
4. Open the Editor, as described in the next section.

If you open Navigator to browse the Web more often than you create or edit documents, you might want to put up with the editing inconveniences of this scenario in order to enjoy the browsing conveniences. But if you open Navigator often to edit, you might want to stifle Navigator's eagerness to connect to the Internet and go home.

When you double-click the icon of an HTML file, Navigator opens automatically only if it is defined in Windows 95's File Types registry as the default application for HTML files.

When opening a pre-existing HTML file, you can get around this problem by not first opening the Browser but by double-clicking the HTML file's icon on the desktop or in a folder. Doing so opens the file in the Browser and prevents the Browser from attempting to access a home page. You can then click the Edit button to edit the file. (To make this approach more convenient, you might want to store pages in progress on your Windows 95 desktop or in a folder on the desktop, for quick-clicking.)

When your object is creating new files, you have two choices for getting around Netscape's habits. You can open an existing file as described above and choose File I **N**ew Document I **B**lank to open the Editor. (You might want to create a new

If you don't know whether you have AutoDial installed, open Navigator without first connecting to the Internet. If your Internet Dial-Up Networking connection opens automatically, you have AutoDial.

document template for this purpose; see the section titled "Working with Templates" later in this chapter.) Alternatively, you can reconfigure Navigator Gold so that it does not attempt to access a home page upon startup, and reconfigure Windows 95 (if necessary) to disable AutoDial. Both techniques are described next.

Preventing Navigator from Connecting to a Home Page

To prevent Navigator from automatically accessing a home page:

1. In the Browser, choose **O**ptions | **G**eneral Preferences. The Properties sheet shown in Figure 3.1 appears. (Make sure the Appearance tab has been selected.)
2. Under Startup, click the radio button next to **B**lank Page (you need not erase the address shown for the Home Page) and then click OK.

Figure 3.1.
Changing Preferences to more quickly open the Editor

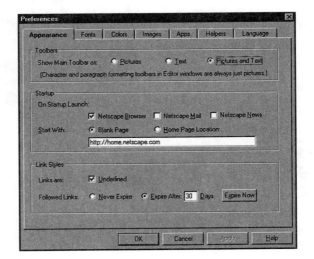

Even after changing the Preferences in this way, the Browser does not attempt to connect to any page upon opening.

NOTE: In Figure 3.1, observe that the default Home Page still appears in the Location field, although Netscape is not attempting to access it. When you really do want to go straight to an online session (instead of authoring), just click the Home button to access that page.

To Disable AutoDial

1. From the Windows 95 Start menu, choose Settings I Control Panel.
2. In the Control Panel, double-click the Internet icon. The Internet Properties opens, as shown in Figure 3.2.
3. Click the checkbox next to **U**se AutoDial to remove the checkmark.
4. Click OK.

Figure 3.2.
Disabling Windows 95's AutoDial.

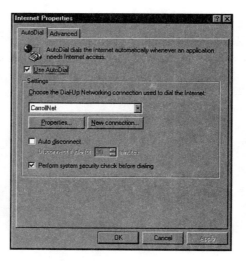

 # Opening the Editor

You can open the Editor in a variety of different ways, all depending upon what you want to do first.

To Open the Editor to Create a New Web Page

From the Browser window, choose **F**ile I **N**ew Document I **B**lank. The Editor opens a new, blank document (and minimizes the Browser on the taskbar), as shown in Figure 3.3. You may start adding text or name and save the document, as described later in this chapter.

Note that when you use this procedure, it does not matter what the Browser shows before you begin (a blank page, a local document, or a page online). After the Editor opens, the Browser stays open, minimized in the taskbar.

To Use the Edit Button

The Edit button in the Browser's toolbar has a special action. It opens the Editor to edit the document that you were viewing in the Browser and closes the Browser behind it.

The Edit button's principle use is to download to your PC and edit a remote Web document—a template file or other remote page (see "Working with Templates" later in this chapter), or a page created by the Page Wizard. (See Chapter 2, "Making the Page Wizard Do the Work.") When viewing a remote document in the Browser, clicking Edit opens the Editor, which immediately prompts you to save the remote document locally before editing it.

If no document appears in the Browser, clicking Edit opens the Editor with a blank document, so you can compose a new page. Finally, if you're viewing a local document (one already stored on your PC) in the Browser, clicking Edit opens the same file in the Editor.

Figure 3.3.
Opening the Editor to create a new document.

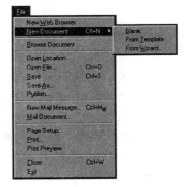

To Open an HTML File on Disk

1. From the browser, choose **F**ile I Open File in **E**ditor. A standard Windows 95 Open dialog opens.

   Note that when you use this procedure, it does not matter what the browser shows before you begin (a blank page, a local document, or a remote document). After the Editor opens, the Browser is minimized on the taskbar.

2. Enter the path and filename, or browse to the file.

Alternatively, you can open an existing file in the Browser first and then edit it by clicking the Edit button. To open a local document in the Browser, choose **F**ile I Open File in **B**rowser. (See Figure 3.4.) Choose the file from the Open dialog and then click the Edit button in the Browser.

You can open Navigator from an HTML file icon only if Navigator is configured as your default browser in Windows 95's File Types registry.

Finally, you can locate the file's icon (or a shortcut to the file) in Windows and then do any of the following to open the file in the Browser. (Note that the Browser can be open or closed when you do any of the following; if closed, it will open automatically.)

❏ Double-click the icon.

❏ Right-click the icon and choose Open from the context menu.

❏ Drag the icon and drop it on the Netscape Navigator Gold icon or on a shortcut to Gold.

Whichever way you choose, the file opens within the Browser (if it is not already open). You can then click the Edit button to edit the file and close the Browser.

Figure 3.4.
Opening the Editor to edit an existing document.

To View a File in Progress in the Browser

As you'll discover throughout this book, the Editor is *mostly* WYSIWYG; that is, in most cases your page will look the same whether viewed through the Editor or the Browser. However, there are a number of page elements that do not appear in the Editor as they would in the Browser—for example, tables and JavaScript routines. To see the proper effects of these page elements, you must switch from the Editor to the Browser to see the way the page will appear to visitors (or to visitors using Netscape, at any rate).

To browse the document you're editing, click the View in Browser button on the Editor's toolbar. The file opens in the Browser. If, before you click View in Browser, the Browser is already open but displays a different file, a new Browser window opens to display the file being edited. If the open Browser already shows the file being edited (as it would if you had clicked View in Browser earlier in your editing session), that window opens.

To return to your editing session after viewing the document in the Browser, click the Edit button.

To Save a File

NOTE: When you save a file, you give it a name. And names can be tricky when it comes time to publish a Web document.

In general, as long as you use an extension of .HTM or .HTML, you can give your page files any name you like. However, the filename must conform to the system the server uses. For example, if the Web server on which you will publish your document (see Chapter 15, "Publishing Web Documents") is a DOS server, your filenames must conform to DOS's 8.3 filename rule: a name of no more than eight characters and an extension of no more than three (.HTM, not .HTML).

Also, when a page is the "top" page of a multipage Web presentation, standard practice is to name it INDEX.HTML. Some servers are configured to open the file INDEX.HTM automatically when a visitor specifies a directory but not a specific file. However, this only works if you have your own directory on the server. Usually, you will. But if you share a directory with others, odds are you won't be the first to post a file called INDEX.HTML, so the server won't accept your document.

The bottom line: Choose your server and find out about its naming guidelines, before settling on final names for your HTML files.

1. From the Editor window, click the Save button (the disk) or choose **F**ile | **S**ave. A standard Windows 95 Save dialog opens.

2. Select a folder if you wish (the default folder is the Program folder within the folder in which you installed Gold) and type a name for your file. You do not need to enter an extension; an extension of .HTM is added automatically.

3. Click OK.

About Document Properties

Everything you would see in a page on the Web (and some things you don't see, like script code), you enter directly into the Editor's document window. But one other standard part of an HTML file—the document title—is entered separately in the Document Properties dialog, along with other descriptive information about the page.

The title entered in Document Properties does not appear on the page itself but in windowing browsers (like most for Windows, Macintosh, and X-Window systems); the title appears in the title bar of the window in which the page is displayed.

A title is not required (although if you don't supply one, the Editor automatically uses the page's filename as its title). It's important that you enter a title, however, because the title describes your page to the Web. For example, when a visitor to your page creates a bookmark for it in his or her browser, the title typically becomes the name of the bookmark. Also, Web directories and crawlers (programs that build Web directories by searching the Web and cataloging its contents) use the title as the primary reference for what the page is about.

Don't confuse the title with the level 1 heading that typically tops your page and serves as its apparent title. Remember, by the time a visitor sees that top-level heading, he or she has already arrived at your page and is presumably already interested in its subject. So that top heading can be more creative than the document title, or even subtle. But the true title must be descriptive, not clever.

An effective true title should accurately describe the contents or purpose of your page. It should also be fairly short, no more than six to eight words, and its most descriptive words should appear first. Remember, in a bookmark list or Web directory, there's often room for only the first few words of a title, so your title needs to be short and those first few words must be meaningful.

Here are some good titles:

> Sammy's Raquetball Directory
>
> The Video Store Online
>
> All About Trout Fishing
>
> Laura Lemay's Awesome Home Page
>
> New Jersey Events for July

In the good examples, notice that the most specific, important descriptor appears within the first three words: Raquetball, Video, Trout, Laura Lemay, New Jersey Events. Notice also that the fewest possible words are used to nail down the page. In the first example, we learn in three words that this page is a directory of Raquetball-related information and that it's Sammy's directory (to distinguish it from any other Raquetball directories). What more do we need to know?

Here, for comparison, are some lousy titles:

> My Homepage
>
> Things to Do
>
> Schedule of Events
>
> A Catalog of Links and Documents Provided as a Public Service for Persons Researching African Population Trends

In the first three crummy examples above, the titles are nondescriptive; they contain nothing about the specific contents of the page. The last example, although containing some useful information at the end, would be trimmed down to its first four or five words in a bookmark list, and those first words say nothing.

Sharing the Document Properties with the title are other descriptive entries that serve mostly to describe your page to crawlers and Web searches. Unlike the title, the other entries are optional and none are as important as the title. But if you supply these items and word them carefully, you'll increase your chances of drawing visitors interested in what you have to say. In other words, when a potential visitor conducts a Web search using any search term that might relate to the topic of your page, the visitor is much more likely to hit on your page if you've used a good, descriptive classification, description, and keywords.

Entering Document Properties

1. In the Editor, open or create the file for which you are entering Document Properties.

2. Choose **P**roperties I **D**ocument. A sheet like the one in Figure 3.5 appears.

Figure 3.5.
Entering document properties.

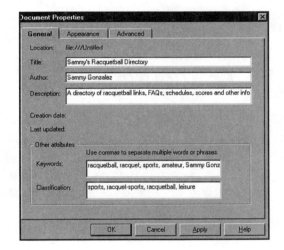

3. In the General tab, enter a title in the Title box, being careful to capitalize and spell it exactly as you want it to appear in a title bar or bookmark list. Do not attempt to use any character formatting, such as bold, italic or super-script. No character formatting is possible within the text-entry areas in the Document Properties dialog, and even if it were, it would not show up anywhere titles typically appear. Titles are functional, not fancy.

4. Enter your name as author. You can enter whatever you feel is most descriptive of you as an author: your name and title, your company name, or even your e-mail address.

5. Fill in any of the remaining fields you wish (all are optional) that are used by various Web directories and search engines as matches for categories or search terms, or to describe your document in the list of search hits.

Description—A brief description of your document. Keep it short, and describe your document simply and accurately. Some Web search

In Editor Preferences, you can enter a default author to show up in Document Properties automatically for every new page. See the section titled "Configuring General Editor Preferences" later in this chapter.

engines, such as InfoSeek, display the Description—along with the title and URL of your page—in the list of search hits it displays.

Keywords—A list of words (separated by commas) descriptive of, or related to, the subject of your page. In the example shown in Figure 3.4, a surfer running a Web search and using as a search term any of the words listed in Keywords should come up with your page in the resulting hit list.

Classification—A list of words (separated by commas) that generally describe the subject of your page. Classification is similar to keywords, except it's used by different search engines and the words used for classification should be words that describe the overall subject of your page, whereas keywords might pertain to only one aspect or section of the Web document.

6. Click OK.

Configuring General Editor Preferences

Using the General Editor Preferences (see Figure 3.6), you can define a default author name for all new documents to save yourself the trouble of typing your author name each time you create a page. (See "Document Properties" earlier in this chapter.) You can also use the General Editor Preferences to set up default applications for editing HTML files (to use HTML tags for which the Editor offers no tools) and image files, and you can change Gold's default template page to any other template file—or directory of template files—you wish.

To edit General Editor Preferences:

1. In the Browser or the Editor (it doesn't matter which), choose **O**ptions I **E**ditor Preferences.

2. Click the General tab (if it is not already selected). A dialog opens like the one in Figure 3.6.

3. Enter a default author name. The name you enter here will be filled in automatically in the Document Properties for each new document you create. For any document, you can override this default selection in the Document Properties. (See the section titled "About Document Properties" earlier in this chapter.)

NOTE: The CD-ROM includes HTML editors, an image editor, and templates—all of which you can point to in the Editor Preferences. See Appendix C, "What's on the CD?"

For more about HTML source editors, see Chapter 9. For more about image editors, see Chapter 6.

4. Enter the full path and filename of the External editors you wish to use:

❏ Your HTML source editor can be any ordinary text editor, one capable of editing and saving files in flat ASCII form, or plain text. The program you specify will open automatically when you choose **V**iew I Edit Document **S**ource in the Editor.

❏ Your image editor should be one that can create, edit, and/or save GIF and/or JPG (JPEG) image files. The program you specify will open automatically when you double-click an image in a page you are editing.

After changing the location of the template page, you can restore the default (Netscape's templates page) at any time by clicking Restore default.

5. Enter the URL of the page containing the template file you want to open when you choose **F**ile I **N**ew Document I From **T**emplate. (See the section titled "Working with Templates," later in this chapter.)

6. Click OK to save your General Editor Preferences.

Figure 3.6.
Configuring Editor Preferences.

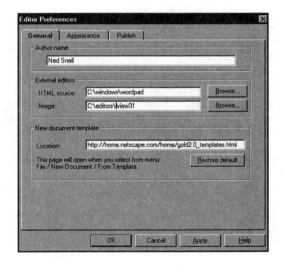

Besides General, there are two other tabs in the Editor Preferences: Appearance is covered in Chapter 4, and Publish is covered in Chapter 15.

Working with the Editor's Toolbars

All functions of the Editor are available from the menubar. Many of the most frequently used functions are also available from one of three toolbars.

Observe in Figure 3.7 that there are three lines of buttons atop the editing window. Each line of buttons is actually a separate toolbar, though the three bars create the impression of a single toolbar when positioned together.

Each individual button on the toolbar is discussed in the chapter covering the action it performs.

The toolbar is as follows:

File/Edit: Contains tools for creating, opening, and saving files; cut, copy, and paste; printing; searching for text; and publishing your page.

Paragraph Properties: Contains tools for determining whether a paragraph is a heading, normal text, and so on; plus tools for making bulleted and numbered lists; and indenting and aligning text.

Character Properties: Contains tools for modifying the appearance of text (font size, superscript/subscript, bold, italic, and so on), plus tools for inserting links, targets, images, and horizontal lines. This toolbar also contains a button for opening a properties dialog for any object in a page—text, image, or link.

Showing/Hiding Toolbars

It's handy to have all the toolbars showing while editing a page. But when they all show, they cut into the size of the edit window, so you can see less of the page you're working on.

You can selectively hide or show any toolbar by choosing **O**ptions and then clicking any of the Show...toolbar choices listed on the **O**ptions menu. (See Figure 3.7.) If the listed toolbar has a checkmark next to it, clicking it removes the checkmark and hides the toolbar. If the listed toolbar has no checkmark next to it, clicking it adds a checkmark and shows the toolbar.

Figure 3.7.
*Showing/hiding
toolbars.*

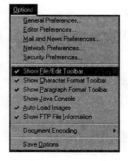

Moving Toolbars

You can drag any toolbar from its home above the edit window to any location on the page. When you drag a toolbar from the toolbar area, it becomes a floating tool palette, as shown in Figure 3.8.

Toolbar settings are file-specific. If you move a toolbar or change show/hide options and then save the document, those settings return whenever you open that document.

To restore a floating palette to the toolbar area, drag it to the toolbar area until the thick outline used to represent the dragged toolbar turns into a thin line; the thin line indicates that the toolbar will snap back into the toolbar area when dropped.

By dragging toolbars around the toolbar area and dropping them at different "snap" locations, you can also change the order in which they appear in the toolbar area.

Figure 3.8.
Moving toolbars.

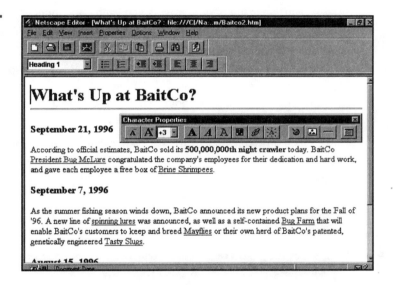

Working with Templates

If Web pages were waffles, templates would be Bisquick. (By extension, I suppose, the Page Wizard is Eggo—but that's another chapter.) Head starts to Web pages, templates offer a quicker and easier way to build documents than starting from scratch, but allow you greater flexibility in the design of your document than is possible with the Page Wizard. Templates are especially valuable when you'll need to create a rather complicated page—perhaps one that you feel exceeds your own authoring skills—and aren't quite sure how to approach it.

NOTE: You can find all of the template files used in examples in this chapter in the Netscape Templates page at

`http://home.netscape.com/home/gold2.0_templates.html`

What's a Template?

A template is simply an HTML file filled mostly with meaningless, boilerplate content instead of the real thing. The pre-fab file has already been organized and formatted with paragraph properties, horizontal rules, and any other bells and whistles, and already includes the basic elements of a Web page: title, headings, body, signature, appropriate links, and so on. (If you don't recognize these parts of a page, see Chapter 1, "Planning Your Page.")

By replacing the boilerplate content with your own content, you can quickly create an attractive, effective Web page without fussing over its organization or formatting. Of course, if you decide you want to change the formatting or organization of a page created from a template, you can, just as you can edit any HTML file in the Editor.

Figure 3.9 shows a template for a human resources department page (HR2.HTML) from the Netscape Templates page. Figure 3.10 shows a page I created by replacing PERS1.HTML's text with my own. Compare the figures and observe that the only difference between the two is content. Observe how I was able to take advantage of the template's organization, fancy horizontal lines, and character formatting while still making it my own.

Figure 3.9.

An unedited template viewed in the browser window.

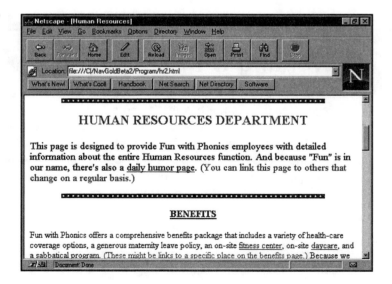

Figure 3.10.

The template edited into a real page with the addition of real content.

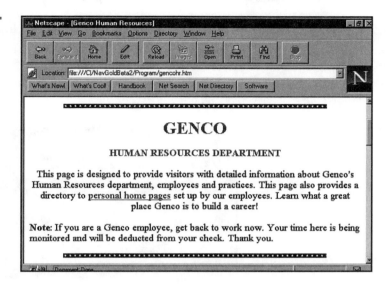

NOTE: The boilerplate content you'll see in templates can take either of two forms. Sometimes, as in Figure 3.9, it represents content; that is, the phony content in the template looks and seems real, but isn't. This approach gives you a clear model to follow in developing your own content. All of the Netscape templates use this approach.

In other templates, descriptions are used where content should go. Set in italics and surrounded by carats (< >), these built-in instructions offer specific suggestions and other guidance to help you determine what type of content to use, and how to present it.

Often, this guidance is based on accepted principles of effective Web design or on emerging traditions for how pages with certain purposes—personal pages, business announcements, and so on—should be organized. Thus, templates not only save beginning authors time but also help ensure that their work conforms to accepted standards and principles for style and content.

Checking Preferences

Two tabs in the Editor Preferences dialog have important effects on your use of templates. To open the Editor Preferences dialog, choose **O**ptions | Editor Preferences. (You can do this from within the Browser or the Editor; it doesn't matter which.)

General Tab

On the General tab (see Figure 3.11) under New document template, you can enter the URL of a template (or directory of templates). The URL entered here will be accessed automatically when you choose **F**ile | **N**ew Document | From **T**emplate to create a new Web document.

Figure 3.11.
The Editor Preferences, General tab.

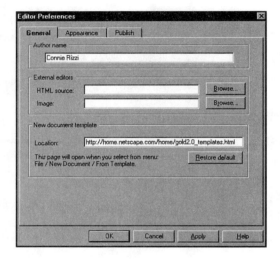

The default URL is

```
http://home.netscape.com/home/gold3.0_templates.html
```

This URL points to Netscape's templates page (see Figure 3.13, later in this chapter), set up specifically to assist authors using Gold. If you leave this default in place, choosing **F**ile | **N**ew Document | From **T**emplate connects to Netscape's directory of templates, from which you can then select the one that most closely matches the page you want to create.

Alternatively, you can change the New document template entry to

❏ The URL of a different directory of templates.

❏ The URL of a specific template page. This may be useful if you compose many similar documents, and often use the same template as your starting point.

❏ A local path and filename (for example, `c:\templates\templates.htm`) for a template file or template directory on your hard disk.

Publish Tab

The settings on the Publish tab (see Figure 3.12) pertain mainly to the publishing of your document and are therefore covered in greater detail in Chapter 15, "Publishing

Web Documents." But before accessing any template files online, you should make sure that the checkbox for Keep images with document is checked. (It's checked by default, so unless you've unchecked it previously, the Publish tab is already properly configured for template access.)

A checkmark next to Keep images with document instructs the editor to save the images in a page along with the HTML file when you save a page (a template or any other page) you've accessed online. This ensures that you'll have copies of any images on your PC, if you choose to keep any of the template's image files in your document. (The image files are saved in the same directory you save the HTML file in.) This same checkmark also ensures that when you send your document to a server to publish it, the images tag along.

Figure 3.12.
The Editor Preferences, Publish tab.

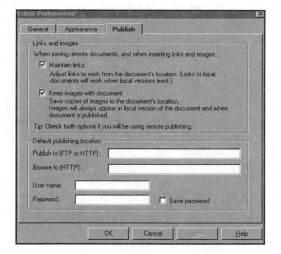

Where to Find Templates

The CD-ROM contains a collection of templates (see Appendix C). Also, many online authoring resources contain templates. (See Chapter 17.)

Netscape's default template page contains a well-varied set of templates, with most of the major page-purposes represented somewhere among them. (See Figure 3.13.) But you can find templates lots of places.

But the set of templates set up by Netscape offers some specific advantages. The templates are specifically designed for use with Netscape Gold and feature such built-in enhancements as

❏ The use of Netscape extensions such as text centering, custom colors, backgrounds, and more. (Extensions have both benefits and drawbacks; see Chapter 1, "Planning Your Page.")

❏ Handy JavaScript routines for common requirements, such as displaying the current date and time on a Web page.

❏ The Netscape Now! button, a GIF graphic linked to Netscape's FTP servers so that visitors to your page can easily download Netscape Navigator, install it, and then revisit your page to view your extension-based formatting and run your JavaScript routines. (If you don't want your page to serve as free advertising for Netscape, you can easily delete the Netscape Now! button as described later in this chapter.)

Note that a copy of any template you find online must be saved to your hard disk (by the Editor, not the browser) before you can edit it in Gold. When a template is already stored on your hard disk, you can simply open it in the Editor.

Of course, you can treat any HTML file as a template. That includes a page you initially created with the Page Wizard, any page on the Web, or any HTML document stored on your hard disk (including those that are cached from your Web sessions, although these will have graphics omitted). Simply use the Editor to replace the existing content of the page with your own content (as described throughout this chapter), leaving intact the page's organization and any formatting or links you wish.

NOTE: Templates are specifically designed to be copied and adapted by Web authors and are therefore copyright-free. You'll typically change most of the content of a template, but you're free to leave any content intact, if you so desire.

Web pages that are not templates, however, might have copyrighted content. If you choose to edit and adapt a Web page (other than one specifically offered as a template) for use as your own, you should replace all content on that page with your own, original content or content you know to be copyright-free.

How Do I Choose the Right Template?

Most templates are designed to match popular approaches to certain types of Web pages. For example, the Netscape Templates page groups templates according to type or purpose, as shown in Figure 3.13.

Before beginning to work with a specific template, open and examine a few different choices that seem like likely candidates. If the available templates seem too far removed from what you want to accomplish, you might be better off finding and using as a template a page that more closely matches what you want to achieve. Your goal is to save yourself time and trouble by choosing a template that requires as little reworking as possible.

Figure 3.13.
The Netscape Templates page, showing links to template files.

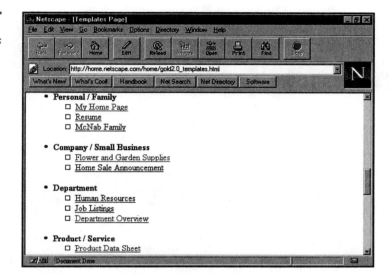

Be aware, however, that every aspect of a template is editable. If you choose a template that requires your content, and some reformatting and/or reorganization, you might still save time and trouble by using it rather than starting with a blank page. By the time they finish adapting a template into their own page, some people end up making so many alterations that the finished document bears no resemblance to the template that spawned it. That doesn't mean the template didn't help; it gave the author a place to start, something to fiddle with, raw material. And often that's exactly what an author needs to stoke the creative fires.

Opening and Saving a Template

Templates found online must be saved by the Editor before you can use them. Templates already on your hard disk can be opened and used immediately.

To Navigate Directly to the Default Template Page

1. From the Browser, choose **F**ile | **N**ew Document | From **T**emplate. Netscape connects to the default templates page, as defined in the General tab of the Editor Preferences dialog. (See Checking Preferences earlier in this chapter.)

2. Choose and open a template from the list, as described in the next section.

To Open a Template Stored on the Web

1. In the Browser window, point to the template file.

2. The two checkboxes in the dialog shown in Figure 3.14 simply confirm entries in the Editor Preferences. (See Chapter 15, "Publishing Web Documents.") Make sure both boxes are checked and click Save. A message appears like the one shown in Figure 3.15.

3. The Hint shown in Figure 3.15 simply reminds you that you shouldn't use copyrighted materials you save from the Web. Template files, by definition, are copyright-free—but Netscape doesn't know you're saving a template. Click OK. A standard Windows 95 Save File dialog appears.

To prevent the Copyright warning shown in Figure 3.15 from appearing in the future, click the checkbox next to Don't display this message again.

Figure 3.14.
Netscape making sure your Publish settings are correct before saving the template page.

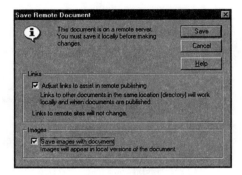

Figure 3.15.
Netscape warning you not to violate copyrights.

4. Enter a new name for the file, but do not change the file extension (.HTML or .HTM).

5. Click OK. You can now edit the file as described in the upcoming sections of this chapter and apply any of the techniques described in the remaining chapters of this book. When finished editing, click the Save button (the disk) or choose File | Save.

NOTE: The first two steps above are the recommended procedure for acquiring a template because they give you a chance to examine it in the browser window before choosing to edit it.

If you don't need to see the template before choosing to edit it, right-click a link that points to the template file (see Figure 3.13) and then choose Open link in Editor from the context menu, as shown in Figure 3.16. Complete the procedure above, beginning with step 3.

Figure 3.16.

A context menu for a link pointing to a template file.

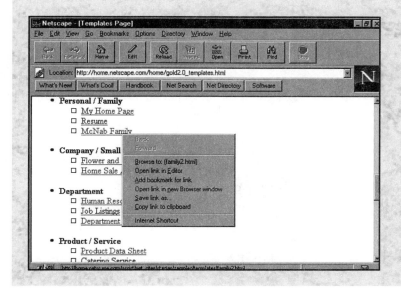

Editing a Template

Once a template has been saved on your hard disk, you can edit, expand, reformat, or delete any part or portion of it. In some cases, you might find that you needn't change something; if it already says what you want it to say, leave it alone. (An example is when templates are copyright-free.) Most of the text you'll see, however, must be replaced or deleted. Also, when you replace descriptive text (in templates that use it), you'll usually want to get rid of the italic character formatting.

You'll learn in detail how to edit Web pages in upcoming chapters. But just to get you started (templates, after all, are for those who want to work quickly), here's a few quick editing techniques:

❑ To replace an entire paragraph, highlight the paragraph from beginning to end by moving the mouse pointer to the left of the paragraph and double-clicking. Then type your new content. The paragraph is instantly deleted and replaced with whatever you type. You new paragraph takes on the same paragraph properties as the one you've replaced.

❑ To replace only a portion of a paragraph, highlight the portion you want to replace (click and hold at the start of the selection, drag to the end and release) and then type your content. The highlighted section is deleted and replaced with what you type.

❑ To delete an image, click it once and press Del.

When editing one of Netscape's templates (see Figure 3.11), your first task it to edit the instructions block at the top of the page. Just click it once and press Del.

NOTE: The only trick to editing a template is to change the content without screwing up the existing formatting. To that end, it's helpful to imagine that, between each paragraph, there are hidden formatting instructions that must not be lost or corrupted during editing. (That's true, actually; see Chapter 9, "Editing HTML Source Code.")

To make sure you don't accidentally alter the formatting, avoid doing anything that would delete the space between paragraphs.

❑ When the edit cursor appears at the very beginning of a block of text, do not press Backspace.

❑ When the edit cursor appears at the very end of a block of text, do not press Del.

❑ If you do change the properties inadvertently, choose **E**dit | **U**ndo. If that doesn't do it, just click anywhere within the paragraph and choose **P**roperties | **P**aragraph, and then choose appropriate paragraph properties from the submenu. (See Chapter 4, "Composing, Editing, and Formatting Text.")

Workshop Wrap-Up

The Navigator Gold Editor does a lot—too much, in fact, for this chapter to cover all of it. (The rest is covered in upcoming chapters.)

The Editor provides simple dialogs and menus for applying properties to paragraphs—the most important activity in building a Web page. When you apply properties to a paragraph, you're actually surrounding the paragraph with the appropriate HTML tags in the underlying HTML source file. The menus and dialogs save you the trouble of remembering what all the tags are, and apply those tags conveniently and accurately. The Editor also supplies a straightforward, simple text-editing environment to make composing your Web document as painless as applying its properties.

But for all that it is, there's one thing the Editor is not: smart. It can't tell you whether the content you've created is well organized, well presented, well written, or even spelled correctly. And while it applies HTML tags to your document dutifully, it cannot tell you whether you've selected the most effective properties for the paragraph at hand.

Thus, the Editor is a replacement only for time and labor, not for judgment. To author an effective Web document, you must acquire a sense of Web aesthetics. You'll pick up much of this sense as you work through this book. But you must also study other pages you see online, and mentally catalog the design aspects and content approaches that sing to you—and those that annoy, bore, or baffle you, as well.

The better you understand what makes Web denizens hit on a site and stay there, the more effectively you'll apply Netscape Gold and the techniques in this book.

Next Steps

Now…

- ❏ To stimulate your thinking about how your page should look and what's involved in making it look that way, see Chapter 8, "Real-Life Examples I."
- ❏ To compose and edit the text for your page or learn how to edit the text in a template, see Chapter 4, "Composing, Editing, and Formatting Text."
- ❏ To add links to your page or to build a multipage Web presentation, see Chapter 5, "Linking Everywhere, Anywhere."
- ❏ To add pictures and rules, see Chapter 6, "Working with Graphics."
- ❏ To add sound and video, see Chapter 7, "Embedding Multimedia."
- ❏ To learn how to apply HTML features not offered by the Editor, see Chapter 9, "Editing HTML Source Code."

Q&A

Q: If text I want to add to my page already exists in a word processing (or plain text) file, how can I get it into the Editor without retyping it?

A: Windows copy and paste (or cut and paste)—described in Chapter 4, "Composing, Editing and Formatting Text," and Chapter 6, "Working with Graphics"—is the most effective way to copy text or pictures from any Windows document into the Editor, because copy and paste is quick and easy, and it prevents compatibility problems by stripping the text of any extraneous formatting not supported in the Editor. But there are other options.

You'll find a few handy conversion utilities on the CD-ROM (see Appendix C). And in Chapter 17, you'll find URLs leading to conversion utilities available online.

You can pick up utilities (often for free) that can convert files in various word processing or other formats into HTML, often preserving some of the page formatting. For example, the conversion program may correctly identify short, bold lines as headings and make them headings in the file. Once you've run a file through a converter to make it an HTML file, you can open it in the Gold Editor, and re-tool it however you wish.

Among the available converters, you'll see several that specialize in specific word processing formats. For example, Microsoft offers a free add-in to Word, called Internet Assistant, that allows you to save (among other things) any Word document in HTML format, straight from the regular Save dialog. After downloading and installing Internet Assistant, you can convert any Word document to HTML simply by opening it in Word and saving it as an HTML file. You can then open it in the Gold Editor. Similar utilities are available for WordPerfect and other applications.

Q: What if I see a page on the Web I can adapt, as you suggest, and there's no mention of copyright anywhere on it? Can I use its content (like its pictures) as well as its format?

A: Technically, if it's someone's original work, it's copyrighted—although that copyright is nearly unenforceable in the absence of a copyright notice. You could probably get away with using such a page. Heck, the way things are on the Web now, you could probably get away with using a copyrighted page. But the issue isn't really enforcement or legality—it's ethics. If a page or other online content is not specifically offered for public use, leave it alone. Roll your own.

Q: Can I make my own templates?

A: Sure. In fact, doing so can save you a lot of time if you create many similar documents. Just build a page containing the elements that you tend to reuse from project to project. You can also set up your custom-built template as your default template page (see the section titled "Checking Preferences" in this chapter), so that it opens automatically when you choose **F**ile | **N**ew Document | From **T**emplate.

FOUR

Composing, Editing, and Formatting Text

Somebody once said to me, "Writing isn't so tough: All you have to do is find a quiet spot, sit down, and open a vein."

How true. But to the extent that writing a Web page can be made less immediately painful and life-threatening, the Editor does just that.

When you work with text in the Editor, your document looks (for the most part) just the way it will look to most visitors on the Web. That's a powerful convenience; without it, Web authors have had to guess about the appearance of the page while fiddling with a page full of HTML code. To check their work, they had to open the file in a browser and then go back to the HTML to make adjustments. With the Gold Editor, it all happens in one window, live and in color.

Perhaps more importantly, the Editor saves time and effort. You would have to type the content of your page or copy it from another source, whether you used the Editor or created an HTML file the traditional way. However, typing a set of HTML tags to specify the properties of a single item in an HTML file usually requires at least 10 keystrokes, whereas the same operation in the Editor takes choosing one item from a menu. Text entry and editing is made still more

In this chapter, you

❏ Learn the basics of entering, editing and formatting the text elements of a Web page

❏ Save time and typing with cut and paste, copy and other text-entry conveniences

❏ Edit and format the text of a page

❏ Check your work to determine how your page will appear to others on the Web, especially those using browsers other than Netscape Navigator

❏ Discover tips for proper and effective page design

Tasks in this chapter:

❏ Entering Paragraphs and Assigning Properties

❏ Formatting Lists

❏ Inserting Extra Space

❏ Checking Your Work

❏ Printing Your Document

❏ Editing Your Web Document

convenient by a complete selection of toolbar buttons, and by the Editor's support for Windows 95 conventions such as cut and paste, drag and drop, and context menus.

About Paragraphs and Their Properties

Other than link names, the Editor calls each discrete chunk of text—all of the text between carriage returns—a *paragraph*, whether it's a heading, one line of a list, or just a bunch of words. That might confuse some authoring veterans because in HTML, *paragraph* generally describes a normal block of text as opposed to a heading or other type of text element—a paragraph in the classic sense. But to get along with software, one must forgive its idiosyncrasies. So in Gold's Editor, any word, line, or block of text standing on its own is a paragraph. Get used to it.

In addition to paragraph properties, there are character properties that control whether text is bold, italic, and so on (covered later in this chapter), and there are link properties that manage the treatment of links. (See Chapter 5.)

What makes a particular paragraph a heading or something else are the *properties* with which you endow the paragraph. Assigning properties to a paragraph is no different than assigning a style in a word processor, and usually it's just as easy. In a nutshell, you type a line or block of text and then assign properties to that paragraph to identify it as a heading, text paragraph, or whatever. *Voila.*

Note that paragraph properties apply only to entire paragraphs, which are text blocks separated by carriage returns just as they are in a word-processing document. For example, you cannot format two words in the middle of a paragraph as an address and the rest of the paragraph as a heading. Either the whole paragraph is one thing or the whole paragraph is something else.

What Each Paragraph Property Does

There are two parts to paragraph properties: paragraph styles and optional, additional styles, or *attributes*, within each style. You'll learn how the styles and attributes work together later in this chapter.

The basic paragraph properties are described below and also shown (as they appear in Netscape) in Figures 4.1 and 4.2.

Normal

Use `Normal` for general-purpose text—like what you're reading right now. Most browsers display Normal paragraphs in a plain font with no special emphasis (such as bold or a special color). Normal is the *meat and potatoes* of your Web page.

Headings

Use headings the way you see them used in this book: to divide and label the logical sections of the page or document. There are six levels of headings, ranging in relative importance from 1 (most important or prominent) to 6 (least important or prominent).

Because the level-1 heading is the most prominent, it is often reserved for the apparent title of your page—one that appears within the page itself (not to be confused with the document title entered in Document Properties). See Chapter 3.

In most browsers, a level-1 heading is displayed as the biggest, boldest text on the page. Level-2 headings are smaller and/or not bold, or are de-emphasized in some other way. Level 3 gets less emphasis than 2 but more than 4, and so on. (Six levels would require a lot of variation, and in some browsers, the difference between headings only one level apart is barely distinguishable, as you can see in Figure 4.5). Text-based browsers (see Chapter 1, "Planning Your Page"), which can't display varying font sizes, use bold, underline, or even numbers to show the varying heading levels.

You can use whatever heading levels you want, but in general, obey the numbers. Subheadings within a section should be of a level that's a higher number than the heading for the section. For example, a section that begins with a level-2 heading may have subheadings within it that are level 3, and the subsections under the level 3 heads may have sub-subsections with level 4 heads.

Address

Use Address for creating an *address block,* a line or many lines identifying someone and usually listing an e-mail address and/or snail mail address or other contact information.

See Chapter 5 to learn how to create a signature for the bottom of your page.

The Address property is used most often for the signature at the bottom of the page, but it can be used to give any address information on your page a unique style that sets it apart from other text. Navigator, for example, displays address blocks in italics; address blocks are the only page element automatically italicized by Navigator.

NOTE: Assigning the Address property to an e-mail address on your page does not, by itself, make the address a mailto link that a visitor could click to send e-mail. However, an e-mail address appearing in the Address property can be a mailto link—You just have to make it one.

To learn how to create a mailto link, see Chapter 5, "Linking Everywhere, Anywhere."

Formatted

The Formatted property applies an HTML style called *preformatted.*

Formatted might seem like a misnomer, because text assigned the Formatted property is less formatted by the browser than any other kind. What formatted means in this context is that you have already lined up and spaced the text in a particular way, and you want browsers to leave that formatting alone.

Figure 4.1.

Paragraphs and their properties: headings, normal text, and an address.

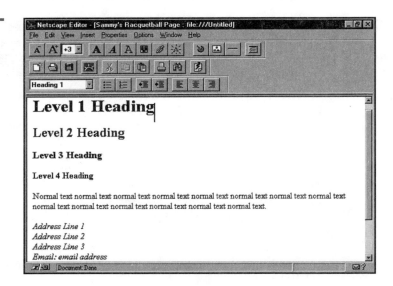

Typically, browsers capable of displaying proportionally spaced fonts (such as TrueType's Arial, or even the snappy font you're reading now) use those fonts for most text, because it looks better than typewriter-style monospaced fonts (such as Courier New). Also, browsers ignore tabs, extra spaces, and blank lines (extra carriage returns) in HTML files. (To create blank lines between paragraphs and extra spaces within paragraphs, you must apply special HTML tags; see the section titled "About Spacing" later in this chapter.)

Suppose you wanted to show a text chart or table on your page, or words arranged in a certain way. Tabs are *verboten*, so you'd need to use spaces and a monospaced font to make the words line up right. But if browsers were permitted to do their regular thing with that text, they'd strip out the extra spaces, display the text in a proportional font, and generally screw up your lovely lining-up job.

You can use the `Formatted` property to create the effect of tables in your document, but you can also create real tables that look much better. See Chapter 10.

For example, observe the careful alignment of columns and the use of a monospaced font in the simple table shown in Figure 4.3. Now look at Figure 4.2, below. Figure 4.2 shows the exact same table as the one in Figure 4.3. The only difference is that the table in Figure 4.3 uses the `Formatted` property, whereas in Figure 4.2 the same paragraph has been assigned the `Normal` property. As it must with a normal paragraph, the browser has wiped out any extra spaces and presented the table in a handsome proportional typeface.

Figure 4.2.
The same table shown in Figure 4.3 but assigned the Normal *property rather than the* Formatted *property.*

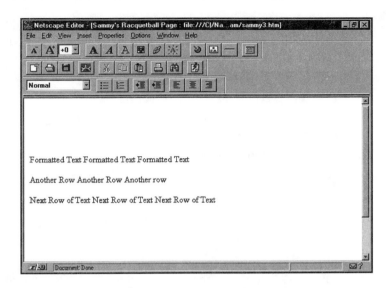

Figure 4.3.
Paragraphs and their properties, The Sequel: formatted text, lists, description titles, and description text.

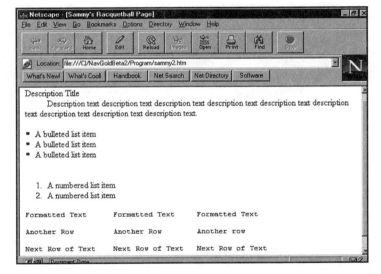

List Item

The List Item property formats lists on your page: bulleted lists, numbered lists, and other types. Each item in a list is a separate paragraph. To build a list, type each item on a separate line (really, a separate paragraph) and assign the List Item property to all the lines.

The Editor gives you a wide range of ways to format lists, including numbered lists with different numbering schemes, bulleted lists with different bullet types, nested lists, and more. See the section titled "Working with Lists" later in this chapter.

Description Title, Description Text

The description properties apply HTML styles called *Definition Term* and *Definition Definition*. The HTML names come from the fact that this property is a great way to build the effect of on-screen glossary entries. Just as in a glossary or dictionary entry, each description (or definition) is made up of two paragraphs: A Description Title, such as the word or phrase being defined, and Description Text, the definition. In Netscape, the Description Text is indented underneath the description title. Other browsers use similar techniques to put the title and text together nicely, so it's clear that they go together as a set.

Although glossary entries are an obvious application for the description properties, you can use Description any time you need to associate a word or phrase with a longer description or definition.

NOTE: You can apply paragraph properties in whatever way suits you. (There are no HTML police—at least not yet....) But it's good practice to think of these properties as a way to determine the role a paragraph plays in your page, *not* its appearance.

For example, there's no technical reason you can't write a lengthy paragraph and then make it a heading, rather than normal text, to make it stand out on the page. But different browsers use different methods to make a heading look like a heading; some make headings big and bold and others underline, and some even number headings according to their levels. Also, some Web search engines catalog pages according to heading contents, since headings generally contain subject information. Putting ordinary paragraph information into a heading might generate some screwy hits on your page from Web searches.

Use properties conservatively, according to their designated roles. Save your artistry for character formatting, images, backgrounds, and other ways you can spice up a page.

Entering Paragraphs and Assigning Properties

You can add text to a page and assign properties to that text in several different ways. All are described below.

When composing your document, do not use tabs, extra carriage returns, or spaces to control the spacing between and within paragraphs. To control spacing, see the section titled "About Spacing" later in this chapter.

To Enter Paragraphs by Typing

When you create a new document, the edit cursor appears automatically at the very top of the document. Type away. To correct mistakes and make changes as you go, use the backspace, Del, and Ins keys just as you would in any Windows document. To end a paragraph and start a new paragraph, press Enter.

By default, your paragraphs are all are set as normal text (unless you select a different paragraph property before you begin typing a paragraph). You can change them to other paragraph properties at any time, as described in the section titled "To Assign Paragraph Properties" later in this chapter.

To Enter Text with Copy and Paste

You can copy text from the Web and paste it into your document. In the Browser, select the text, then choose **E**dit I **C**opy. Switch to the Editor and click the Paste button. (Do not do this with copyrighted text if you intend to publish the resulting page.)

This procedure describes how to copy text from another document in Windows—such as a word processing file and spreadsheet file—into the editor so it can be incorporated in your Web page. This is a convenient way to use pre-existing text, such as your resume or a description of your business, in your Web page without retyping it.

1. Open the application normally used to edit or display the document and open the document.

2. Highlight the desired text. (To copy an entire document into your Web page, choose **E**dit I Select All, in the application used to open the document.)

3. Press Ctrl+Ins to copy the selection to the Windows clipboard. (Alternatively, you can click the Copy button on the toolbar or choose **E**dit I **C**opy.)

4. Open the Editor and open (or create) the Web document into which you want to copy the text.

5. Click the spot on the page where you want to copy the text. If you've just created the document, the text must be copied to the top of the document where the edit cursor is already located. In a document that already has other paragraphs in it, you can click at the start or end of any paragraph to add the selection to that paragraph, or press Enter between paragraphs to start a new paragraph for the selection.)

6. Press Shift+Ins to copy the selection into the page. (Alternatively, you can click the Paste button on the Editor's toolbar or choose **E**dit I **P**aste.)

NOTE: When pasted into a blank document, the text is automatically assigned the Normal paragraph property. You can then change it to any other paragraph property.

When pasted into a document with other paragraphs in it, the text is automatically assigned the same property as the paragraph it is inserted into or adjacent to.

To Assign Paragraph Properties

There are two steps to assigning properties: First, you select the paragraph or paragraphs.

❏ To select a paragraph, position the edit cursor anywhere within it (either by clicking within the paragraph or by pressing the arrow keys until the cursor arrives within the paragraph). Note that positioning the cursor within the paragraph is sufficient; you needn't highlight the whole paragraph.

❏ To select two or more paragraphs, click anywhere in the first paragraph and then drag to anywhere in the last paragraph and release, as shown in Figure 4.4.

Figure 4.4.
Selecting multiple paragraphs to assign them all the same paragraph property.

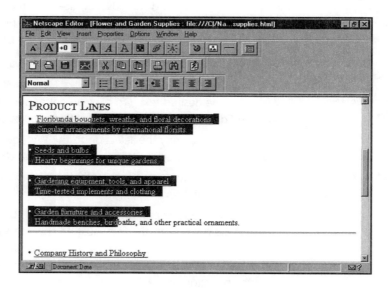

You can assign List Item as the paragraph property and choose a bulleted list or a numbered list by clicking the Bullet list or Number list button on the toolbar.

Once the paragraph or paragraphs are selected, you can assign a paragraph property in any of three ways:

❏ Click the drop-down list in the Paragraph Properties toolbar (usually appearing in the lower-left corner of the toolbar area) and select a paragraph style.

❏ Choose **P**roperties and then **P**aragraph to display a submenu of paragraph properties, as shown in Figure 4.5. Click the name of the desired style to apply it to the selection.

Figure 4.5.

Choosing paragraph properties from the Properties menu.

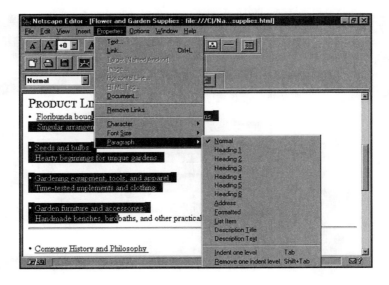

Observe in Figure 4.5 that two additional paragraph properties for indenting appear at the bottom of the menu. These options are covered later in this chapter.

❏ Click the Object Properties toolbar button (or choose **P**roperties | T**e**xt) to open the Properties dialog and then click the Paragraph tab, as shown in Figure 4.6. Select the name of the desired property from the Paragraph style drop-down list. Click Apply to apply the property without closing the dialog or click OK to apply the property and close the dialog.

Figure 4.6.

Choosing paragraph properties from the Properties dialog.

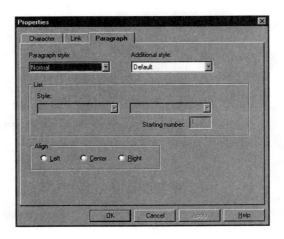

The other features of the Paragraph tab shown in Figure 4.6, and the Character Tab, as well, are covered later in this chapter. The Link tab of the Properties dialog is covered in Chapter 5.

❏ Finally, you can right-click the selection to display a context menu (see Figure 4.7), and then choose Paragraph/List properties to display the Paragraph properties dialog shown earlier in Figure 4.6.

Figure 4.7.
Opening the Properties dialog from a context menu.

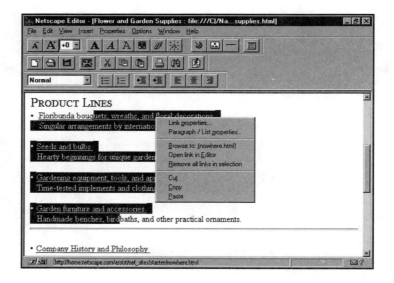

To Assign Properties and Attributes as You Type

Although there's a certain logic in entering your paragraphs and then assigning properties, you can do the opposite.

To assign properties as you type a paragraph:

1. Click the spot you want the paragraph to go.
2. Click the drop-down list in the Paragraph Properties toolbar (usually in the lower-left corner of the toolbar area) and select a paragraph style. Or click the Object Properties toolbar button (or choose **P**roperties I **T**ext), click the **P**aragraph tab to open the Paragraph Properties dialog, and assign Styles, Additional styles, and/or List styles.
3. Type your paragraph. It will appear on the page as you type it, showing the properties you selected.

About Attributes

Figure 4.6 reveals that choosing a paragraph style is not all you can do to a paragraph in the Paragraph Properties dialog. You can also choose an additional style from a drop-down list. When List Item is selected as the Paragraph style, you can choose from different List styles, as well.

Even though nothing on the Paragraph Properties dialog says so, these extra selections apply HTML *attributes*, special codes that modify the effects of some HTML tags. When you select a paragraph style, you apply the HTML tags for that style to the selection. When you choose an additional style or list style, you're applying attributes that modify the effect of the HTML paragraph style tags.

Under Additional styles, you'll find three choices:

Default: The default style. This option adds no attributes to the selected paragraph style, so that the paragraph appears in its regular way.

List: List is available as an additional style only if the Paragraph style is List Item. The List Additional style is fairly pointless, except that it enables the List styles on the Paragraph Properties dialog. The List styles let you choose a type of bullets for bulleted lists, or a type of numbers for numbered lists. (See the section titled "Working With Lists," later in this chapter.)

Block Quote: Block quote identifies the selected paragraph as a block quote, a quote long enough that it needs to be set apart from other text. When you select Block quote, the selected paragraph retains whatever Paragraph style you set it in, but is displayed in most browsers in a slightly different way from other paragraphs of the same style. Most browsers indent a block quote, just as block quotes are traditionally indented in books. Figure 4.8 shows two block quotes: The first (Shakespeare) is in the heading 3 style, and the second (Walt Kelly) uses normal text. But both use the Block Quote Additional style.

If List Item is the paragraph style and Default is the additional style, the list is automatically an unnumbered (bulleted) list, and no List styles are available for modifying the bullets.

Figure 4.8.
Two block quotes: heading 3 style above, normal paragraph style below, use the Block Quote Additional style.

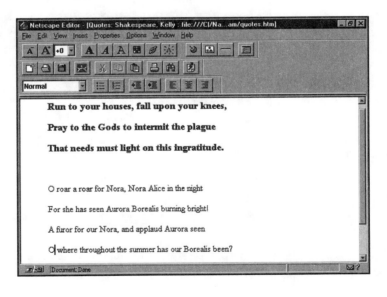

Working with Lists

The numbers in numbered lists do not appear in the Editor. Instead, placeholders (# for Arabic, *X* for Roman, *a* for upper-case, *A* for lowercase) appear. To see the actual numbering, click the View in Browser button.

When creating a list, the formatting options do not stop with the mere assignment of the List Item paragraph style. Within that style, you can easily create a variety of optional list styles. All of these can be selected as List styles (See Figure 4.9) on the Paragraph Properties page.

Unnumbered lists (default): An ordinary indented bulleted list. If you assign the List Item paragraph property (or click the Bullet List button on the toolbar), this is what you get. Using the List styles, you can choose the look of the bullet.

You cannot change the List style (or bullet or number style) in the middle of a list, unless you *nest* (indent) the list items to which you want to apply a different style. See the section titled "Nesting Lists" later in this chapter.

Numbered lists: A list whose items are numbered from top to bottom with Arabic numerals (1, 2, 3), Roman numerals (III, IV, V), or letters (A, B, C or a, b, c).

Directory: A bulleted, un-indented list of short items. The items must be short (a word or two) because some browsers wrap directory lists into columns.

Menu list: A bulleted, indented list of short items.

Description list: Longer items (even short paragraphs) formatted in an indented, bulleted list.

Figure 4.9.
List styles.

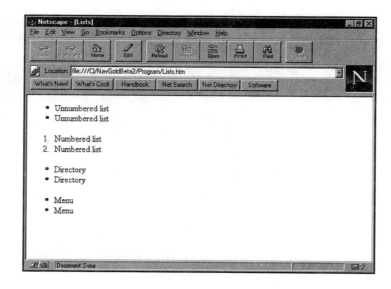

In some pages you'll see online, and in pages built by the Page Wizard (see Chapter 2), you'll see cool, geometrical (often multicolored) bullets on lists. These are not real bullets assigned by an attribute but images inserted right before each line of text. See Chapter 6.

Finally, if the List style you select is unnumbered or numbered, you can choose Bullet styles and Number styles. (See Figure 4.10.)

When you select Unnumbered list, a drop-down list for Bullet style appears to the right of the List Style selection. You may choose the following:

Automatic: The Editor picks the bullet style; the default choice is the Solid circle. (See the section titled "Nesting Lists" later in this chapter to learn when Automatic selects other bullet styles.)

Solid circle: The default bullet type, an ordinary black dot.

Solid square: A filled-in little square.

Open square: An empty square, like a checkbox.

When you select Numbered list, a drop-down list for Number style appears to the right of the List Style selection. You may choose the following:

Automatic: The Editor picks the number style; the default choice is 1,2,3. (See Nesting Lists later in this chapter to learn when Automatic selects other number styles.)

Arabic numerals: 1,2,3,4, and so on.

Roman numerals: (uppercase only): I,II,III,IV, and on.

Uppercase letters: A,B,C,D, and so on.

Lowercase letters: a,b,c,d, and on.

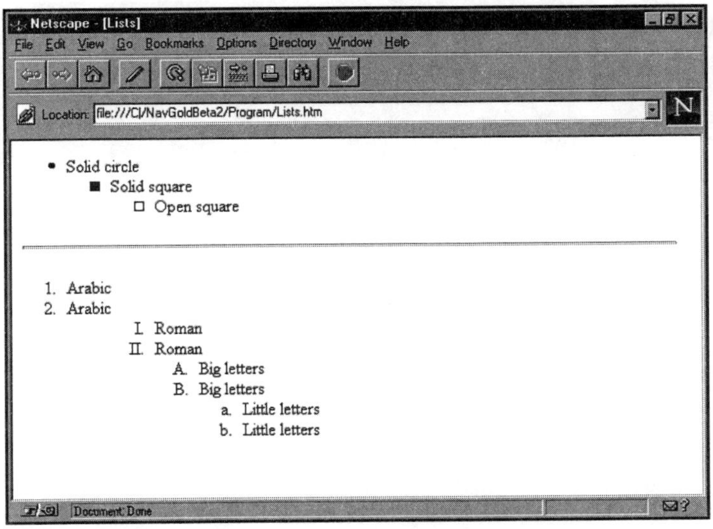

For a Numbered list, you can enter a starting number in the box under the Number style. (The default is 1.) Always use Arabic numerals to choose a starting number; for example, to begin a list with E, enter 5 as the starting number. For IV, enter 4.

Figure 4.10.
Bullet/numbering styles.

The number styles, bullet styles, and starting number are all enabled by Netscape extensions. In browsers that don't support extensions, a single style of bullets is chosen by the browser, and all numbered lists use Arabic numbering, beginning with 1.

Formatting Lists

To choose List styles and bullet/number styles:

1. Select the List Item text.

2. Click the Object Properties button on the toolbar (or choose **P**roperties I T**e**xt).

3. Click the **P**aragraph tab. (See Figure 4.6 earlier in this chapter.)

4. For the paragraph style, choose List item.

5. To create a default bulleted list with no optional style attributes, choose Default as the Additional style. Otherwise, choose List as the Additional style.

6. Under List, choose a style. If you choose Unnumbered or Numbered as the style, choose a Bullet/Number style.

7. Click OK.

Nesting Lists

The Editor gives you still one more way to use lists. You can nest lists within lists, as shown in Figure 4.11.

Figure 4.11.
Nested lists.

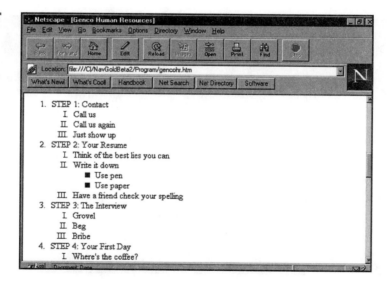

To nest a list within a list, simply indent items to be nested. The easiest way to build a nested list is to enter all of the items in one flat list, and then go back and selectively indent the nested parts. To indent a group of items in a list, select them and click the

Indent button on the toolbar, or press the Tab key. (See the section titled "Aligning and Indenting Text" later in this chapter.)

The Editor forces all list entries at the same indent level to use the same properties; you cannot, for example, switch from bullets to numbers in the middle of a list, unless you first indent the numbered section of the list. When you nest lists, you can switch List styles in the nested items, making them different from the un-indented list in which they nest. You can also change Bullet or Number styles in the nested items.

When you nest numbered lists, each nested list automatically restarts the numbering at 1, unless you specify a starting number for each nested list. (See Figure 4.11.)

When Automatic is selected as the bullet or number style, the Editor automatically changes the bullet or number style for each indent level in the list. For example, if you nest items in a bulleted list whose bullet type is a solid circle, the nested items whose bullet type is automatic are automatically assigned solid squares. If that nested list contains within it another nested list that uses the Automatic Bullet style, the nested-nested list automatically uses empty squares. The same happens with numbered lists nested and assigned the Automatic Number style. If the main list uses Arabic numerals (1,2,3), the first level of indenting automatically uses Roman numerals, the next level uses A,B,C, and so on.

In a nested list, you cannot use a higher level of number or bullet style than that of the list above. For example, if the main list used Roman numerals, a list nested within it would use upper- or lowercase letters (not Arabic numbers).

Aligning and Indenting Text

On the Paragraph Properties toolbar are buttons for aligning left, aligning right, and centering. The Paragraph Properties dialog (see Figure 4.6, earlier in this chapter) offers radio buttons for the same three choices. These can be applied to any paragraph in any style; you can select normal text, paragraphs, headings, lists—anything—and center it on the page or align it on the left or right side. (See Figure 4.12.)

Left alignment is the default selection for all paragraph styles. You need to select left alignment only when undoing another alignment selection.

When applying alignment, restrain yourself. Centering and right alignment are enabled by HTML 3 tags; in browsers that don't support HTML 3, your centered or right-aligned text will appear left-aligned anyway.

More importantly, our eyes are accustomed to left-aligned text, especially for *body copy,* or normal text. A big centered heading looks good on some pages, and right alignment can create a nice effect when text is put to the right of a graphic. (See Chapter 6.) Normal centered paragraphs can appear a bit off, and centered lists look downright strange (try one).

You can indent paragraphs, just as you would in a word processor. This capability is most useful when nesting lists (see the section titled "Nesting Lists" earlier in this chapter), but you can indent any paragraph.

As with alignment, don't go overboard with indents. Many browsers don't support indenting, so whatever structural or aesthetic impression you achieve with indents will be lost to many visitors. It's far better to select paragraph styles or attributes that are naturally indented, such as description text or a block quote. In browsers that don't support indenting, such paragraphs will still be set off in some unique way, so some of your intention may be preserved.

Figure 4.12.
Left (default), center, and right-aligned text.

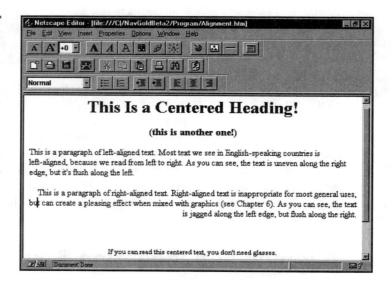

Indenting is enabled by a Netscape extension. In browsers that don't support indenting, the selection appears left-aligned.

To indent a paragraph, select it and do any of the following. (Repeat the procedure to indent further or to decrease the indent further.)

To indent to the right:

1. Click the Increase indent button on the toolbar.
2. Press Tab once.
3. Choose **P**roperties I **P**aragraph I **I**ndent one level.

To decrease the indent (move back to the left):

1. Click the Decrease indent button on the toolbar.
2. Press Shift+Tab.
3. Choose **P**roperties I **P**aragraph I **R**emove one indent level.

Character Properties

Paragraph properties always apply to the whole paragraph; you cannot make part of a paragraph a heading and another part normal, for example. But character properties can be applied to a single character in a paragraph, words, whole paragraph, or whole document. The most common (and best) use of character properties is to make words bold or italic. But you can also change the color of characters, make them blink, change the font size, and so on.

NOTE:

The following character properties are based on Netscape extensions or preliminary HTML 3 specifications. (See Chapter 1.) These properties will have no effect when displayed through browsers that do not support HTML 3 or the extensions.

If you use these properties, before publishing view your page through a non-HTML 3, nonextension-supporting browser to evaluate the appearance of the page with these properties ignored. (See the section titled "Task: Checking Your Work" later in this chapter.)

Netscape extensions: Custom text colors, blinking text style, font sizing, and JavaScript.

HTML 3: Superscript/subscript and strikethrough.

In Figure 4.13, the Clear Style Settings button reverts the Style choices for the selected text to their defaults for the paragraph style. The Clear **A**ll Settings button restores defaults for all character formatting: color, style, JavaScript, and so on.

Most of the character properties appear in the Character Properties toolbar and in the submenu under **P**roperties I **C**haracter. All of these, plus a few more options, appear on the Character Properties dialog. (See Figure 4.13.)

Figure 4.13.
The Character Properties dialog.

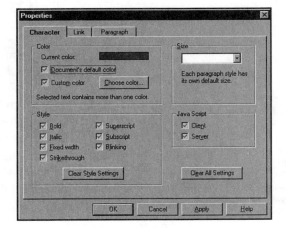

To apply character properties, you must highlight the selection rather than simply clicking it (as you can to select paragraph properties). If you don't know how to select text, see the section titled "Editing Text" later in this chapter.

To apply character properties, highlight the character, characters, paragraph, or paragraphs to which you want the properties applied. Then open the Character Properties dialog by clicking the Object Properties button on the toolbar (or choosing **P**roperties I **Te**xt) and then clicking the Character tab.

To help you understand how the character properties are applied, I'll explain them here as they appear on the Character Properties dialog (in Figure 4.13). Just keep in mind that most of these properties may also be selected by clicking buttons in the Character Properties toolbar or by choosing **P**roperties I **C**haracter.

You may choose custom text colors only if you have selected Use custom colors in the Appearance tab of the Document Properties or Editor Preferences dialog. See Chapter 3.

Color: The default color for the text you've select appears in the color box. To make the selection conform to the default color selections for the document (see Chapter 3, "Using the Netscape Editor"), check the checkbox next to **D**ocument's default color.

To change the color of the selection from default colors for the document to custom colors, check the checkbox next to Custom color. Then click the Choose color button. A Windows 95 Color dialog opens like the one shown in Figure 4.14. You can click any color box to select a text color or click Define Custom Colors to create a new color by choosing a spot within a two-dimensional color spectrum.

Figure 4.14.
Choosing custom colors.

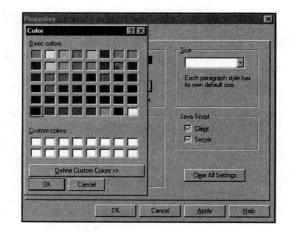

The bold and italic styles come through as bold and italic in most browsers; but really, these styles indicate emphasis only. Some browsers interpret your emphasis in their own way, with underlining, for example.

Style: Choose a character style by clicking one or more checkboxes. Most Styles can be mixed; for example, characters can be both bold and italic. The **F**ixed Width style sets the characters in a typewriter-style, monospaced font (just as the Formatted paragraph property does), which can be useful for lining up text elements or showing a line of program code. The B**l**inking style makes the selection blink on and off (in extension-supporting browsers).

Size: You can increase or decrease the size of the font used for the characters. The size is indicated not by points, as it would be in a word processor, but by relative steps above or below the size of normal text, which is size 0. Note that all paragraph styles start out at a default size: Normal text is 0, a level-1 heading is a 3, and so on.

JavaScript: The JavaScript character format designates a string of characters as a line of JavaScript code. See Chapter 13, "Using JavaScript."

About Spacing

Because the Editor is a WYSIWYG (what you see is what you get) editor, whatever you do in the Editor is supposed to appear in the editing window exactly as it would appear to a visitor using Netscape, and generally the way it would appear to visitors using other graphical browsers.

In real life, however, what you see is not always what you get. For example, scripts (see Chapter 13) may have code that appears in the Editor, while the result of the code's execution appears through browsers.

You can force browsers to recognize extra carriage returns and blank spaces within a block of text by assigning the Formatted property. See the section titled "Formatted," earlier in this chapter.

The other exception is extra white space on the page. HTML does not recognize carriage returns as blank lines or extra blank spaces as extra blank spaces. Thus, browsers ignore these characters when displaying a page. When you add extra spaces or carriage returns in the Editor, they create extra space on the page in the editing window, which may make you think they'll add the same space on the Web. But if you add extra space in the Editor and then view the same document through the browser (see the Task section titled "Checking Your Work," later in this chapter), you'll see those lines and spaces wiped out. When you return to the Editor, the lines and spaces return. Weird, man.

There's rarely any need to add extra space between paragraphs. When displaying your page, browsers will decide how much space to put between page elements to produce a pleasing result. If you want to force browsers to put some extra space between paragraphs, you must insert a new line break. To add extra character spaces within a paragraph, you must insert a nonbreaking space. Both techniques are described in the following task section.

Inserting Extra Space

Use the techniques shown in this section to insert extra blank space in your document to achieve a desired effect.

To Insert a New Line Break Between Paragraphs

1. Position the edit cursor at the very end or very beginning of a paragraph.
2. Press Shift+Enter or choose Insert | New Line Break.

You may add as many lines this way as you wish.

To Insert a Non-Breaking Space Within a Paragraph

1. Position the edit cursor at the spot within a paragraph that you want to add extra spaces.
2. Press Shift+Space or choose Insert I Nonbreaking Space.

You may add as many spaces this way as you wish.

Checking Your Work

Again, the Gold Editor is supposed to be WYSIWYG, so there shouldn't be any need to view your document through a browser to verify its appearance on the Web. But as earlier sections of this chapter have demonstrated, some things can change between the Editor view of a document and the Browser view. Also, the browser has a different toolbar, and a different look overall, which means that even when the formatting of your page is identical in the Editor and the Browser, you may make new discoveries about its appearance while in Browser view because it is in a different environment, with a difference *ambiance*.

So from time to time and certainly before publishing your page on the Web, view it through the Browser. In the Editor, click the View in Browser button or choose Window I Netscape Browser. When you finish viewing the document, return to the Editor by clicking its button on the Windows 95 taskbar or by clicking the Edit button on the Browser's toolbar.

The Multibrowser Test

The Browser shows you only how your page will appear to visitors using Netscape. What about the other 10 to 20 percent of the Web population?

It's a good idea to keep some other browsers around to see how the other half sees you. NCSA's Mosaic and Microsoft's Internet Explorer, for example, can both be downloaded from the Web for free. You can open your new page in either (check their help files to learn how to open an HTML file on disk), and see how it looks outside Navigator.

Although these two browsers are good choices because they're popular, they're both graphical browsers—similar to Netscape in most respects—and support many Netscape extensions. So your page is likely to look very similar in Netscape, Mosaic, and Internet Explorer. Given that, try to get your hands on a worst-case scenario browser, preferably a text-only browser and certainly one that does not support Netscape extensions. Viewing your documents through this browser will help you determine how your cool page really looks—with its fancy formatting down around its ankles.

You might decide, based on what you see, to moderate your use of extensions or make other changes to ensure that all visitors to your page see something they can appreciate. Or you might decide that you'd rather show a state-of-the-art page to most of the Web than dumb it down for a few obsolete stragglers. It's all up to you.

TASK ## Printing Your Document

Click the Print button on the toolbar or choose **F**ile | **P**rint. The document is printed exactly as it would be from the Browser. The general formatting is retained, but the page is broken up into appropriate-sized chunks to fit on paper pages.

TASK ## Editing Your Web Document

Editing a Web page is straightforward, very much like editing any word processing document. To do almost anything, highlight the text you want to change and then make the change.

You can also search for a text string using the Editor's Find tool. Finally, you can print your page.

To Highlight Text

To highlight text with your mouse, position the cursor at the start of the area you want to highlight, and then click and hold the left mouse button. Drag to the end of the selection and then release the mouse button. Note that you can select as much text as you want in this way: a few characters, a word, a whole paragraph, or a group of paragraphs.

Here are other ways to highlight a selection for editing:

- ❏ Double-click a word to select the word.
- ❏ Double-click at the very beginning of a line to select the first word.
- ❏ Double-click at the very end of a line to select the last word.
- ❏ Position the pointer to the left of a paragraph and double-click to select the entire paragraph, or single-click to select just the line the cursor is next to.

When you drag through an area that includes both text and images, only the text is selected. Images must be selected separately. See Chapter 6.

You can right-click selected text to display a context menu with choices for changing properties, creating links, and for cut, copy, and paste. See Figure 4.7, shown earlier.

To Replace Selected Text

Begin typing. The selection is deleted immediately and replaced with whatever you type. Any surrounding text that was not highlighted remains unaffected.

You can also replace a highlighted selection with the contents of the clipboard by clicking the Paste button on the toolbar or by choosing **E**dit | **P**aste. (Of course, you must previously have cut or copied something to the Clipboard; see the section titled "To Copy or Move Selected Text.")

To Delete Selected Text

Press the Del key to delete the selection.

To delete the selection from its current location but copy it to the Windows Clipboard so that it can be pasted elsewhere in the page or into another page or another Windows document, click the Cut button on the toolbar or choose **E**dit | Cu**t**.

To Copy or Move Selected Text

To copy a highlighted selection, click the Copy button on the toolbar or choose **E**dit | **C**opy. Then click in the location where you want the copy to go and click the Paste button or choose **E**dit | **P**aste.

To move a highlighted selection, click the Cut button on the toolbar or choose **E**dit | Cu**t**. Then click in the location where you want the selection moved to and click the Paste button or choose **E**dit | **P**aste.

To Find Text

To find a text string anywhere within your Web document:

1. Click the Find button on the toolbar or choose **E**dit | **F**ind. The Find dialog opens, as shown in Figure 4.15.
2. Enter the exact text string in Find What.
3. To search just for text in your Web document that matches not only the text string but its precise capitalization, check the checkbox for Match Case. To search from the spot where the edit cursor is located back to the beginning of the page, click the Up radio button. To search from the spot where the edit cursor is located to the end of the page, click the Down radio button.
4. Click Find Next.

Figure 4.15.
The Find dialog.

To Undo Previous Actions

If you goof, you can undo the last edit you made by choosing **E**dit I **U**ndo or pressing Ctrl+Z.

Tips for Good Text Design

It's your page, and far be it from me to tell you what it should look like. I once the had the hands-down, stankiest, homeliest little dog that ever lived, but I loved her dearly. So I understand the subjectivity involved in making aesthetic judgments.

Nevertheless, if you are interested in some of the accumulated wisdom of the Web masters, here are a few things to keep in mind when working with text on your page.

❑ Write clearly and be brief. Web surfers are an immediate-gratification, fast-food-type lot. To hold them, you must dole out your message in quick, efficient bites.

❑ Break up your message into pages (or rule-divided sections) of reasonable length, and break up pages into at least two or three sections each (three is best) delineated by headings, pictures, or rules. This makes your page more attractive and inviting, and also allows visitors to easily scan your page for items of interest.

❑ Don't overdo emphasis. Look through your page, and watch for overuse of bold and italics or custom font sizes and colors. Watch also for using headings, block quotes, or other properties just to pump up a paragraph that really belongs in normal text. Let your page's organization (and pictures) create visual interest and let your choice of words emphasize important ideas. Use bold to light up a word or two and use italics for things that belong in italics, such as book titles or foreign phrases.

❑ Proofread carefully before publishing. Have someone else check your spelling, as well, and critique your writing and layout.

❑ Always use a signature (see Chapter 5, "Linking Everywhere, Anywhere") as a matter of courtesy, and to benefit from feedback and criticism that visitors might want to share with you.

Workshop Wrap-Up

The Editor provides simple toolbar buttons, dialogs, and menus for applying properties to paragraphs—the most important activity in building a Web page. When you apply properties to a paragraph, you're actually surrounding the paragraph with the appropriate HTML tags in the underlying HTML source file. The menus and dialogs save you the trouble of remembering what all the tags are and apply those tags conveniently and accurately. The Editor also supplies a straightforward, simple text-editing environment to make composing your Web document as painless as applying its properties.

But for all that it is, there's one thing the Editor is not: smart. It can't tell you whether the content you've created is well-organized, well-presented, well-written, or even spelled correctly. And although it applies HTML tags to your document dutifully, it cannot tell you whether you've selected the most effective properties for the paragraph at hand.

Thus, the Editor is a replacement only for time and labor, not for judgment. To author an effective Web document, you must acquire a sense of Web aesthetics. You'll pick up much of this sense as you work through this book. But you must also study other pages you see online, and mentally catalog the design aspects and content approaches that sing to you—and those that annoy, bore, or baffle you, as well.

The better you understand what makes Web denizens hit on a site and stay there, the more effectively you'll apply Netscape Gold and the techniques in this book.

Next Steps

Now…

❑ To stimulate your thinking about how you want your page to look and what's involved in making it look that way, see Chapter 8, "Real-Life Examples I."

❑ To add links, or to build a multipage Web presentation, see Chapter 5, "Linking Everywhere, Anywhere."

❑ To add pictures, backgrounds and rules, see Chapter 6, "Working with Graphics."

❑ To add sound and video, see Chapter 7, "Embedding Multimedia."

❑ To learn how to apply HTML features not offered by the Editor, see Chapter 9, "Editing HTML Source Code."

❑ To endow your page with special functions and capabilities, see Chapter 13, "Using JavaScript."

❑ To publish your page on the Web, see Chapter 15, "Publishing Web Documents."

Q&A

Q: Looking over the toolbar and menu items in the Editor, I see the stuff described in this chapter, plus other stuff I know you'll cover in later chapters, such as images and JavaScript. But where are the menu items or toolbar buttons for frames, tables, and some other page elements I've seen on the Web?

A: The Editor is pretty full-featured, supplying tools for 90 percent of the things 99 percent of Web authors do. But it is not a universal, all-encompassing Web authoring system. It does not do everything.

That's why this chapter and others remind you at appropriate points that no matter what you do in the Editor, you're building an HTML document underneath. When you move onto the page elements for which the Editor supplies no tools, you'll need to switch off the cruise control and press the HTML pedals directly. You'll begin that experience in Chapter 9, "Editing HTML Source Code," and I think you'll discover it's not so challenging. Until then, explore and enjoy the things the Editor *does* do, all coming up in Chapters 5 through 8.

FIVE

Linking Everywhere, Anywhere

Except for scripts, links are the one great mystery of Web authoring. Everything else is up front and visible; everything else just has to *look* right. A link, on the other hand, has to *do* something—has to *act* right. Links are mysterious because what they do when activated is not immediately visible to the naked eye.

Fortunately, creating links in the Editor is surprisingly simple. The only tricky part is phrasing the underlying URL exactly right. As you know from your own Web travels, any mistake in an URL means you're dead in the water. Put a flawed URL under a link in your document, and your page distributes frustration—globally. Just remember: "Your page is only as strong as its weakest link," or something like that. ("Links that touch liquor will never touch mine"? "You're nobody 'til somebody links you"?)

With an eye to where the real linking pitfalls are, this chapter focuses first on the basics of URLs, and *then* shows you how to fuse URLs into links. If you don't get the URL right, it doesn't matter whether you construct the link properly.

In this chapter, you

- ❏ Learn how to properly phrase URLs for linking to all types of remote Internet resources, including Web pages, newsgroups, Gopher, and FTP
- ❏ Use copy and paste, drag and drop, and other techniques to conveniently copy links into your page so you don't *have to* phrase the URL yourself
- ❏ Link to other pages on the same server (to build a multipage document) or files
- ❏ Create and link to *targets* (*anchors*), which are specific spots anywhere within a Web page
- ❏ Build a signature with a mailto link that enables visitors to conveniently send you e-mail

Tasks in this chapter:

- ❏ Copying Links from other Documents
- ❏ Inserting a New Link
- ❏ Making Existing Text into a Link
- ❏ Creating Targets
- ❏ Linking to a Target
- ❏ Creating a Signature
- ❏ De-linking Text

What's in a Link?

This chapter shows how to build links activated by text on the page. You can also use a graphic to activate a link (see Chapter 6), or different areas of a graphic to activate multiple links (see Chapter 12).

Every link has two parts. Creating links is a simple matter of choosing a spot on the page for the link and then supplying both parts:

❏ The *link source*, the actual text (or graphic) that appears on the page to represent the link. When a visitor activates a link, he or she clicks the link source to activate the unseen URL below.

❏ The URL describing the page, file, or Internet service to be accessed when the link is activated.

You can create menus or directories (see Figure 5.1) of links by making each link a separate line in the List Item paragraph property. But links needn't be on separate lines. As Figure 5.1 shows, you can use any words or phrases in your page, including headings (or words in headings), words in normal paragraphs, list items, or even single characters in any paragraph property.

Figure 5.1.
Links (underlined) in text and by themselves in a menu.

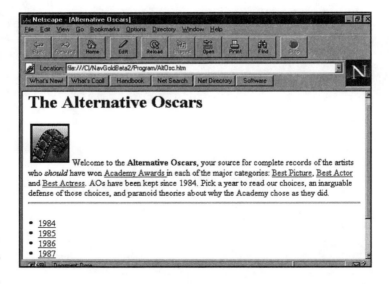

You can edit the character properties (see Chapter 4) of link source text, making them bold or italic, for example. But most browsers override such formatting to keep links identifiable. Netscape browsers show the formatting but always insist on underlining links, no matter what else you do to them.

The link source takes on the paragraph properties of the text it is inserted into or closest to, but you can change the paragraph properties (see Chapter 4, "Composing, Editing, and Formatting Text ") of the link source at any time, just as you would for any other text. The underlying link is undisturbed by such changes.

What's Linkable?

A link can point to any resource that can be expressed in a URL or to *local files* (files residing on the same server as the page containing the link). That includes not only remote Web pages and other pages and files residing on the same Web server as your document, but also newsgroups and articles within them, e-mail messages, and Gopher and FTP servers. In your travels on the Web, you've already encountered links pointing to all such resources.

Also, a link can point to a specific location within a Web page—even to a specific location within the same page containing the link. For example, in a long Web page (such as the one-page, linear type described in Chapter 1, "Planning Your Page"), each entry in a table of contents (see Figure 5.2) can be a link pointing to a specific section of the page. This allows visitors to navigate quickly and easily within the page. The spots within pages to which a link can point are called *anchors,* or *targets.*

Figure 5.2.
A menu (table of contents) made up of links to targets within the same document.

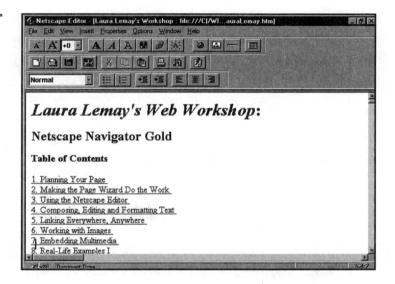

To create a link, you use the same procedure, regardless of the type of resource the link points to. However, for each type of resource, there are issues you must consider when composing the URL for the link. The next several sections describe in detail the special considerations for each type of URL.

Web Pages

Web pages are the most commonly linked resource, and for good reason; you can bet that anybody viewing your Web page can view any other Web page, so links to Web pages are a reliable way to provide information. Linking to Web pages also allows your visitors to apply a consistent set of navigation techniques; many newer Web surfers are a little baffled by Gopher directories, for example.

URLs pointing to Web pages always begin with the protocol designator `http://`. The protocol is followed by the Web server hostname, the directory path to the page file, and the actual HTML file of the page. For example:

`http://`*hostname*`/`*pathname*`/`*file*`.HTM`

In some cases, you can omit the filename. Some Web servers have default files they display automatically whenever someone accesses the server or a directory without specifying a filename. For example:

`http://www.mcp.com/`

accesses the default page for the server `www.mcp.com`.

`http://www.mcp.com/publications/`

accesses the default page for the directory `publications` on the server `www.mcp.com`.

Note that the directory examples above each end in a slash. You should always use a slash to end an HTTP URL that does not end with a filename, to instruct the server to access the default file (usually `INDEX.HTML`). Some servers can still access the default file if you leave off the slash, but some won't—so in a link, use the slash for safety's sake.

Finally, always be careful to follow the exact capitalization of the URL as you would see it in Navigator's Location box when viewing the page. Many Web servers are case-sensitive and won't recognize the directory or filename if it is not properly capitalized.

> The easiest way to ensure that a URL is properly expressed is to copy it directly from the Web. See the section titled "Copying a Link from Another Document" later in this chapter.

Targets in Pages (Anchors)

Web pages can contain predefined locations to which links can point. These spots are called *anchors* in HTML (and are created with the `<A>` tag—*A* for *Anchor*). But in the Editor, they're called *targets*. You'd think Netscape, with its salty ship's wheel logo, would have kept the nicely nautical anchor nomenclature, but target it is. Go with it.

You can add targets to your own Web pages and then link to those targets from elsewhere in the same page or from other pages you create. Also, you can create links to point to any existing targets in other pages on the Web.

> The URLs for links to targets must spell and capitalize the name of the target exactly as it was spelled and capitalized when the target was created. Otherwise, they miss their target.

When you create a target (see the section titled "Creating Targets" later in this chapter), you give the target a name. You create links to targets as you do to a Web page, with one difference: You add the name of the target to the URL you enter for the link.

In the Editor, the correct combination of the URL and the target name is automatically handled for you when you select targets from a list the Editor produces. But just for your general URL education, you should know that the precise phrasing depends upon

To avoid having to worry about the proper phrasing of URLs to other servers, simply copy them straight from the Web as described in the Task section titled "Copying Links from Other Documents."

You can use a *relative pathname* to point to a target in another file stored on the same server; for example, to link from one page of a multipage document to a target in another page in the document. See the section titled "Local Files."

Technically, the pathnames you enter to create links to local files are not URLs. But when creating a link, you enter these pathnames in the same place you'd enter an URL for linking to a remote resource. So I refer to them generically as URLs.

whether you're linking to a target in the same document in which the link appears or to a target in another document:

❏ The URL for a link to a target in another document includes the full path to that document, a hash sign (#), and the target's name. For example:

`http://www.mcp.com/directory.html#Chap4`

opens the file Chap4 in the document DIRECTORY.HTML and then scrolls to the target named Chap4.

❏ The URL (actually, it's not technically a URL, but it takes the place of one) for a link to a target in the same document is made out of nothing but the target's name, preceded by a hash sign (#). For example:

`#Fish`

scrolls to the target named Fish in the document that contains the link.

Local Files

Just as you can link to resources on any server, you can also link to resources residing on the same server as your Web document. Obviously, this is what you would do when linking among the pages of a multipage presentation. But you might also choose to link to anything on your local Web server that relates to the topic of your page, such as another Web document or a text file containing related information.

When you phrase the URLs to create links to local resources, you need to consider the differences between *relative* pathnames and *absolute* pathnames.

NOTE:
If you use Gold to publish your document on the server (instead of using FTP separately), don't worry much about relative and local pathnames. Gold pretty much takes care of that, as explained in Chapter 15, "Publishing Web Documents." Still, to assert full control over your Web project and to be able to resolve any problems that might arise, it's important that you understand the principles behind these pathnames.

Relative Pathnames

Relative pathnames include only the information necessary to find the linked resource from the location of the document containing the link. In other words, the path given to the file is *relative* to the file containing the link; from outside that file, the information supplied as the URL for the link is insufficient to locate the file.

Use relative pathnames to link together the pages of a multipage document on your PC. Because the paths are relative, when you publish that document to a server, the inter-page links will still work properly. See Chapter 15.

For example, suppose all of the pages of your multipage document share the same directory on the server and one of those pages is called FLORIDA.HTM. To link from any page in your document to FLORIDA.HTM, you need enter only the filename as the URL for the link. For example:

FLORIDA.HTM

Now suppose all pages but the top page reside in a folder or directory called STATES, and that this folder is within the same folder containing the top page. To link from the top page to FLORIDA.HTM in the states directory, you would enter the directory and filename, separated by a slash. For example:

STATES/FLORIDA.HTM

This approach works as far into the folder hierarchy as you wish. Just be sure to separate each step in the path with a slash. For a file several levels beneath the file containing the link, you might enter

ENVIRO/US/STATES/FLORIDA.HTM

Now suppose you're linking from a page lower in the directory hierarchy to a page that's higher. To do that, you must describe a path that moves up in the hierarchy. As in DOS and in FTP servers, a double period (..) is used in a path to move up one level. For example, link from the FLORIDA page back to the top page (call it TOP.HTM), which we'll assume is one level above FLORIDA. For the URL portions of the link, you would enter

../TOP.HTM

If TOP.HTM were three levels above FLORIDA, you would type

../../../TOP.HTM

Finally, suppose you want to link to a local file that resides in a folder that is not above or below the file containing the link but is somewhere else in the hierarchy. This would require a path that moves up the hierarchy and then down a different branch to the file. In such a case you use the double periods to move up and then specify the full directory path down to the file.

For example, suppose you want to link from

ENVIRO/US/STATES/FLORIDA.HTM

to

ENVIRO/CANADA/PROVINCE/QUEBEC.HTM

The phrasing you need is

`../../../CANADA/PROVINCE/QUEBEC.HTM`

The three sets of double periods move up to the ENVIRO directory; then the path down from ENVIRO to QUEBEC.HTM follows.

NOTE:
On DOS and Windows systems, a relative or absolute path might include the letter of the hard disk, but it must be followed by a vertical bar (¦) rather than the standard colon. For example:

`C¦/STATS/ENVIRO/CANADA/PROVINCE/QUEBEC.HTM`

Absolute Pathnames

Absolute pathnames give the complete path to a file, from the top level of the directory hierarchy of the system. Absolute pathnames are not portable from one system to another. In other words, while composing a multipage document on your PC, you may use absolute pathnames in links among the pages. But once you publish that document, all of the links become invalid because the server's directory hierarchy is not identical to your PC's.

In general, you'll use absolute pathnames only when linking to specific local resources (other than your own pages), such as FAQs, residing on the server where your page will be published.

Absolute pathnames are phrased just like relative pathnames, except that they always begin with a slash (/) and always contain the full path from the top of the directory hierarchy to the file. For example:

`/STATS/ENVIRO/CANADA/PROVINCE/QUEBEC.HTM`

Other Internet Services

In addition to Web pages and their targets, links point to any other browser-accessible servers. But before linking to anything other than a Web page or a target, keep in mind that not all browsers—hence not all visitors—can access all of these other server types.

Nearly all browsers can handle Gopher and FTP. Less common is mail access, and even less common is newsgroup access. Netscape Navigator has native support for both. Other browsers open helper applications for mail; for example, Internet Explorer opens Windows 95's Exchange mail client when a mailto link is activated. Still, many browsers have no news or mail access at all.

Gopher

Pointing straight to a Gopher server to display the main directory there is pretty simple. Simply build the URL out of the `gopher://` protocol designator and the gopher server hostname; for example:

`gopher://gopher.umn.edu`

Beyond that, pointing to a specific file or subdirectory on a Gopher server gets tricky, often involving port numbers and complex system of paths, so there's no simple set of rules for specifying the path to a Gopher file in a URL. Therefore, the best way to point a particular Gopher file is to

- ❏ Explain in your Web page the menu choices required to navigate from the main directory to the file and then link only to the server.
- ❏ Using Navigator, connect to the Gopher server and click menu items to navigate all the way to the Gopher resource; then copy the link from the Location box to your document. (See the Task section titled "Copying Links from Other Documents," later in this chapter.)
- ❏ Search for a Web page that carries the same information as the Gopher resource (increasingly, you'll find one), so you can avoid linking to the Gopher server at all.

FTP

If you create a link to an HTML file residing on an FTP server, clicking the link downloads the file and displays it, just as if it were on an HTTP server.

Using a link to an FTP server, you can point to a directory or to a specific file. If the link points to a directory, clicking the link displays the list of files and subdirectories there (see Figure 5.3), and each listing is itself a link the visitor can click to navigate the directories or download a file. If the link points to a file, the file is downloaded to the visitor's PC when he or she activates the link.

To link to an anonymous FTP server, use the protocol designator `ftp://`, followed by the name of the FTP server, the path, and the filename (if linking to a file). For example:

Observe that you do not end an FTP URL with a slash when linking to a directory. This differs from an HTTP URL, where a slash is always advisable except when accessing a specific HTML file.

`ftp://ftp.mcp.com`—Links to Macmillan's anonymous FTP server and displays the top-level directory.

`ftp://ftp.mcp.com/pub`—Links to Macmillan's anonymous FTP server and displays the contents of the PUB directory.

`ftp://ftp.mcp.com/pub/review.doc`—Links to Macmillan's anonymous FTP server and downloads the file REVIEW.DOC from the PUB directory.

Figure 5.3.
An FTP directory.

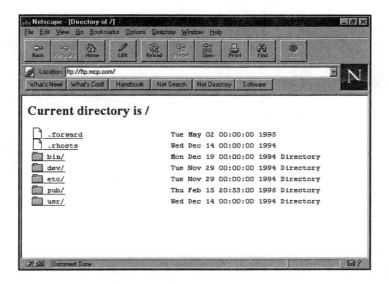

Linking to Locked FTP Servers

You can link to nonanonymous, password-protected FTP servers. But in most cases, such servers have been set up precisely to prevent public access. A URL to a nonanonymous FTP server includes a username and password for accessing that server, so anyone who accesses your page can access the FTP server—or read the URL activated by the link to learn the password.

Obviously, you should never create a link to a nonanonymous server unless you have express permission to do so from the server's administrators. And getting such permission is unlikely.

To link to a nonanonymous FTP server for which you have permission to publish a link, you phrase the URL exactly as you would for anonymous FTP, except that you insert the username and password (separated by a colon), and an @ sign, between the protocol and the path, as shown:

`ftp://username:password@ftp.mcp.com/pub/secrets.doc`

downloads the file secrets.doc from a password-protected server for which the actual username and password in the URL are valid.

News

A link can open a newsgroup article list or point to a specific article within that list. While both newsgroups and the articles they carry come and go, a link to the article list might be valid for years, whereas a link to a specific article might be valid for only a few days, until the article ages past the limit and is automatically deleted from the server.

Thus, the best use of news links is to point to the article list of a newsgroup whose topic relates to that of the Web document. If a newsgroup contains an article that you want to make a long-term part of the page, copy it into a separate file and link to that file, or simply copy it into a Web page.

Before copying a news article into a page, check for any copyright notice in the article. Whether it's copyrighted or not, e-mail the author and request permission to use the article.

To link to a newsgroup to display the current article list, use the protocol designator `news:` followed by the name of the newsgroup. (Note that a `news:` URL omits the double slashes used in HTTP, FTP, and Gopher URLs.) For example:

```
news:alt.video.laserdisc
```

or

```
news:news.announce.newusers
```

To link to an article, find the message ID in the article's header; it's enclosed between carats (`< >`) and labeled `message ID` by most newsreaders (including Navigator's; see Figure 5.4). To phrase the URL, use the protocol designator `news:` followed by the message ID. Note that you do not include the carats, and you do not need to include the newsgroup name in the URL. For example:

```
news:Do5D18.7Hs@deshaw.com
```

Figure 5.4.

A news article header (bottom pane) in Navigator's News window, showing the message ID and the newsgroups to which the message is posted.

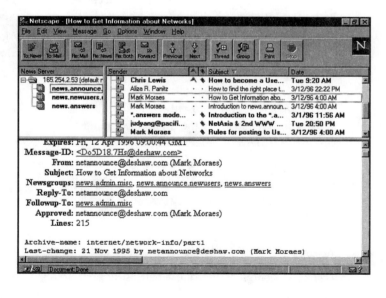

Mail

Mail URLs can be the most difficult ones to goof up. You enter `mailto:`, followed by an e-mail address. That's it. (Note that a mailto: URL omits the double slashes used in HTTP, FTP, and Gopher URLs.) For example:

```
mailto:nsnell@carroll.com
```

The most common use of mailto: links is in a signature at the bottom of a page. (See the section titled "Creating a Signature" later in this chapter.) But you can use a mailto: link anywhere it makes sense to offer your readers a way to contact you or someone else.

Observe in Figure 5.4 that the newsgroup names and Message ID are underlined in the article header. They're links and can be copied directly into a page in the Editor with copy and paste or drag and drop. See the Task section titled "Copying Links from Other Documents."

Copying Links from Other Documents

Anywhere you see a link, you can easily copy it into your document using copy and paste or drag and drop. For example, you can copy the URL of a document you're currently viewing on the Web—call it the *source document*—and paste it as a link into your document in the Editor—the *target document.*

In fact, a page you've just accessed on the Web makes the most reliable source for a link. If you copy the URL of a file while viewing it and paste it as a link into a document you're creating, you can pretty much bet that the link will work properly (until and unless the page or other resource is moved or removed).

Before putting any e-mail address—other than your own—in a link, ask permission from the addressee.

In other places you can pick up links, the links might be accurate and up-to-date, or they might not be. Obviously, if the link is faulty where you get it, it won't work in your document, either. Test, test, test. (See Chapter 16, "Testing and Maintaining Web Documents.")

Sources for copying links include

The links you can copy from news and mail message headers appear there only if you select **O**ptions I Show All Headers in the News or Mail window.

- ❑ The Browser's Location box (where the URL of the current page appears)
- ❑ The Bookmarks folder
- ❑ The header of a news article in Navigator's News window
- ❑ The header of a mail message in Navigator's Mail window
- ❑ Any link appearing in a Web page through the browser

Before publishing a link to anything other than your own document, e-mail the Webmaster or server administrator of the resource to request permission. Servers have limits, and some administrators want to discourage the proliferation of links to overtaxed systems.

NOTE: When copying a link into your document, keep in mind the following:

❑ Except when copying from the Bookmarks folder, the link source is not copied; instead, the link source that appears in the Editor shows the URL as the link source. To give the link a name to appear instead of its URL, edit the Link Properties as described in later in this chapter. (When you copy a bookmark as a link, the link source is the name of the bookmark.)

❑ The link takes on the paragraph properties of the paragraph it is inserted into or closest to. But remember, a link can accept any paragraph properties or character properties—though in most browsers, the character properties cannot override the default way links are displayed. That's a good thing, actually; you don't want your formatting to disguise the fact that a link is a link.

To Copy and Paste a Link

Copying and pasting, in case you've forgotten, is a two-part deal. First, you copy something to the Windows Clipboard and then you paste it from the Clipboard into the place you want it to go. You can accomplish each half of the job in several ways. There are several ways to copy, and several to paste, and you can combine any copy method with any paste method and get the same results.

From the lists below, pick a copy method you like, pick a paste method you like, and put 'em together.

To copy to the Clipboard:

❑ A link to the Web page currently appearing in the Browser: Double-click the link icon to the left of the Browser's Location box.

❑ A link shown in a Web document: Right-click the link, and choose **C**opy link to clipboard from the context menu. (See Figure 5.5.)

❑ A link appearing in the Bookmarks folder: Open the folder in the Browser by choosing **B**ookmarks | **G**o to Bookmarks. Right-click the desired bookmark and choose **C**opy link to clipboard from the context menu or click the bookmark to highlight it. Then choose **E**dit | **C**opy.

❑ A link appearing in the header of a news or mail message: Open the message and locate the desired link in the message header. Right-click the link, and choose **C**opy link to clipboard from the context menu, or click the link to highlight it, then choose **E**dit, **C**opy.

Figure 5.5.

Copying a link to the Clipboard by right-clicking.

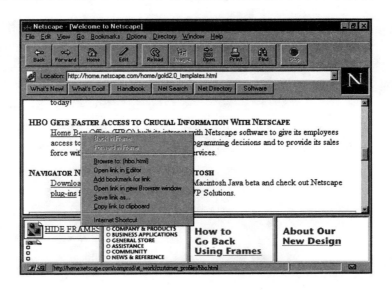

If the link for Message ID does not appear in your news or mail message headers, you must select **O**ptions I Show All Headers to make it appear.

To paste a link from the Clipboard into your document:

1. In the open document in the Editor, click where you want to insert the link.

2. Choose **E**dit I **P**aste (or press Shift+Ins).

Alternatively, you can right-click the spot where you want to paste the link and then choose **P**aste link from the context menu.

To Drag and Drop a Link

Unfortunately, you can't copy and paste or drag and drop a Windows 95 Internet shortcut to make a link. You can, however, highlight the shortcut's URL in its properties sheet, copy it, and then paste it into the Editor's Link Properties dialog.

1. In the Browser, open the document (local or remote) containing the desired link, or open the Bookmark folder or news or mail message containing the link.

2. Open the target document in the Editor.

3. Position the open windows so that both are visible on the Windows desktop. One way is to right-click an open spot on the Windows 95 taskbar and choose one of the Tile Windows options. (See Figure 5.6.)

4. Scroll in the browser (or folder window) until the desired link is visible.

5. Click and hold the left mouse button on the link and drag to the Editor window. As you drag, the pointer becomes a link pointer, to indicate that you're dragging a link.

To drag a link pointing to the document currently open in the browser, drag the link icon that appears next to Location.

6. When the chain pointer moves into the Editor window, the edit cursor follows its movements. If you drag to any edge of the window, the window scrolls in that direction. Pull the mouse through the document until the edit cursor arrives at the spot where you want to insert the link.

Figure 5.6.
Windows tiled for dragging and dropping a link.

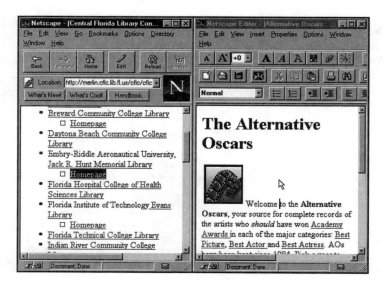

7. Release the mouse button to drop the link.

 Inserting a New Link

1. In the Editor, click at the spot in the document where you want the link to appear.

2. Click the link button on the toolbar. (Alternatively, you can choose Insert I Link or right-click the spot and choose Insert link from the context menu.) The Link Properties dialog opens, as shown in Figure 5.7.

When inserting a new link, make sure nothing is highlighted before you open the Link Properties dialog. Any highlighted text becomes the link source; see the section titled "Making Existing Text into a Link" later in this chapter.

3. Fill in the Link source (the words you want to appear on the page to represent the link). If you leave Link source blank, the URL will appear in the document as the link source.

4. Under Link to a page location or file, fill in the URL of a remote resource or a local pathname. (See the section titled "What's Linkable" earlier in this chapter for specifics on phrasing the URL or pathname).

To link to a local file, click **Browse**, browse to the file, and select it. The Editor completes the Link to box for you, with a *relative* pathname. If you want an absolute pathname instead, insert a slash (/) before the pathname in the Link to box.

5. Click OK. The link source appears in the document at the edit point. The link source is underlined and displayed in the document's link text color. (See Chapter 4, "Composing, Editing, and Formatting Text.")

Figure 5.7.
Inserting a new link.

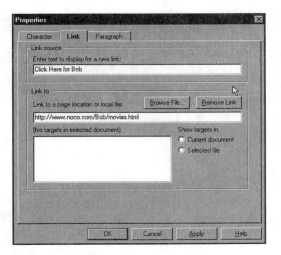

Figure 5.8.
The link is ready to go.

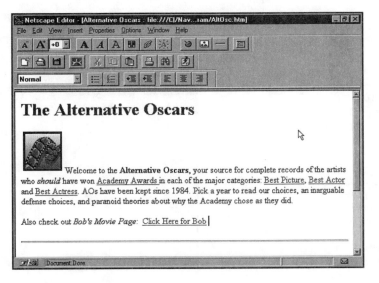

When editing a template (see Chapter 3), you must delete the template's "dummy" link sources, or create new links. See the sections "Inserting a New Link" to add a new link to a template or "Making Existing Text into a Link" to build a real link beneath the dummy link source.

Making Existing Text into a Link

To make an existing paragraph (including normal text, a heading, a list item, and so on) or any text within a paragraph, into a link:

1. In the document, highlight the words you want to use as the link source.

2. Open the Link Properties dialog by right-clicking the highlighted text and choosing Create Link using selected, as shown in Figure 5.9. (Alternatively, you can open the dialog using any of the methods described in the Task section titled "Inserting a New Link.")

Figure 5.9.

Using a context menu to create a link from existing text.

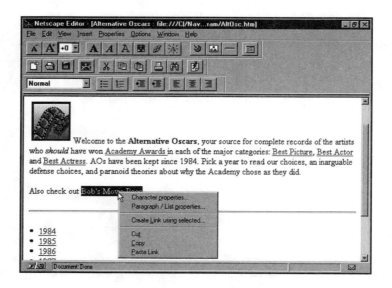

When the Link Properties dialog opens, note that the selected text appears as the Link source. (See Figure 5.10.)

Figure 5.10.

Link properties for a link made from existing text.

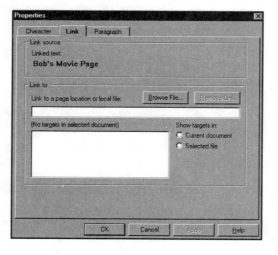

When making a link from existing text, you cannot edit the link source in the Link Properties dialog. To change the link source, click Cancel and then change the selection in the document or create a new link.

On every page in a hierarchical or Web-structured document (see Chapter 1), it's a good idea to insert a link leading back to the top page.

3. Complete the URL or pathname in Link to a page location or file and click OK.

TASK

Creating Targets

Unlike links, targets are not connected to any words appearing on the page. Instead, they mark an exact spot between words or paragraphs. Targets have names, but the name does not appear on the page; it's used only as a reference for links. (Of course, you can create the effect of an on-page target name by using a bit of on-screen text as the name for a nearby target.)

To create a target in a document:

1. Click the spot in the document where a link pointing to the target should take a visitor.

2. Click the Target button on the toolbar. (Alternatively, choose **I**nsert | **T**arget from the menu bar.) The Target dialog opens, as shown in Figure 5.11.

3. Supply a name for the target. The name needn't be long, but it must be different from the name of any other target in the file.

Figure 5.11.
The Target Properties dialog.

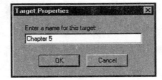

4. Click OK. A target icon appears in the document, as shown in Figure 5.12. (The target icon is visible in the Editor but not through the Browser or any other browser.)

Figure 5.12.
The finished target, as seen through the editor.

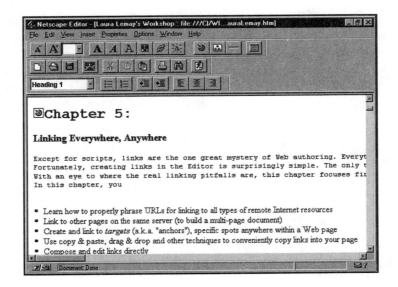

To create the target name automatically out of existing text, highlight the text before opening the target dialog. The text will appear in the dialog as the name, and the target will be positioned immediately following the selected text.

Linking to a Target

Follow the steps described earlier for creating a link (either with new or existing text). Then, in the Link Properties dialog, complete the link to the target:

❏ For a target within the same page as the link, leave the Link to a page or file box empty and click the radio button next to Current file. A list of the target names in the current file appears, shown in the same order in which they appear in the document. (See Figure 5.13.) Click the desired target. Its name appears in the Link to a page box preceded by a # mark. Click OK.

Figure 5.13.
Linking to a target.

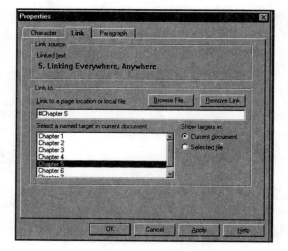

❏ For a target located within another local document, enter the URL for the local file in Link to a page location or local file (see Figure 5.13) and then click the radio button next to Selected file. A list of the target names in the selected file appears, shown in the same order in which they appear in the document. Click the desired target. Its name appears in the Link to a page box preceded by a # mark. Click OK.

Creating a Signature

A signature is really nothing more than some sort of generic sign-off message that has an e-mail address embedded within it. A few stock wording choices, in popular flavors, are

Inviting: Comments? Questions? E-mail me at `nsnell@carroll.com`

Formal: If you have any comments or questions regarding this page, contact `nsnell@carroll.com`

Efficient: Feedback: `nsnell@carroll.com`

Traditionally, the paragraph containing the signature uses the `Address` property, though that is not required. The e-mail address itself is also a mailto: link, in addition to being part of the address paragraph.

To Create a Signature

1. Click where you want the signature located (usually at or near the very end of the page, and only on the top page of a multipage document).

2. Type the signature message, including the e-mail address.

3. Choose paragraph properties for the signature. (In Figure 5.14, the `Address` property is used, according to standard practice.)

4. Highlight just the e-mail address and click the Link button on the toolbar.

5. In Link to a page location or file, enter the mailto link. For example:

   `mailto:nsnell@carroll.com`

6. Click OK.

Figure 5.14.
A signature, with a mailto link under the e-mail address.

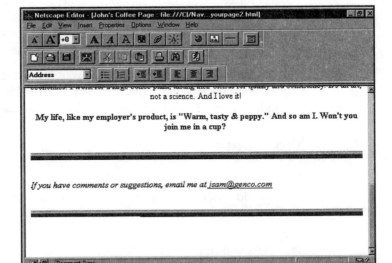

De-linking Text

Suppose you want to remove a link from your page but keep its link source text on the page. You could simply delete the link and retype the text. That's a solution for a link or two, but if you want to kill all the links in a large section or entire document, you'd find all the retyping tedious.

Instead, you can highlight the text and choose **P**roperties | **R**emove Links. This works even if you highlight whole blocks of text or whole documents. All the text, including words or paragraphs that were once link sources, remains. But the link beneath is removed, as is the link color and underlining.

Workshop Wrap-Up

Links are links, and as you can see, they're not all that complicated. In fact, making the link is the easiest part, especially if you copy the link from elsewhere. Phrasing the URL just right is the hardest part, and even that can be accomplished reliably with cut and paste, drag and drop, or some careful note-taking and typing (gasp! *typing*!). Targets are also simple to create and to link to, and provide a great way to help your visitors navigate the material you offer.

Remember, though, that just because you *can* link everywhere doesn't mean you *should*. Pages with extraneous links are no more useful than linkless ones. Check out carefully each place you'll link to. Is it really useful to your readers? Does it provide something new, or simply duplicate material your other links already lead to? Does it appear to be on a reliable server, or one that's often inaccessible or slow?

Your goal should be to provide your readers not with as many links as possible but with a choice selection. And it goes without saying that you must check, update, and add to your links often. Do that, and your visitors will return often, too.

Next Steps

Now…

- ❏ To add images and then embed links beneath them, see Chapter 6, "Working with Graphics."
- ❏ To link to video clips, sound clips or other external media, see Chapter 7, "Embedding Multimedia."
- ❏ To pepper an image with links, see Chapter 12, "Creating Interactive Forms and Image Maps."

Q&A

Q: If I want to offer quick access to other resources related to my page, can I link directly to a category listing in a Web directory, such as Yahoo or the WWW Virtual Library?

A: Sure, and many people do that. As always, it's proper to e-mail the Webmaster of any directory you link to and request permission.

Also, try not to get too specific; link at the most general point in a directory's hierarchy that pertains to your topic, and let the visitor navigate down to the specifics. Broad categories in directories are fairly stable and remain in place for years. Very specific directory listings low in the hierarchy might disappear or change names, invalidating any links to them.

Q: I'm still fuzzy on this whole relative/absolute path business, and I have a headache. Can I just stay stupid on this one, and hope everything works out in the morning?

A: To some extent, you can. Just trust Gold. When making links to local documents, use the Browse button in the Link Properties dialog to choose files, so that the Editor can phrase the path for you. Then use Gold's publishing features (see Chapter 15, "Publishing Web Documents") to publish your document, instead of handling the uploading on your own. Gold automatically adjusts the local file links and uploads all the linked files, so that the links still work on the server.

SIX

Working with Graphics

Hey, pal, you can keep your linky-dinky hypertext—*images* made the Web. Hypertext and the Web were around for years, and nobody outside the veteran online fold much cared. Then Mosaic opened the browser to pictures, hypertext became hypermedia, the vice president discovered the Internet, the press discovered the vice president, and all heck broke loose. Odds are pretty good that, had Web images not captured the world's imagination, you wouldn't be authoring Web pages today.

So it is with great and sober respect for that history that I announce the ugly truth: Images are a nuisance. They slow down access to Web documents and bottleneck servers. They pack pages with pretty but pointless pictures so that guests must scroll or link someplace just to read what they came for. They've forced millions to shell out hundreds of dollars for 28.8 kbps modems when, before the pictures, a $49, 9600 bps modem worked great. They clutter the screens of non-graphical browsers with empty little blips saying `[image]`. Most important, while images do nothing to lure any-body *to* your page—by the time a guest sees the images, he's there already—images can drive people *away*, by exceeding their patience.

There's no escaping the fact that incorporating inline images into the layout of a Web page is an important part of every Web author's goal—and to be fair, most Web surfers like and expect a little visual stimulation. So in this chapter, you'll learn how to do whatever you

In this chapter, you

- ❏ Learn how to break up your page with horizontal rules— eh, sorry, break it up with *lines*
- ❏ Discover the types of graphics files to use for inline images, and where to get them
- ❏ Insert images into documents in the Editor
- ❏ Change the alignment, spacing, and even the size of images in your pages
- ❏ Provide alternatives to images, for those whose browsers can't display images
- ❏ Use images as links
- ❏ Add a background color or pattern to a page
- ❏ Create fancy bullets and lines, like those used in the Page Wizard

Tasks in this chapter:

- ❏ Adding Horizontal Lines (Rules)
- ❏ Inserting an Image
- ❏ Formatting an Image
- ❏ Creating Alternatives
- ❏ Editing Images
- ❏ Deleting Images
- ❏ Using an Image as a Link
- ❏ Adding a Background

want to do with inline images in Navigator Gold. But you'll also get occasional, small doses of tough love. You'll learn when *not* to use images, how to avoid some picture pitfalls, and when less is more.

Adding Horizontal Lines (Rules)

Once again, we find ourselves at the mercy of Netscape's rewriting of Web taxonomy. The straight lines running horizontally across most Web pages (see Figure 6.2, later in this chapter) have always been known as *horizontal rules,* especially since they're created by the HTML tag <HR>—*HR* for *Horizontal Rule.*

Horizontal lines are not images. They're only in this otherwise image-centric chapter because they affect the page in a graphical way, not a textual way, and because there wasn't any room in Chapter 4.

But Netscape thinks the term *rule* is confusing, so in the Editor, it's a horizontal *line.* If you're trying to develop a non-Netscape-specific understanding of authoring terms, just remember that rules are rules, except in Netscape, where rules are broken. Creating a horizontal line in the Editor inserts the <HR> tag into your document to draw a rule.

Virtually any browser can handle horizontal lines, because any computer system can draw one across the screen (if even with underscores or dashes). So lines are a universal way to add some visual interest to your page, and to break up logical sections of a page or document to communicate more effectively.

To Add a Horizontal Line

1. In your document, position the edit cursor where you want to insert the rule.
2. Click the Insert Horiz. Line button on the toolbar or choose **I**nsert I **H**orizontal Line.

The line appears at the insertion point. You can leave it like it is or change its appearance by choosing Horizontal Line Properties, as shown in the next section.

To Choose Line Properties

Everything you can do in the Horizontal Line Properties dialog is based on Netscape extensions. Browsers that don't support extensions display an ordinary, 2-D rule across the full window, regardless of what the properties say.

This procedure describes how to alter the appearance of a horizontal line in your document. After the procedure, Figure 6.2 shows some of the lines you can create by applying different properties.

1. Double-click the line to open the Horizontal Line Properties dialog. (See Figure 6.1.) (You can also single-click the line and then click the Object Properties button on the toolbar or click the line and choose **P**roperties I **H**orizontal Line.)

Figure 6.1.
*Choosing Horizontal
Line Properties.*

2. Under Dimensions, enter the **H**eight (thickness) of the line in pixels. The
   default is 2 pixels, which creates a line that's very fine but clearly visible
   (classy and understated). Then choose the **W**idth of the line as a percentage
   of the width of the browser window. The default, 100%, draws a line
   across the entire window. A width of 50% draws a line half as wide as the
   window.

The choice you make
under Align is irrelevant
if you have selected
100% of window as the
width.

NOTE: In the Width field, you can open the drop-down list to choose Pixels
instead of % of window and then enter the number of pixels wide that you
want the line to be.

This approach is inadvisable, though, because even among guests using
Netscape, the apparent line width may vary noticeably with the resolution
settings for the visitor's display. For example, the line will appear to be wider
in a 640×480 display than in an 800×600 display.

Instead of bona fide
horizontal lines, you can
insert images that look
like stylized, colored
horizontal lines (like
those appearing in
pages built with the
Page Wizard, as shown
in Chapter 1). See the
section titled "Fancy
Bullets and Rules" later
in this chapter.

3. Under Align, click a radio button to align the line along the **L**eft edge of the
   screen, **C**enter the line, or align it on the **R**ight.

4. To create a shadow below the line to give it a 3-D look (see Figure 6.2), click
   the checkbox next to 3-D **s**hading.

5. Click OK.

Figure 6.2.
Horizontal lines with various properties.

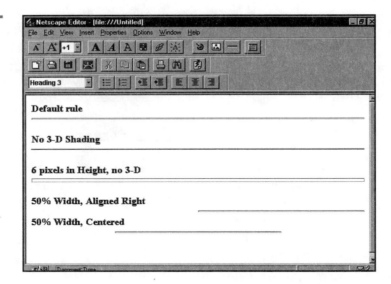

About Inline Images

Inline images are those that automatically appear within the layout of the page when the page is accessed by a graphical browser. In this section, you'll learn about inline images.

Don't confuse inline images with *external* media—images, video clips, sound clips, animations—which display or play in the browser or in a helper application when the visitor hits a link. External media—including external images—are covered in Chapter 7, "Embedding Multimedia."

Types of Image Files

The CD at the back of this book includes several great viewers for image files, including ACDSee, Graphics Workshop, and VidVUE. (See Appendix C.)

Image files come in many types: The .PCX and .BMP files are used most often in Windows, TIFF (.TIF) files are used in publishing, and so on. But by far, the most common type of image file used for inline graphics is GIF (pronounced *jif* and using the file extension .GIF). The next most popular type is JPEG (file extension .JPG in most Windows systems).

GIF files offer certain advantages (see the section titled "Interlacing" later in this chapter), but are limited to 256 colors (or 256 shades of gray in black and white images). For most graphics, especially those originally drawn on a computer, this "8-bit" color is plenty. But for photographs, paintings, and other images taken "from life," 256 colors does not permit enough variation in color or shade to present a realistically shaded image; the results can look computerish.

However, GIFs 256-color limitation is not necessarily a big disadvantage, for two reasons:

❏ Images in 16-bit color (65,000 colors) or 24-bit "true color" (16 million colors) tend to be much larger than 256-color graphics—so much so that they might be inappropriate as inline images. (See the section titled "File Size" later in this chapter.)

❏ A large proportion of your audience will be running their browsers in 256-color mode anyway which cannot display the extra color depth and detail possible in 16-bit and 24-bit color graphics.

Although images in file types other than GIF or JPEG are inappropriate for inline images, other file types may be used as external images, those that appear only when the visitor clicks a link. See Chapter 8, "Real-Life Examples I."

However, if you want or need to display more than 256 colors or grays, a JPEG file can handle it.

All graphical Web browsers can display inline GIF images, and most can display *only* GIF images. Netscape Navigator, Internet Explorer, and a few others can also display JPEG images. Inline support for other image file formats is almost non-existent. Unless and until things change, all of your inline graphics should be GIF or JPEG files.

Where Image Files Come From

Where can you get images? You can make (or acquire them) in the following ways. The important issue is not where they come from, but their file type, size and other factors, as described in the next section.

Paint/Draw: You can use a paint or draw program to create your inline graphics. Ideally, the program should be able to save your picture as a GIF (or, optionally JPEG) graphic. If not, you can find conversion utilities on the Web to convert most graphics file types to GIF. (See Chapter 17, "Developing Your Authoring Skills," and Appendix C, "What's on the CD?"

Handy graphics programs that can convert many types of image files is included on the CD-ROM at the back of this book. See Appendix C.

Convert: If you have existing graphics you want to use in your page, but they're not in GIF or JPEG format, you can convert them to GIF or JPEG using a graphics conversion utility.

Scan: Using a hand scanner, sheetfed scanner, or flatbed scanner, you can scan photographs or other images and save them (using the scanning software) as GIF or JPEG images.

Clip: Collections of clip art are available on the Web and in commercial and shareware software packages. As a rule, clip art is offered copyright-free, and you can use it any way you want to. Some clip art collections are copyright-protected for some uses; be sure to read any copyright notices accompanying any clip art before you publish it in a Web page.

The CD-ROM at the back of this book contains a selection of copyright-free clip art for your Web pages. Chapter 17 shows the URLs of clip art collections on the Web.

NOTE: Clip art collections on the Web generally offer their wares by displaying the images in a Web page. You can copy these images directly from the Web page into your document, using the following steps:

1. Viewing the page in the browser, right-click the desired image and choose Save this Image as from the context menu, as shown in Figure 6.3. A standard Windows 95 Save As dialog opens.

2. Save the file using the path and filename desired. (The image's current filename has been supplied for you, but you can change it. Do not change the extension, which informs browsers of the image's type.)

3. Switch to the Editor and insert the image into your document as described later in the Task section titled "Inserting an Image."

You can use the same procedure to download any image you see on the Web, in any page. But be careful not to download and then publish copyrighted images.

Finally, recall from Chapter 3, "Using the Netscape Editor," that you can capture any Web page, including its graphics, by viewing it in the browser and clicking the Edit button. Using this technique, you can quickly capture whole pages of clip art in one step.

Figure 6.3.
Copying an image from the Web.

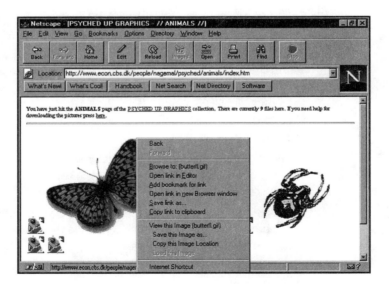

Important Inline Image Considerations

Before inserting an image into your document, consider the following issues.

File Type

As a rule, try to use GIF files whenever possible. Doing so ensures that almost any visitor using a graphical browser can see the image.

When using JPEG, it's a good idea to show thumbnails—small, low-resolution versions—of the images inline and then link the inline thumbnails to the full JPEG file as an external image. See Chapter 8.

When you want to publish a more photorealistic image or have a JPEG file you can't get converted to GIF, you can use a JPEG file as an inline image. If you do, be aware that you're hiding your picture from anyone not using Netscape Navigator or one of a handful of other browsers that do not support inline JPEG.

For either GIF or JPEG, when your image editor gives you a choice of color model and resolution, choose RGB as the color model and 72 dpi as the resolution. These settings offer the best balance between appearance and file size.

File Size

In theory, it takes roughly 20 seconds for a 20KB image file to travel from a server to a browser over a 14.4 kbps Internet connection. Over a 28.8 kbps connection, the image should show up twice as fast (10 seconds), but in practice, it would more likely take about 3/4 the time (7-8 seconds). A host of factors affect the speed with which an image makes it to a visitor's optic nerve, including the disc access speed of the server, processor speed of the client PC, performance of the browser, and multitasking speed.

Still, the one-second-per-KB rule of thumb is a good way to estimate the speed with which your page will materialize on most visitor's screens. Given that, consider how long you want to make visitors wait to see your whole creation. Popular wisdom says a typical Web surfer won't wait 30 seconds before moving on—and, of course, popular wisdom is usually wrong. You might lose visitors if your page takes as few as 20 seconds to shape up.

Add up the size of your HTML file and all the inline images you plan to add to it. The recommended maximum is 30KB—such a page appears, images and all, in about 30 seconds. Realistically, though, it's wise to try to keep the whole package to around 20KB or less.

The obviously solution is to use fewer images. Other than that, here are some ways to keep your document compact:

Use images that take up less area on the page: Smaller pictures generally mean smaller files.

Use fewer colors: When drawing or painting an image, use as few colors as you can to achieve the desired effect. When working with clip art or scanned images that contain many colors, use an image editor to reduce the number of colors, or the size of the *color palette*. Most editors offer options for making color images black and white, or for posterizing a photograph to give it a graphical look. Either of these options tends to reduce file size dramatically and can result in some nifty effects.

Create text-only alternative Web pages: When your document is heavily graphical, create a second set of all pages beyond the top page, using the same general content but no graphics. On the top page, provide a link to this text-only version of your document. Visitors with text-only browsers and others who simply don't care to wait for images can use the text version instead.

Use thumbnails and external media: Instead of displaying large GIF or JPEG images inline, use inline thumbnails or text as link sources to external versions of the images. That way, visitors have the option of viewing or ignoring the images. Visitors wait more patiently for images they actually choose to view.

Copyrights

The ease with which images can be scanned, converted, copied, or even captured from the Web itself is a natural invitation to copyright infringement—and, in fact, the Web today is rampant with copyright violations.

Regardless of whether it was accompanied by a copyright notice, do not publish any image unless

❏ You created it yourself by drawing or painting it, or by photographing it with a digital camera.

❏ You scanned it from artwork you created or artwork you know to be copyright free.

❏ You acquired it from a clip art collection whose copyright notice specifically calls the images contained therein "copyright-free" or states clearly that you are authorized to publish the images. (If the copyright notice requires that you label the image with information about its creator, do it.)

If you do publish your own artwork on the Web, include on your page a link to a copyright notice in which you reserve the rights to your artwork.

Interlacing and Low-Resolution Versions

Interlacing and low-resolution alternatives are two ways to speed up the apparent display of images on your page.

Interlacing, which works only for GIF graphics, does not affect the final look of the image in your page at all and requires no changes to the steps used to insert or format the image in your page. But interlacing does change the way the image materializes on the screen in some browsers.

Typically, when retrieving a non-interlaced GIF image, a browser displays an image placeholder until the entire GIF image has been downloaded and then displays the image. If you save your GIF image in interlaced format, browsers that support interlacing can begin to display the image while downloading it. As the image is retrieved, it appears quickly as a blurry rendition of itself and then incrementally sharpens up as more of the image is retrieved.

Interlacing allows visitors to your page to get an idea of what your images look like before they've finished downloading. If the visitor sees what he or she needs to see before the image comes into focus, the visitor can move on without waiting for the finished graphic.

Another way to give visitors something to look at before the graphics show up is to use your image editor to save an alternate version of the image in a very low resolution (and with a different name from the high-res version). You can then define the low resolution version as the Image alternative representation when choosing Image Properties (see the Task section titled "Creating Alternatives" later in this chapter) for the high-resolution version.

In browsers that support alternative representations, the low-res, alternative image displays first—and quickly, because decreasing resolution makes the image file smaller. Although the visitor examines the low-res version, the browser loads the full resolution image in the background and prepares it for display. When the full resolution image is ready, it replaces the low resolution version on the page. Like interlacing GIF images, this technique allows visitors to get an idea of what the image represents well before the final image shows up. You can use low-res alternatives for both GIF and JPEG images.

Obviously, the larger the file size of your images, the more important interlacing and low-res alternatives become.

Inserting an Image

The Publish tab of the Editor Preferences dialog allows you to instruct the Editor to automatically keep image files together with the document when publishing and to adjust links in the process. See Chapter 15.

Before beginning, prepare your image file(s). Ideally, any image files should be stored in the same directory as the HTML file for the document in which they will appear. If images reside in other directories, the Editor can copy them automatically to the same directory. (See the section titled "Keeping Images and Documents Together" later in this chapter.)

1. Position the edit cursor in your document where you want to insert the image.

2. Click the Insert Image button on the toolbar or choose Insert | Image. The Image Properties dialog opens, as shown in Figure 6.4.

Figure 6.4.
Image properties.

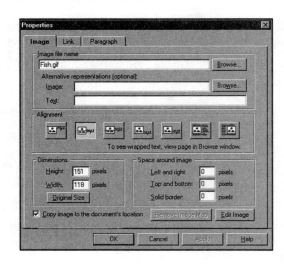

The image alignment options are enabled by Netscape extensions. In browsers that do not support extensions, all images appear directly above adjacent text and on the left side of the page, regardless of your alignment choices.

You can also insert an image by dragging an image file icon from a Windows 95 folder and dropping it at the desired insert location in your document.

To use the same image multiple times in a document, you don't need multiple copies of the image. With one copy of the file available on the server, you can enter the same Image file name in as many Image Properties dialogs as you want to.

3. Enter the image filename or click **B**rowse to find it.

4. Click OK. The image appears in the document with no Alternative representations, and with the default settings for Alignment, Dimensions, and Space around image (none).

To change the properties for Alignment, Dimensions, and Space around image, see the next section. To create alternative representations, see the Task section titled "Creating Alternatives."

Formatting an Image

Using the Image Properties dialog, you can change the way an inline image is displayed and treated in a variety of ways. You can make these changes in the dialog while inserting the image (see the preceding section), or you can open the Properties dialog for an image at any time by

❑ Double-clicking the image

❑ Single-clicking the image and clicking the Object Properties button on the toolbar

❑ Single-clicking the image and choosing **P**roperties | **I**mage.

To Change Alignment

The buttons under alignment enable you to choose how the image should be positioned relative to adjacent text. You can position the text in five different ways to the right of the image. You can also wrap paragraphs around the image, on either side of the image.

To choose Alignment, click any of the six alignment buttons. The choices (in button order, from left to right) are

❏ The first line of text goes to the right of the image, and any remaining text starts beneath the image. The top of the first line of text aligns with the top of the image. (See Figure 6.5.)

❏ The first line of text goes to the right of the image, and any remaining text starts beneath the image. The horizontal centerline of the first line of text aligns with the center of the image.

❏ The first line of text goes to the right of the image, and any remaining text starts beneath the image. The first line of text sits on top of the centerline of the image. (See Figure 6.6.)

❏ The first line of text goes to the right of the image, and any remaining text starts beneath the image. The first line of text aligns with the bottom of the image (descenders in text hang below line).

❏ The first line of text goes to the right of the image, and any remaining text starts beneath the image. The first line of text, including descenders, sits above the bottom line of the image.

❏ Text wraps around the right side of the image. The first line of text starts directly above the image.

❏ Text wraps around the left side of the image. The first line of text starts directly above the image. (See Figure 6.7.)

Figure 6.5.
An image aligned by the first alignment button from the left.

Descenders are the parts of letters that hang down below the baseline, like the tails on *y* and *j*.

If you choose either of the two text-wrapping alignment buttons, you must browse the document to see the results. Text wrapping around an image does not display properly in the Editor.

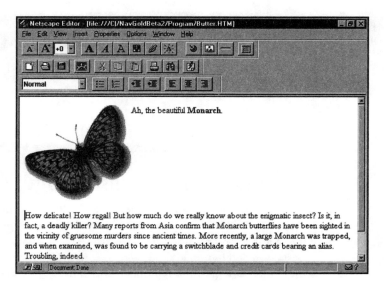

Figure 6.6.
An image aligned by the third alignment button from the left.

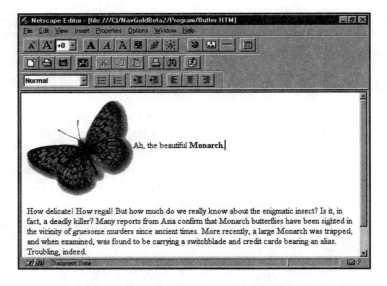

Figure 6.7.
An image aligned by the alignment button farthest to the right.

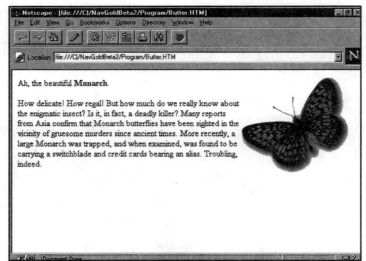

Be sure to test your page in a variety of browsers to see how your image choices come out in those that don't support extensions or differ from Navigator in other ways. See Chapter 3 and Chapter 16.

To Change the Dimensions of the Image

As a rule, images should be properly sized before you insert them. For example, you'll get better results if you size a new image in the application used to create it, or in a good image-editing program, than in the Editor. Scanned images come out best if size is determined before in the scanning software before the scan even happens; after that, you're better off sizing the image in the scanning software than in the Editor.

Why? First, the Editor can't really change the dimensions of an image. Instead, it applies tags to the HTML file that Netscape uses to resize the image when displaying it. Netscape is not as sophisticated a graphics scaler as a real image-editing program, and the likelihood of unattractive "artifacts" in the scaled image, such as streaks through the image, is high. Also, when you scale an image in most image-editing programs, you can optionally preserve the original aspect ratio of the image. In the Editor, to preserve the original ratio, you must calculate it yourself.

But most importantly, using the Dimensions box in Image **P**roperties is inadvisable because the scaling relies on a Netscape extension. If you use dimensions to scale your image, the image will still appear in its original size in all graphical browsers that don't support Netscape extensions. On the other hand, if you scale the image in an image editor and leave the Dimensions box in Image Properties alone, the image will appear in the proper size in any graphical browser.

If you decide to change dimensions anyway, choose a height and width, in pixels, for the image. The default you see when you first open the Image Properties dialog is the image's original size.

You can restore the original size at any time by clicking **O**riginal Size.

To Change Spacing and Add Borders

You can add extra space all around the image, just on the sides, or just on the top and bottom. You can also add a black border all around the image, and choose the border's width (in pixels).

Note that there's a reasonable amount of space around the image even when the default choices in these fields—0 pixels for space and 0 for border (no border)—are selected. Take a look at Figure 6.7. The image in that picture uses the default selections for spacing around and does not butt hard against the text.

> To increase the space between the sides of the image and adjacent text, enter the number of pixels in **L**eft and right.

> To increase the space between the top and bottom of the image and adjacent text, enter the number of pixels in **T**op and bottom.

> To add a black border all around the image (see Figure 6.8), enter a number of pixels for the thickness of the border in **S**olid border.

Figure 6.8.

The same page shown in Figure 6.7 but with additional Space around image (30 pixels Left and Right) and a 4-pixel border.

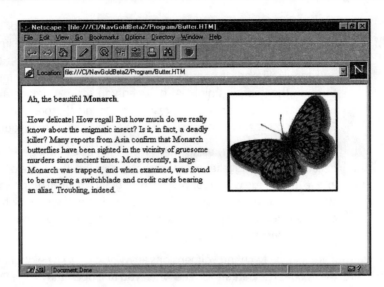

Keeping Images and Documents Together

At the bottom of the Image Properties dialog, check the checkbox next to **C**opy image to the document's location to automatically copy the file specified in Image file name to the same directory as the current HTML document. When you click OK, the image is copied and the path in the Image file name box is removed (leaving just the filename, which is all that's required for pointing to an image file in the same directory as the document).

Even though storing your images and HTML files together is advisable, it's not essential. If you have checked the two checkboxes in the Publish tab of the Editor Preferences dialog, all image files will automatically be stored in the same server directory as the document when you publish. (See Chapter 15, "Publishing Web Documents.") The pointers in the document specifying the locations of image files are automatically updated, as well, so that browsers know where to find the image files when reading your document.

So if you prefer to keep your documents and images in separate directories while creating them on your PC, that's fine: Netscape Gold can straighten everything out when you publish.

Creating Alternatives

The Alternative representations fields in the Image Properties dialog each do two very different things:

If you enter an empty string—two quotation marks together (" ")—as the text alternative, text-only browsers display no text alternative, but don't display an image placeholder either; they just ignore the whole image issue.

In I**m**age, you enter (or browse for) the filename of a low-resolution version of the image appearing above in Image file name.

In Te**x**t, you enter some text to appear instead of the graphic, in browsers that do not support graphics. This allows you to supply some informative text to replace the idea that was originally communicated by the picture. Also, many browsers that support text alternatives will display an image placeholder, something like <image>, if you don't supply a text alternative representation. The text alternative would not only be more informative in such browsers, but also better looking.

Editing Images

The Edit Image button near the bottom of the Image Properties dialog (refer back to Figure 6.4) opens the image editor defined in the Editor Preferences. (See Chapter 3, "Using the Netscape Editor.")

In the Editor Preferences, you can enter the path and filename of any image editor you like. On the CD-ROM accompanying this book, you'll find two terrific editors: Paint Shop Pro and Graphics workshop. Use these programs to create, convert, or edit images you'll put in your pages.

Deleting Images

To delete an image, click it once to highlight it and then press Del or click the Cut button on the toolbar.

Using an Image as a Link

You cannot move an image within a document with drag and drop or cut and paste. You must delete it one place and reinsert it in the other.

When you use an image as a link source, always supply the same link nearby on the page, using descriptive text as the link source. That way, visitors who cannot display the image still have a descriptive link source to select.

Every link has two parts: the link source (the thing a visitor sees and clicks) and the URL (or local path and filename) to which the browser points when the link source is clicked.

When you make an image into a link, all you're really doing is using an image as the link source, instead of text. To do that:

1. Insert the image into the document, as described earlier in this chapter, and format it as desired.

2. Right-click the image and choose Create **L**ink using selected from the context menu. (Alternatively, you can single-click the image to highlight it and then click the Insert Link button on the toolbar or choose **I**nsert I **L**ink.) A screen appears like the one in Figure 6.9, showing the image's filename as the Link source.

3. Enter a URL, local pathname, or target name in the Link to a page location or file, as described in Chapter 5, "Linking Everywhere, Anywhere."

Figure 6.9.
The Link Properties dialog, with an image as the link source.

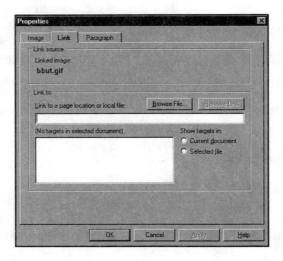

Image maps are another way to use images as links. In an image map, different spots on an image activate different links. You'll create image maps in Chapter 12.

Fancy Bullets and Rules

You'll find a great selection of GIF image files for fancy bullets and rules on the CD-ROM at the back of this book. See Appendix C.

If you've seen the pages created by the Netscape page Wizard (see Chapter 2, "Making the Page Wizard Do the Work") or some other highfalutin' pages, you might have seen cool, multicolored graphical bullets and rules. These are not actual bullets and rules, the kind you create with the Unnumbered List property and Insert Horizontal Line, respectively. Instead, they're images that look like bullets and rules.

Chapter 17 shows where you can find bullet and rule images on the Web.

Rule-type images, sometimes called *bars,* are simply inserted between paragraphs. The bullets are inserted before individual lines of text, using any paragraph style other than List. (If you use List, you get your cool bullets plus the List's bullets or numbers. Icky.) To get the best results when inserting a bullet image next to a line of text, choose the second button from the left under Alignment in the Image Properties dialog.

Figure 6.10.
Cool rules and bullets.

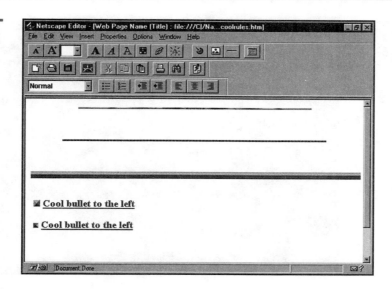

Adding a Background

You'll find a selection of GIF and JPEG image files for background textures on the CD-ROM at the back of this book. See Appendix C.

You can add a *background*—a solid color, graphical texture, or repeated graphic that covers the entire page but stays behind your text and images—in two ways:

Backgrounds are enabled by Netscape extensions. In browsers that don't support extensions, the background does not appear at all.

A solid color: A flat color (other than the visitor's browser's default background color) appears behind all of your text and graphics.

A tiled image: An image file (GIF or JPEG) repeated across the entire background. When this image has been designed carefully to match up perfectly with its mates at all four corners, the tiling creates a seamless, "texture," effect, as if one enormous image covered the background. (See Figure 6.11.) Fortunately, the effect is created out of only one small image; accessing an image file large enough to cover a page would choke most Internet connections.

As an alternative to a background texture, you can choose to tile an image that doesn't match up perfectly with its copies at the edges. Using this technique, you can create some fun background effects, as shown in Figure 6.12.

Finally, you can use as a background a single, large image file that covers the entire page background (and thus requires no tiling). But doing so is not advisable, since such a large image would take a *very* long time to download. Many visitors would jump to another page before your background ever showed up.

Figure 6.11.
A tiled background texture.

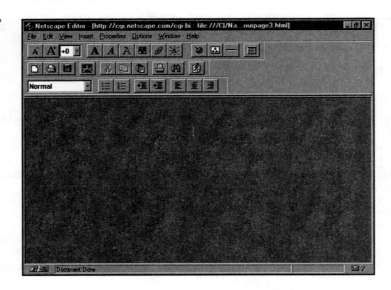

Figure 6.12.
A fun background made of a tiled image.

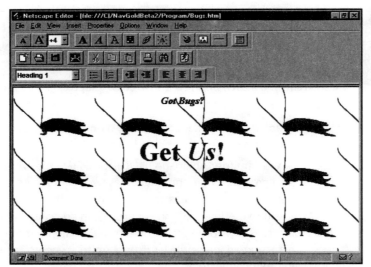

NOTE: Be careful with backgrounds. If you don't choose carefully, you'll wind up making your text illegible, or at least hard on the eyes.

Use custom text colors (see Chapter 4, "Composing, Editing, and Formatting Text") to contrast the text with the background. Use light colors to stand out against dark backgrounds, and dark to stand out against light backgrounds.

Chapter 17 shows where you can find background images on the Web.

To collect some free backgrounds, run the Page Wizard (see Chapter 2) multiple times, choosing a different background texture each time. Each time, you'll save a different copyright-free background texture on your PC, which you can use for other pages you create.

Even with those precautions, a tiled-image background is usually too much when seen behind a page with lots of text on it. A way around this is to use a snazzy tile background behind your logo or brief text on a top page, then switch to a solid color or no background on text-heavy pages to which the top page links.

To add a background:

1. Open the Document Properties dialog by choosing **P**roperties | **D**ocument.
2. Click the Appearance tab.
3. Under Background:
   - ❏ To create a solid color background, click the radio button for Solid **c**olor. Then click Ch**o**ose Color to select a color.
   - ❏ To create a tiled image background, click the radio button for **I**mage file. Enter the filename of the image to tile or **B**rowse for it.

Figure 6.13.
Choosing a background in Document Properties.

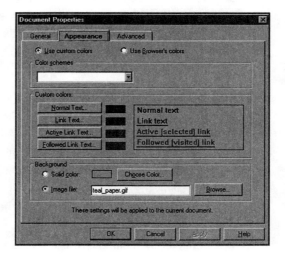

NOTE: In the Appearance tab of the Editor Preferences dialog (see Chapter 3, "Using the Netscape Editor"), you can select a default background for all documents you create in the Editor. The steps for specifying a default background in Editor Preferences are the same as those for the Document Properties dialog. (See the Task section titled "Adding a Background" earlier in this chapter.)

After you choose a default background in Editor Preferences, it appears automatically in every document you create (but not in documents you created before you defined the default background). For any document, you can override the default background by choosing a new background (or no background) in Document Properties.

Workshop Wrap-Up

In the cookie that is a Web page, images are the chocolate chips. And as we all know, the best cookie strikes just the right chip-to-cookie ratio—too many chips is as bad as none at all. (Replace with your favorite ratio-balancing analogy: pizza crust:cheese, peanut butter:jelly, RAM:processor speed, longevity:fun, and so on.)

The issue is not just whether you use graphics, or how many, but why. Do the images add something useful to your page—like photos of people the page is by or about, or images of products and places described—or are they mere decoration? An image or two added for the sake of style is worthwhile, but only if the image succeeds in actually conveying style. If it seems like a generic image dropped there for the mere sake of having an image, dump it. Dress your page with careful text formatting, and the natural beauty of solid organization and strong writing.

Next Steps

Now...

❏ To learn how to add links to external images, video, audio and animation, see Chapter 7, "Embedding Multimedia."

❏ To see examples of pages created using the techniques introduced in Part I of this book, see Chapter 8, "Real-Life Examples I."

❏ To learn how to apply Web page techniques not supported in the Editor, see Chapter 9, "Editing HTML Source Code."

❏ To pepper an image map with links, see Chapter 12, "Creating Interactive Forms and Image Maps."

Q&A

Q: I've seen graphics software packages that let you create wonderful stylized graphics out of words, letters, and numbers. Can I use these to create Web graphics?

A: Of course, provided the program saves files as GIF or JPEG, or as something that can be converted into GIF or JPEG. That's a great way to make a snazzy title for your page.

But watch out: If you make pictures out of words, and those words are important, you must be sure to provide the same text elsewhere in nongraphical form (for the graphics-impaired). Use an alternative representation or repeat the text nearby on the page.

Q: You sure are a downer about images. But on the coolest, award-winning pages out there, I see lots of graphics. Aren't you being a little puritanical here?

A: Perhaps—and yes, there are some great, highly graphical sites out there. But for every slickly produced, award-winning site, there are a hundred others that overuse pointless graphics or obliterate text with poorly chosen background textures. The award winners use all their graphics smartly, and to a purpose. My point is not to discourage the use of images. I just want you to ask yourself the right questions before dumping any old picture on your page. You can bet the award winners do.

SEVEN

Embedding Multimedia

You might expect multimedia to be one of the most challenging aspects of Web authoring. But in truth, embedding multimedia is mostly a matter of inserting an ordinary link that points to a multimedia file; if you know how to make a link, you know how to embed multimedia. (See Chapter 5, "Linking Everywhere, Anywhere.")

Your only responsibility is creating the link and getting your page and the multimedia file properly published on the server. (See Chapter 15, "Publishing Web Documents.") After that, making multimedia work is the visitor's problem. If the file type the link points to can be played or displayed in the visitor's browser (or, more commonly, in a helper application), the file works. If not, not. Either way, there's not much you can do about it other than trying to stick with the most widely supported file types.

But that doesn't mean there's nothing to learn about adding external media to your Web pages. In particular, it's essential to understand which types of external media are best supported in the browser world so that you can reach the widest possible audience.

In this chapter, you

- ❑ Discover how external media works and what you can do with it
- ❑ Learn about the most common types of files offered as external media
- ❑ Choose media types to serve the widest possible Web audience or a targeted audience
- ❑ Insert links to external media in your Web document
- ❑ Learn how to present your links to external media in ways visitors will find attractive and functional

Tasks in this chapter:

- ❑ Linking to External Media

About External Media

External media are media files—images, video clips, sound clips—to which links in a document point. External media files do not display or play automatically when a visitor accesses a Web page; rather, they are downloaded to the visitor's PC and displayed or played there only when the visitor executes a link.

In most cases, the browser does not play or display the file itself. Instead, a helper application opens to do the job. Some browsers have native support for some types of files, but when the file is set up as external media, the effect is the same as if a helper application was used. For example, Netscape Navigator has native support for JPEG image files; it can handle them as inline or external media. But when a JPEG image is supplied as an external file, it has no home on the page—Netscape doesn't know where to put it. So despite its ability to display a JPEG image inline, Netscape always opens an empty window (see Figure 7.1) to show an image accessed as an external file.

Figure 7.1.

Viewing an external JPEG image through Netscape Navigator Gold.

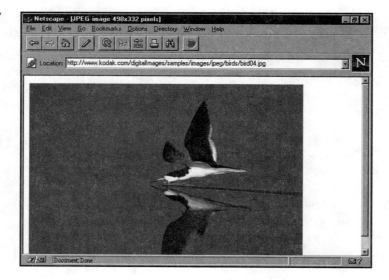

But what if the visitor's browser has no native support and no helper application for a particular external media file? When the visitor clicks the link, the browser downloads and saves the file on disk. (See Figure 7.2.) That way, the visitor can install an appropriate application later to play the file offline. Because unplayable files are downloaded and saved, text-only browser users can still capture media files from the Web and then play them later in an application or a system that supports them.

Figure 7.2.
When it lacks support for an external file type, Navigator offers to download and save the file or let you configure a new helper application.

Understanding Media Types

(Yes, I know, Dan Rather is a "Media Type"… but you won't learn about him here. Stay with me.)

Using the techniques for embedding external media, you can build links to any type of file in the world, from video and sound clips to the dynamic link library (.DLL) files used by Microsoft Golf.

But video and sound clips may be playable by the visitor, whereas the .DLL files from Golf are useless (except to Golf). So the important question is not, "What can I supply as external media," but "What can the browsers and helper applications out there actually play or display?"

You can help your visitors deal with whatever media you supply by including links to sites where they can download helper applications to play the files. See the section titled "Tips for Proper Presentation" later in this chapter.

Unfortunately, there's a tendency for external media file types to be system-specific, or at least favored by certain systems. Some types of files will play only in Windows, others only in Macintosh, and so on. More commonly, a type of file will work across multiple systems but is favored by one system. For example, Video for Windows (.AVI) video clips play natively in Windows but require a special player on a Mac. When faced with a choice between formats that don't reach everyone, you have three options:

❑ Use the most widely supported format, even if it is not universally supported.

❑ Choose the file type most easily supported by your target audience. For example, most artists (not all, of course) use Macs. If your page and its external media files are aimed at the arts community, favor file types that favor the Mac.

❑ Offer multiple versions of your media files, each in a different format. (See the section titled "Tips for Proper Presentation" later in this chapter.)

Finally, although inline images are lost on those using text-only browsers, keep in mind that the text-only crowd often can use external media. When a browser doesn't know how to display or play an external file, it simply downloads the file to disk and saves it. That gives the text-only visitor the ability to play or display that file outside the browser in a compatible application, or to copy the file to disk and take it to another computer properly equipped to display or play the file.

NOTE: In the descriptions of the various types of external media, the standard file extension for each type is shown. These file types are extremely important, because they help the browser determine which helper application (or internal program) to open to display or play the file.

If you publish an external media file and violate the extension conventions— for example, using an extension of .VID on an AVI video clip—the file will almost certainly fail to appear or play to visitors, although it will still be downloaded to the visitor's computer.

Images

As explained in Chapter 6, "Working with Graphics," the main image file format for inline graphics in Web pages is GIF. Also appearing inline, but much less frequently than GIF, are JPEG graphics, which can look better than GIF images but are only supported as inline images by a handful of browsers. (Netscape Navigator is one.) Although GIF and JPEG images can be used inline, there's no reason why you couldn't offer them as external media instead; in fact, there are some good reasons to do so.

Suppose you had many graphics you wanted to show—for example, pictures of products you sell or headshots of your employees or family. Inserting many such images inline, even in GIF format, will dramatically increase the time required to transmit your full page to a visitor. The longer the page takes to shape up on screen, the more likely a visitor is to jump elsewhere without fully appreciating your message. In such a case, consider using a minimum of inline images in a page that's compellingly organized and written. Then offer your images as external media, from a menu or from thumbnails. (See the section titled "Tips for Proper Presentation" later in this chapter.)

Offering images as external media has other advantages as well. When using inline images, in order to avoid building a page that takes a week to appear on the visitor's screen, you often must compromise the appearance of the images by using few colors and by making images fairly small (covering a small area). When images are external, you can publish the highest quality images you want to—even full-screen, photorealistic, 24-bit color JPEG images. (True, when the visitor clicks the link to view such images, the wait for such a picture to appear can be long. But by the time a visitor chooses to see external media, he or she has already been pulled into your document and is much more likely to wait patiently.) Professional artists who publish their portfolios on the Web nearly always offer their work as external JPEGs so they can show the best.

Although GIF and JPEG are the only image formats supported inline, any other image format may be used externally. There is, however, one caveat: GIF and JPEG have been

On the CD at the back of this book, you'll find two great utilities for editing and converting image files—Graphics Workshop and Paintshop Pro—plus two great image file viewers—ACDSee and VidVUE. See Appendix C.

favored for a reason. They are broadly supported across the principle graphical systems—Windows, Macintosh, and X Window. Other image file types tend to be supported by applications on one or two systems but rarely on all three. So although you may offer these alternative image formats, you should convert these and publish them as GIF or JPEG files whenever possible.

Publisher's Paintbrush (PCX) and Windows Bitmap (BMP): The principle graphics formats used in Windows (3.1 and 95). Graphics created in Windows 95's Paint program can be saved in either format. Any Windows-based graphical browser that uses helper applications can display external PCX and BMP files because Paint can be used as the helper. In the Mac world, there is some application support for PCX files but very little for BMP. As a rule, use PCX or BMP formats only when your intended audience includes only Windows users.

Tagged-Image File Format (TIF, or TIFF): TIFF files are a longtime standard for scanned images, and most scanning software saves TIFF files (along with other formats). TIFF files are great for high-resolution images destined for printing but tend to be rather large as external media in comparison to other formats. TIFF files are used on all types of systems but are not widely supported by applications other than desktop publishing programs.

Macintosh Picture (PIC, or PICT): A Macintosh picture file. The Mac has native support for PICT, so any Mac visitor to your page can display PICT files. But PICT support is rare beyond the Mac world.

XBM: An X Window bitmap image. X Window systems, and most other graphical interfaces to UNIX environments, have native support for XBM, so almost any visitor using a UNIX system with a graphical interface can display XBM files. But XBM support is rare beyond the UNIX world.

Video

On the CD at the back of this book, you'll find two great players for video clips: VidVUE and MPEGPlay 32. See Appendix C.

Three principle video file formats appear on the Web. Each offers acceptable video quality (by the standards of computer-based viewing), and all three can include audio with the video. MPEG offers the best overall quality, but MPEG files are generally larger than comparable files for similar clips in the other formats.

Video for Windows (AVI, or Audio-Video Interleave): AVI files, which include both picture and sound, are the standard for video clips in Windows 3.1 and Windows 95. Windows 95's Media Player applet has native support for AVI, whereas Windows 3.1 users must install a Video for Windows player to play AVI files. Mac users can install players for AVI, as well, but outside of the Windows world, MPEG and MOV files are far better supported.

Motion-Picture Experts Group (MPG, or MPEG): An independent standard for high-quality audio and video. An MPEG player is required on any system type. Because MPEG offers such high quality and because there are so many MPEG clips on the Web, most surfers interested in using video have installed an MPEG player.

QuickTime (MOV, or Movie): QuickTime is the Macintosh video standard, Apple's counterpart to Video for Windows. All Macs have native support for QuickTime, whereas users of other systems must install a player. Windows users can install a QuickTime player or add an extension to Windows 95's Media Player that enables it to play QuickTime files.

Chapter 17, "Developing Your Authoring Skills," lists good places to find video clips, players or other information.

Audio

Audio is perhaps the most confusing area of Web multimedia. There are many formats now, and a few more emerge each year as developers try to improve the quality or download speed of audio information.

Although some browsers contain native support for some sound formats, the effect is the same as when a helper application is used. A pop-up window opens with controls for the sound, such as Play or Rewind.

On the CD at the back of this book, you'll find two great players/ converters for sound clips: VidVUE and GoldWave. See Appendix C.

Basic audio (AU or SND): The most common sound format, basic audio is supported natively by several browsers and by most audio player helpers. Although Basic audio offers only so-so sound, its combination of wide support and relatively small file size make it the recommended media type except when high audio quality is required.

Windows Sound Clip (WAV): The sound clip standard for Windows 3.1 and 95. The audio quality is about the same as Basic audio, but the format is not well supported outside of Windows. WAV is best used for distributing sounds to Windows users.

To learn more about using RealAudio and TrueSpeech, visit their home pages. The URLs appear in Chapter 17.

RealAudio and TrueSpeech: These are two competing standards for realtime, audio over the Web. What *realtime* means in this context is that audio data can play as it arrives at the client; the surfer needn't wait for the whole file to download before hearing it. As a result, much longer sound files can be published in these formats, including whole radio programs and live broadcasts. To supply RealAudio or TrueSpeech as external media on your Web page, you must set up special proprietary software on the Web server. Free players are available for these formats, but you must pay for the server.

Chapter 17, "Developing Your Authoring Skills," lists good places to find sound clips, players, and other information.

Other File Types

Although the principle use of the techniques described in this chapter is to offer links to multimedia files through your Web pages, note that the steps described in the next section can be used to offer any file to your visitors. Again, supplying a file to visitors through an external link is always the same process, regardless of what the file contains. Your task is to determine whether your target audience has the appropriate hardware or software to use what you offer.

Some of the other file types commonly offered through the Web as external media include

Adobe Acrobat (PDF): Adobe Acrobat is an effort to create a cross-platform document format. A PDF file—including its fonts, formatting, and colors—is readable across many different systems, including Windows, Macintosh, and X Window. It works, but still relatively few people have the required Acrobat viewer.

Adobe PostScript (PS): Adobe's page description language, used primarily for printed documents. Few people have the necessary viewers to read a PostScript file on-screen, but many—especially Mac users—have PostScript printers and can print PostScript files. PostScript is an excellent way to distribute manuals or books intended for printing.

Flat ASCII text (TXT): Not the prettiest way to offer information, but unquestionably the most widely supported. Everybody on the Net can read a text file. The only thing you have to worry about is whether your intended audience reads English.

 ## Linking to External Media

The following procedure assumes you understand the basics of linking. If you don't, see Chapter 5, "Linking Everywhere, Anywhere."

To link to external media:

1. Prepare the external media file. Ideally, the file should share the same directory as the document file so the link to it can be phrased as a relative pathname.

CAUTION: When naming a file intended for use as external media, you must use the standard filename extension for the file's type. See the section titled "Understanding Media Types" earlier in this chapter.

2. Create the link source in either of two ways:

   Compose text for the link source. (See Chapter 4, "Composing, Editing, and Formatting Text.")

   Insert an image for the link source. (See Chapter 6, "Working with Graphics.")

3. Highlight the link source (by highlighting the text or single-clicking the image).

4. Click the Insert Link button on the toolbar. The Link Properties dialog opens. (See Figure 7.3.) The selected link source is shown in the upper half of the dialog.

Figure 7.3.
Setting up a link to external media.

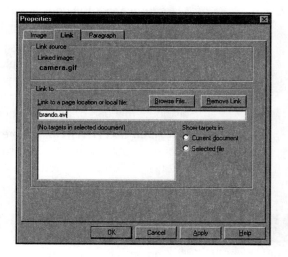

If the file is not in the same directory as the document, you'll have to include a path before the filename. But you should put the document and media file in the same directory, and then enter just the filename, as shown in Figure 7.3.

5. In Link to a page location or file, enter the full filename of the external media file.

6. Click OK. The link is complete.

7. Click the View in Browser button on the Editor's toolbar to see the document in the Navigator Browser.

After linking to any external media, test the page and media thoroughly as described in Chapter 16, "Testing and Maintaining Web Documents."

8. Execute the link to make sure it and the file work properly in your Navigator configuration. That won't tell you whether the media will function properly in a different environment, but it's a start.

Tips for Proper Presentation

As you can see, simply making the link to external media is simple—much simpler, usually—than creating or acquiring the media file in the first place. But the secret to effective use of external media isn't setting up the link and file. The secret is presenting the link to external media in an attractive, inviting, useful way.

The next few pages offer tips for properly presenting your external media.

Show File Type and Size

Whenever offering external media, always show the file type and its size as part of the link (or very close to it), so that visitors can make two decisions before clicking a link in your document:

❏ Do I have the necessary software to play, display, or run a file of this type?

❏ Do I have the time/patience to download a file of this size?

Keep in mind that many Web surfers today are still novices, especially when it comes to dealing with external media types. (See Figure 7.4 for an example.) Configuring helper applications baffles many browser users, so they just don't do it. You'll make your document to be newbie-friendly if, in addition to showing the file size and type, you

❏ Describe what the file type means and what's required to use the file. Don't just say the file is AVI; say the file is a Video for Windows (AVI) file, which requires Windows 95, or a Video for Windows player in Windows 3.1 or Macintosh systems.

In Chapter 17, you'll find URLs of sites for downloading helper applications. You can offer links to these sites from pages on which you use external media, to help any helper-deficient visitors.

❏ Tell visitors where they can find the helper applications they need to play or display your file. If you know of a good source online, you can even provide a link to that source. That way, a visitor who wants to use your external media file but lacks the right software can jump to the helper application source, get the right helper, and then return to your page. (The visitor can also simply download and save your external media file, and go get the helper, and then play or display the file later, offline.)

❏ Offer media in multiple formats, as described later in this chapter.

Figure 7.4.
File type and size of an image linked to external media.

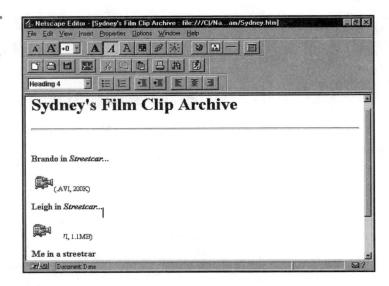

Use Descriptive Images as Link Sources

In addition to labeling a link to external media with its file type, it's a good idea to use as the link source an image that represents the file type. For example:

A camera makes a great link source for any video clip.

Sound visually informs visitors that the link leads to a sound file. Note that using these images is not a replacement for properly labeling the link with text describing the file. For one thing, a little movie projector indicates a video clip but doesn't communicate whether that clip is an AVI, MPEG, or MOV file. Also, text descriptions are essential for the text-only crowd.

Remember: Under certain circumstances, text-only browser users can still use external media. If you use an image as a link source, be sure to provide a text link as well. (See Chapter 5.)

Show Inline Thumbnails for Large External Images

As mentioned earlier in this chapter, thumbnails are a great way to create meaningful link sources for external images. A thumbnail is a very small, low-resolution version of a larger image. The thumbnail appears on the page as an inline image and also serves as the link source to the larger, full-resolution image. Thumbnails provide visitors with a general sense of what the full image looks like, so they can decide whether to bother downloading the full image.

As with any link to external media, you must provide the file type and size along with the thumbnail. If a group of thumbnails all link to files of the same type and of about the same size, you can describe the files once for the group, as shown in Figure 7.5.

Figure 7.5.

Thumbnails linked to larger JPEG images.

Using an editor or converter, you can create GIF thumbnails of JPEG images and use the GIFs inline as links to their external JPEG versions. This lets you exploit the wide support for inline GIFs when offering high-quality external JPEGs.

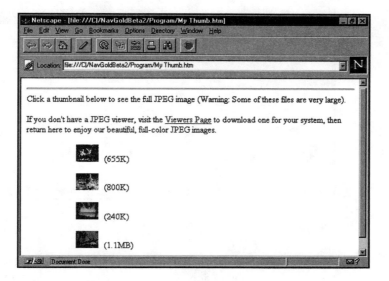

Supply Media in Multiple Formats

You can convert images between different file formats either by using image editing software or graphics converters. You can also convert video and sound files converted between formats, although doing so is tricky and the converted versions are often inferior to the original. Still, to the extent that you can acquire or create multiple versions of an external media file, each in a different format, you expand the visitor's options.

For example, if you offer the same video clip in both MOV and AVI versions, you can rest assured that almost any Windows or Macintosh visitor can play it. If you offer an external image in both JPEG and GIF versions, you provide the higher image quality of JPEG to those who can display JPEG images, while still offering the GIF-only world something to look at. Figure 7.6 shows links to different formats of the same video clips.

Figure 7.6.

Links to the same video clip in differing file formats.

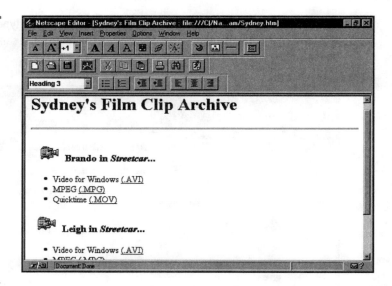

Workshop Wrap-Up

Embedding external media files in Gold is a snap: Make sure the file is the right place, build a link, and you're done. The only way you can blow it after that is if you forget to copy the media file to the server when you publish your page—and Gold can even make sure you get that right. (See Chapter 15, "Publishing Web Documents.")

The tricky part is creating or choosing the right type of file to reach either the broadest possible audience or the specific audience you want to reach most. PCs are more common in homes than Macs, so if you're trying to reach homes, it helps to slant your file choices to whatever makes Windows happy. Many, many corporate users, especially those in engineering and technical departments, are on UNIX systems with X Window interfaces. Web authors often overlook the UNIX crowd when choosing media types. If your message is aimed at that crowd, try to aim your media files that way, too.

Next Steps

Now...

❏ To learn more about linking, the fundamental task in embedding external media, see Chapter 5, "Linking Everywhere, Anywhere."

❏ To learn how to edit an HTML file—which you'll need to do to take on any of the tasks in Chapters 10 through 14—see Chapter 9, "Editing HTML Source Code."

Q&A

Q: If a video clip or other file I like is already available through a link on another Web page, can I simply link to it instead of supplying my own file?

A: Sure you can, and in fact, doing so is quite common. There are, however, a couple of rules:

> First, as always, e-mail the Webmaster of the site to which you will link, and ask permission to link to the site and file.

> Second, avoid linking directly to the file. Instead, link to the page on which the link appears. After all, the site providing the file is doing you a favor—the least you can do is give visitors a glimpse of the site's message before retrieving the link. Also, if the site is using the file in violation of a copyright (something that's difficult for you to find out), linking to the page rather than the file better insulates you from sharing the blame for the violation.

When you do create the link, you can use Gold's support for drag and drop or cut and paste to easily insert the link into your document. See Chapter 5, "Linking Everywhere, Anywhere."

Q: There seem to be an awful lot of file formats, and no one type seems to be universally right. No matter what I do, I'm either shutting out visitors with certain equipment or compromising the quality of what I offer. Is this gonna get better or worse?

A: Worse. Although there are efforts underway to better standardize file formats on the Web, the historical pattern of the Web is that evolution always outpaces standards. The HTML extensions developed by Netscape and Microsoft serve as object lessons: When real standards evolve slower than the demand for new capabilities, visionaries step in with nonstandard solutions, and compatibility problems inevitably result.

Just when it seems everybody's got the right helpers for all the types of media files, some enterprising programmer comes up with a better way to play audio or show images, and everybody jumps on the bandwagon. Because the Internet (thankfully) is loosely overseen by committees—rather than ruled by a governing body or corporation—nothing on the horizon will change the pace of new files and formats, and any actual standards will tend to be very loosely defined and very slow in coming.

EIGHT

Real-Life Examples I

This chapter describes a variety of sample Web pages created entirely in Netscape Navigator Gold with authoring techniques introduced in Part I (Chapters 1 through 6). The examples include

Example 1. A personal home page (created with the Netscape Page Wizard)

Example 2. A professional business page (created with the Netscape Page Wizard)

Example 3. A Human Resources department information sheet (created from a Netscape template)

Example 4. A company profile document

Example 5. An online catalog document

Example 6. An online book document

Example 1: Harry Boone's Home Page

Document title: Harry Boone's Home Page (Figures 8.1 and 8.2).

Files: Page file `Harry.HTML`, GIF images `Rule08.GIF`, `Pattern08.GIF`, `Now8.GIF`.

Description: A run-of-the-mill personal home page as produced by the Netscape Page Wizard.

Techniques applied: Page created entirely with the Page Wizard (see Chapter 2, "Making the Page Wizard Do the Work"); no post-Wizard editing performed.

Figure 8.1.
The upper half of
Harry.HTML.

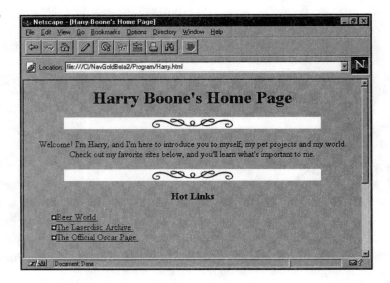

Figure 8.2.
The lower half of
Harry.HTML.

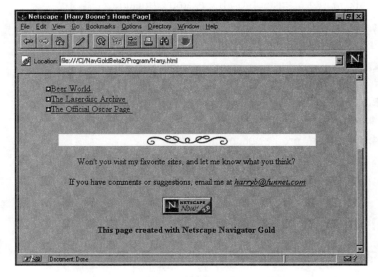

Example 2: Carol Baugh, Atty.

Document title: Carol Baugh, Atty. (Figures 8.3 and 8.4).

Files: Page file `Baugh.HTM`, GIF image `Rule10.GIF`.

Description: A professional page created initially with the Netscape Page Wizard (see Chapter 2, "Making the Page Wizard Do the Work"), and then edited and fine-tuned in the Editor to make it more serious and professional (befitting its subject).

Techniques applied:

Inline Image. (See Chapter 6.) A graphical rule (`Rule08.GIF`) was copied from below the level 1 heading and pasted below the second paragraph, and a new paragraph was added beneath it to introduce the links.

Background color. (See Chapter 6.) A flat background color was applied (no background texture).

Delete text. (See Chapter 4, "Composing, Editing and Formatting Text.") The words `Hot Links` were removed from above the list of links (see Figure 8.3) to make it read more professionally (compared to Figure 8.1). Also, the words `me at` removed from signature (see Figure 8.4) to make it read more professionally (compared to signature in Figure 8.2).

Delete inline image. (See Chapter 6,) and text. Netscape Now! button and associated text deleted.

Figure 8.3.
The upper half of
Baugh.HTM.

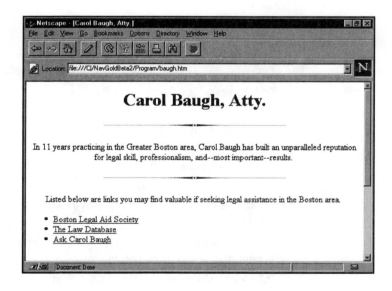

Figure 8.4.
The lower half of
Baugh.HTM.

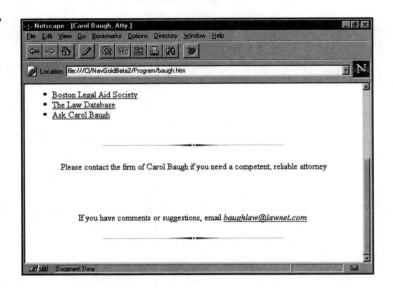

Example 3: Genco Human Resources

Document title: Genco Human Resources (Figure 8.5).

Files: Page GencoHR.HTM, GIF image RULE02.GIF.

Description: An information sheet about the Human Resources department of a large corporation.

Techniques applied:

> **Template.** (See Chapter 3, "Using the Netscape Editor.") Page built from template HR2.HTM, found at the Netscape templates page.

> **Delete text.** (See Chapter 4.) The template instruction block at top of page was deleted.

> **Character properties.** (See Chapter 4.) Italics applied to level 1 heading (GENCO).

> **Custom text colors.** (See Chapter 4.) Text colors were applied to top two paragraphs for emphasis.

> **Link.** (See Chapter 5, "Linking Anywhere, Everywhere.") An in-text link points to directory of home pages.

> **Text alignment.** (See Chapter 4.) The Center alignment property was applied to the top three paragraphs.

> **Inline images.** (See Chapter 6.) A GIF image, Rule02.GIF, was inserted twice to form stylized rules.

Figure 8.5.

GencoHR.HTM.

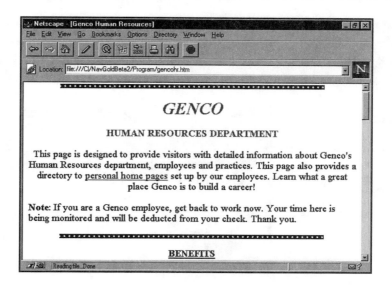

Example 4: BaitCo, Inc., Home Page

Document title: BaitCo, Inc., Home Page. (See Figures 8.6 and 8.7.)

Files: Pages BaitCo.HTM (top), BaitCo2.HTM, BaitCo3.HTM, BaitCo4.HTM, BaitCo5.HTM; GIF image FISH.GIF.

BaitCo.HTM

Description: The top page of a basic company home page document. The simple top page welcomes the visitor, announces the company slogan, and offers links to four informative pages about the company. The page bottom (scrolled out of the figure) features an e-mail link to BaitCo's Public Relations department.

Techniques applied:

Heading. (See Chapter 4.) A level 1 heading was used for an on-page title, and a level 3 heading for the slogan.

Inline image. (See Chapter 6.) A simple GIF image was inserted, with text aligned with the centerline of the image.

Character properties. (See Chapter 4.) Italic character properties were applied to the slogan (fresh).

Horizontal line. (See Chapter 6.) A horizontal line was inserted, and its thickness was expanded in the horizontal line properties to 6 pixels in height. (2 pixels is the default.)

List. (See Chapter 4.) An unnumbered list was created, with the solid square bullet style.

Links. (See Chapter 5.) Each list item is a link source for a link to another BaitCo page.

Figure 8.6.
BaitCo.HTM, *the top page of BaitCo's home page.*

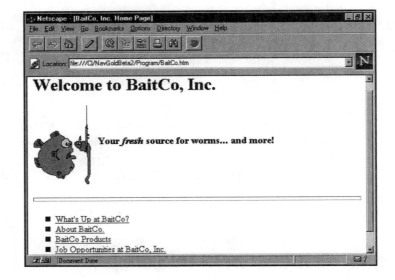

Figure 8.6.
BaitCo.HTM, *the top page of BaitCo's home page.*

BaitCo2.HTM

Description. An events page for BaitCo, linked to the list Item What's Up at BaitCo, on top page Baitco.HTM. The events page traces important events and milestones at BaitCo, in reverse chronological order. The page is regularly updated with recent events at the top, but earlier events remain beneath. Visitors can scroll down the list to read about earlier BaitCo events. At the page bottom (scrolled out of figure), a link back to the top page (BaitCo.HTM) appears.

Techniques applied:

Headings. (See Chapter 4.) A level 1 heading was used for an on-page title and level 3 headings are used for the dates.

Horizontal line. (See Chapter 6.) A default horizontal line was inserted.

Character properties. (See Chapter 4.) Bold character properties were applied to **500,000,000th night crawler**.

Links. (See Chapter 5.) In-text references to important persons or products are linked to targets in other pages of document where descriptions of persons/products are located.

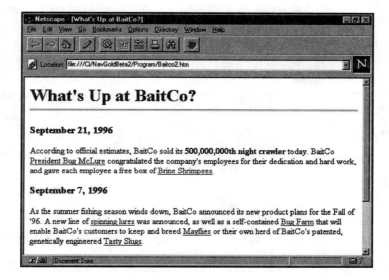

Example 5: Nancy's Discount Lab Supply

Document title: Nancy's Discount Lab Supply. (See Figures 8.8 and 8.9.)

Files: Pages NDLS.HTM (top), NDLSCatalog.HTM, OrderInfo.HTM, OrderForm.HTM; GIF image SCOPE.GIF.

NDLS.HTM

Description: The top page of an online catalog and sales document. The top page announces the company name and slogan, and offers links to the catalog page, ordering instructions, and an order form. The page bottom (scrolled out of the figure) features an e-mail link to NDLS's Sales department.

Techniques applied:

Inline image. (See Chapter 6.) A simple GIF image was inserted before the first text on the page. The text alignment with the graphic is the Editor's default.

Image properties. (See Chapter 6.) A 2-pixel border was applied around graphic in Image Properties.

Headings. (See Chapter 4.) A level 1 heading was used for an one-page title, and a level 3 heading for the slogan.

Horizontal line. (See Chapter 6.) A default horizontal line was inserted.

List. (See Chapter 4.) An unnumbered list was created, with the solid circle (default) bullet style.

Links. (See Chapter 5.) Each list item is a link source for a link to another NDLS page.

Figure 8.8.
NDLS.HTM, *the top page of NDLS's catalog document.*

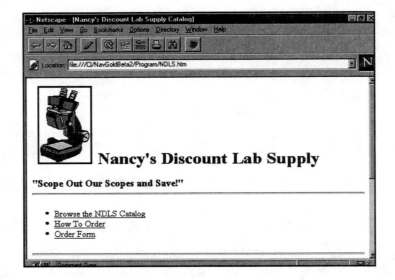

NDLSCatalog.HTM

Description: A category directory for an online catalog. The catalog text has been broken down into nine different pages, each showcasing a different type of product. Each line in the directory is a link to a product page. The page bottom (scrolled out of the figure) features a link back to the top page.

Techniques applied:

Headings. (See Chapter 4.) A level 2 heading labels the page.

List. (See Chapter 4.) An unnumbered list was created with solid circle bullet style (default), for stylistic consistency with top page of document.

Links. (See Chapter 5.) Each list item is a link source for a link to a product page.

Figure 8.9.
NDLSCatalog.HTM, *the directory for the NDLS catalog.*

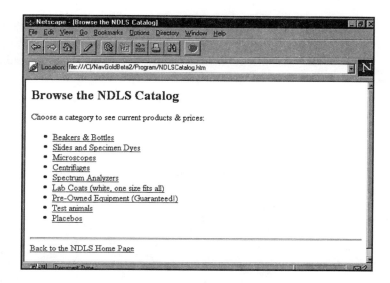

Figure 8.9.
NDLSCatalog.HTM, *the directory for the NDLS catalog.*

Example 6: Ghost Train

Document title: Ghost Train. (See Figures 8.10 and 8.11.)

Files: Pages GhostTrain.HTM (top), Train1.HTM, Train1.HTM, Train1.HTM, Train1.HTM, Train1.HTM; GIF image RULE03.GIF, TRAIN.GIF.

GhostTrain.HTM

Description: The top page (and table of contents) for an online book. A light background dresses the page and does not interfere with the text because the text is simple and the page's title is so large. The top page announces the book's title and author, and offers a link to each chapter. Observe that the subheadings with chapters are not links; the author has chosen to make jumping into a chapter easy (to facilitate returning to the book after a break) but wants to encourage reading each chapter straight through. The page bottom (scrolled out of the figure) includes a mailto link to the book's author.

Techniques applied:

Character properties (font size). (See Chapter 4.) The on-page title "The Ghost Train" is a level 1 heading, but has its font size pumped to +4.

Text alignment. (See Chapter 4.) The Center alignment property was applied to the top three paragraphs.

Inline image. (See Chapter 6.) A GIF rule image (centered) takes the place of a regular horizontal line to help balance oversized heading.

Character properties. (See Chapter 4.) The bold character property was applied to author's name (Angie Neer).

List. (See Chapter 4.) A numbered list was created with the Arabic (1,2,3) number style.

Nested list. (See Chapter 4.) Nested unnumbered lists were created within a numbered list.

Links. (See Chapter 5.) Numbered list items are link sources, but not unnumbered items.

Figure 8.10.
GhostTrain.HTM, *the top page, and table of contents to an online book.*

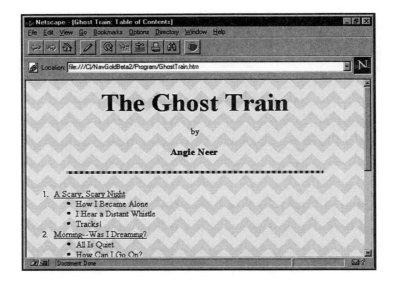

Train2.HTM

Description: One chapter file in the online book, linked to `1. A Scary, Scary Night` on top page (`GhostTrain.HTM`) The page bottom (scrolled out of the figure) features a link back to the top page.

Techniques applied:

Headings. (See Chapter 4.) A level 2 heading labels the page.

Character properties (font size). (See Chapter 4.) The second "Scary" in the heading is increased in size by +1.

Text alignment. (See Chapter 4.) The center alignment property was applied to the top heading.

Inline image. (See Chapter 6.) A GIF rule image (centered) takes the place of a regular horizontal line for stylistic consistency with top page.

Inline image. (See Chapter 6.) A GIF image was inserted and given the `align` property for wrapping to allow text to wrap to the left of the image.

Headings. (See Chapter 4.) A level 3 heading, How I Became Alone, was inserted after GIF image. The insertion of the heading after the image allows the normal paragraph that follows the heading to begin beside, not over, the image.

Character properties (font size, bold). (See Chapter 4.) Font sizing and the bold character property were applied to the first letter of the Normal text to create a *drop cap* effect.

Figure 8.11.

Train1.HTM, *the first chapter of The Ghost Train.*

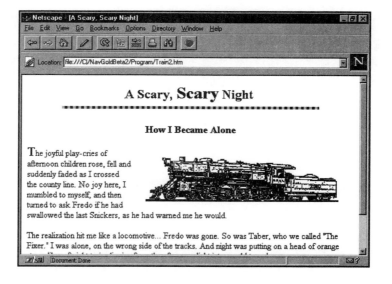

P A R T

III

Advanced Authoring and Scripting

NINE

Editing HTML Source Code

The title of this book implies an oxymoron.

The title tells you that the book is about Web authoring and that it's about Netscape Navigator Gold. All of that's fine, except that the authoring part of Navigator Gold—the Netscape Editor—does not directly support a number of important aspects of Web authoring. To create full-featured tables, write scripts, make forms and image maps, and do a number of other advanced things in your Web document, you need to move beyond the Editor into the realm of the HTML source file itself.

This chapter introduces you to HTML source files and to how new tags and attributes can be applied. Armed with that knowledge, you're ready to take on the tasks in the next several chapters.

Note that knowing how to edit HTML directly in no way diminishes the Editor's value to you. The Editor's role is not to create the impression that an HTML file doesn't exist beneath the pretty interface. Rather, the Editor saves you time by applying HTML tags and attributes in a click or two that would otherwise require a dozen keystrokes, by applying those tags consistently and accurately, and by showing you the on-screen results (most of the time) instantly, so you needn't keep hopping between an editor and a browser to check your work. These benefits remain, even after you know HTML coding inside and out.

In this chapter, you

- ❏ Learn how to read and understand an HTML source file
- ❏ Learn how to view the HTML source file of any document
- ❏ Use the Editor's menus to insert HTML codes, called *tags*, into a document
- ❏ Discover the different types of programs you can use to edit HTML source code outside of the Editor
- ❏ Learn about the HTML editing tools included on the CD-ROM at the back of this book
- ❏ Define a specific program in the Editor as your default HTML editing tool, so you can access it quickly from within Gold

Tasks in this chapter:

- ❏ Viewing the HTML Source Code of a Document
- ❏ Using the Editor to Insert an HTML Tag
- ❏ Setting up an HTML Editor

Following this chapter, the remainder of this book generally assumes that your approach to Web authoring is to lay out your page and perform most of the formatting in the Netscape Editor, and to code directly only those features and functions for which the Editor offers no direct support.

How to Read an HTML File

Recall from Chapter 1, "Planning Your Page," that an HTML source file consists of four basic elements:

- ❏ The text to appear on the page
- ❏ The filenames of inline images
- ❏ The URLs or filenames for links (and the text or image filenames for the link source)
- ❏ HTML tags and attributes, which tell browsers which lines are images, which are links, which are headings or normal paragraphs, and so on

The best way to learn about HTML is to study HTML files and compare them to the output in a browser. Figure 9.1 shows a very basic Web page displayed in Navigator, and Figure 9.2 shows the HTML source file for the page.

In Figure 9.2, notice that HTML tags are always enclosed within carats (< >), and that each content element of the page—a paragraph or image filename—is surrounded by a pair of tags. Compare Figures 9.1 and 9.2 carefully, and you'll quickly see how HTML tags tell a browser what to do with the text and files that make up a Web page.

NOTE:
Most Web pages contain more elaborate coding than you see in the example illustrated by Figures 9.1 and 9.2. However, this example contains all of the basics and shows how HTML tags are applied. Once you understand this example, you know enough to apply almost any other HTML tag.

You can find a complete directory to all of the HTML tags and attributes, and the Netscape extensions to HTML, in Appendix B, "HTML Reference."

If you're wondering why you see some tags in uppercase letters and some in lowercase letters, see the Q&A section at the end of this chapter.

While examining Figure 9.2, observe that you typically (but not always) need two HTML tags to identify a page element: one tag that has no slash (/) inside the first carat and another that has a slash there. The no-slash version is used to mark the beginning of a page element, and the slash version (sometimes called the *close* tag) marks the end. For example, the tag <HTML> at the very top of the file marks the very beginning of the entire HTML document, and the close tag </HTML> marks the end.

Figure 9.1.

A basic Web page, as interpreted by a browser.

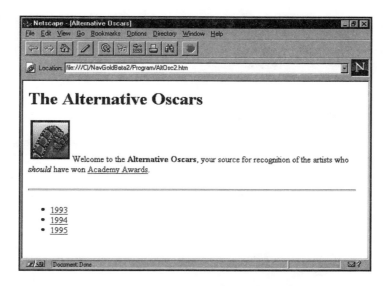

Figure 9.2.

The HTML source code for the Web page shown in Figure 9.1.

Now take a look at how the tags, text, and filenames work together to build a page. Every HTML document begins with the command

<HTML>

which tells the browser that it's reading an HTML document and should interpret it as such. Typically (but not always), the next tag is

<HEAD>

which informs the browser that what follows <HEAD> is header information. Information entered in the header does not appear as part of the page, but is important because it describes your document to the browser and to Web search engines and directories.

> # NOTE:
> The header portion of an HTML file created in the Editor contains all of the information you entered in the Document Properties dialog. (See Chapter 3, "Using the Netscape Editor.") This includes not only such standard elements as the document title, but also header elements created by Netscape extensions. These are indicated with either of two tags, both of which contain text you entered on the General and Advanced tabs of the Document Properties:
>
> ```
> <meta name=...>
> <HTTP-equiv>
> ```
>
> To learn more about these header elements, see Chapter 15, "Publishing Web Documents."

The next two tags, <TITLE> and </TITLE>, surround the text of the title. After the title and any other header lines, the tag </HEAD>, informs the browser that the header is over. Next comes the body of the page, kicked off by the tag <BODY>. The body contains everything that actually appears on the page itself.

The first element of the body in Figure 9.2 is a heading. The heading tags are easy to remember: <H1> is a level 1 heading, <H2> is a level 2 heading, and so on. The first heading in the example is a level 1 heading.

```
<H1>The Alternative Oscars</H1>
```

Notice that the end of the heading is marked with </H1>.

The inline image (GIF file movies.gif) is indicated with the <IMG SRC...> tag.

```
<img src="movies.gif"...>
```

Observe that the <IMG SRC...> tag requires no close tag.

Note that the image filename must be enclosed in quotes. In Figure 9.2, between the beginning of the <IMG SRC...> tag and the close carat (>) that ends it, appear optional *attributes* for spacing, image dimensions, and a border around the image. Attributes are always optional and go inside the tag itself (between the carats).

Immediately following the end of the <IMG SRC...> tag comes a normal text paragraph (beginning with Welcome). Note that no tag is required to identify it; any text appearing in an HTML document is assumed to be a normal paragraph unless tags appear to say otherwise. However, keep in mind that while entering normal text you cannot simply type a carriage return to start a new paragraph. To break a paragraph and begin a new one, you must enter the new paragraph tag (`<P>`). It's proper to end a paragraph with a close paragraph tag (`</P>`), but doing so is not required.

Embedded within the normal paragraph, you can see a few more tags:

❏ The set of `<b>` and `</b>` surrounding `Alternative Oscars` applies bold character formatting.

❏ The set of `<i>` and `</i>` surrounding `should` applies italic character formatting.

❏ The tag beginning with `<a href...` creates a link to another page, using the text `Academy Awards` as the link source. In the link, the `<a href=` portion indicates that, when activated by a reader, the link should open the file or URL named in quotes. The text between the close carat following the filename and the close tag `</A>` is the text that appears in the page as the link source.

Following the normal paragraph is a new paragraph tag that inserts a blank line before the horizontal line (`<hr>`) that follows. All by itself, the tag `<hr>` inserts a line; the `width=100%` is an attribute, one of Netscape's line properties extensions. (See Chapter 6, "Working with Graphics.")

The `<ul>` tag starts an unnumbered list. (Look for the `</ul>` tag that closes the list.) Each list item is surrounded by `<li>` and `</li>`, and contains a link (`<a href`) to another page in the document.

At the bottom of the file, the `</BODY>` tag closes off the body, and the `</HTML>` tag indicates the end of the HTML document.

That's it. To learn more about the HTML source code of pages you've created in the Editor, or any page you see on the Web, follow the steps in the next section.

 # Viewing the HTML Source Code of a Document

A great way to learn more about HTML is to study the source for Web documents. You can study the source code for pages you view on the Web or look at the underlying source for documents you create in the Editor. You can even view the source for a document you're editing, make a small change in the Editor, and then view the source code again to see how the source file has been changed.

❏ To view the HTML source for the current document in the Browser, choose **V**iew I Document **S**ource.

❏ To view the HTML source for the current document in the Editor, choose **V**iew I View Document **S**ource.

TASK

Using the Editor to Insert an HTML Tag

Chapters 10 through 14 describe tags you might want to add with **I**nsert I **H**TML Tag or with an HTML editor. In addition, Appendix B describes all of the tags and attributes you may apply.

To edit a tag, double-click the tag icon. The HTML Tag dialog opens so you can edit the tag and verify your changes. To delete a tag, single-click it and press Del.

When you've built a document in the Editor but need to add a tag here or there for which the Editor offers no button or menu, the Editor's Insert tag function allows you to do that conveniently, without you having to exit the Editor and edit the document in another program.

In addition to making tag insertion convenient, the Insert I HTML Tag function offers another benefit: It checks your work. The Verify button on the HTML Tag dialog reads your tag to make sure you've phrased it properly. (The Verify button can check whether you've accurately coded a particular HTML or Netscape extension tag, not whether you've chosen the right tag for the right job.)

NOTE: In the Editor, Insert I HTML Tag can be used to insert any HTML tag—even those that the Editor inserts automatically when you apply properties to text or an image. However, it's wise to use Insert I HTML Tag only for tags not supported by another menu item or button in the Editor.

The reason isn't just convenience—though using the Editor's menus and buttons is generally more convenient than using Insert I HTML Tag. When you use Insert I HTML Tag, the results appear as a tag icon in the document instead of appearing in the Editor window as they would through a browser; you do not get WYSIWYG results with Insert Tag, even when the tag you insert is one the Editor can display.

For example, if you click the Insert Horiz. line button, a line appears in the document in the Editor window (just as it would appear in the browser) and an <hr> tag is added to the HTML source file. But if you use Insert I HTML Tag to insert the <hr> tag, a tag icon appears in the Editor window, not a line, even though the same <hr> tag has been added to the HTML source. To see the line you've created (instead of the tag icon), you have to switch to the browser.

The example that follows inserts the horizontal line (<hr>) tag, which is supported by the Editor's buttons and menus. The <hr> tag is used in the example only to provide an easy-to-follow test case without introducing a tag not yet covered in this book.

To insert an HTML tag with the Editor:

1. Position the edit cursor in the document at the spot where you want the tag to go.
2. Choose Insert I **H**TML Tag. The HTML Tag dialog opens. (See Figure 9.3.)

Figure 9.3.
Inserting an HTML tag.

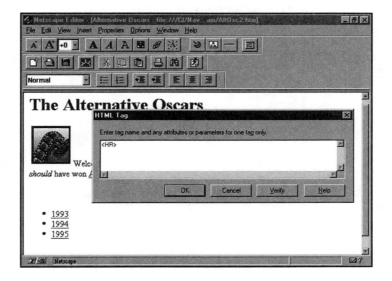

The HTML Tag dialog supports long entries (by including scrollbars) not so you can enter multiple tags but so you can enter a very long tag (one with many attributes or long text strings or paths inside it) when you need to.

3. Type the complete text of your tag entry. Note that you can enter only a single tag this way (one set of carats at the beginning and end).
4. Click **V**erify so the Editor can check your tag for proper phrasing. If you've phrased the page correctly, nothing happens and you can continue. If you've made an error (for example, leaving the closing carat off the tag), an error message appears describing your mistake.
5. Click OK. A tag icon appears in the document at the spot where you positioned the edit cursor. (See Figure 9.4.) To see the effects of the tag, click the View in Browser button.

Figure 9.4.
The tag icon in the Editor.

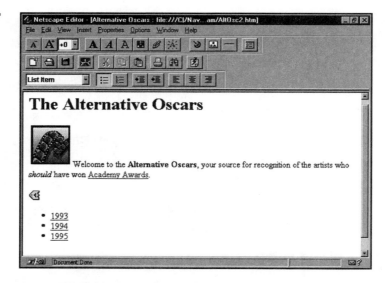

Figure 9.5.
The effects of the tag shown in Figures 9.3 and 9.4, as seen in the browser.

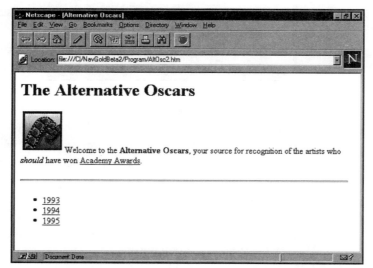

Using an HTML Editor

The Editor's Insert HTML Tag function is terrific for inserting a tag or two in a file, but for more serious work, you'll find it easier to open your HTML file in an HTML editor, perform any major work there, and return to the Editor to finish up and fine-tune.

In principle, for your HTML editor you may use any program capable of saving flat ASCII text files. Windows's Notepad is ideal, because it edits and saves *only* flat text files and it's small; it opens and closes quickly so you can get in, make your edits, and get out.

Windows 95's WordPad (see Figure 9.6) also works fine for editing HTML, although you must be sure to choose Text document in Save as **t**ype when saving the file (and use the extension .HTM or .HTML).

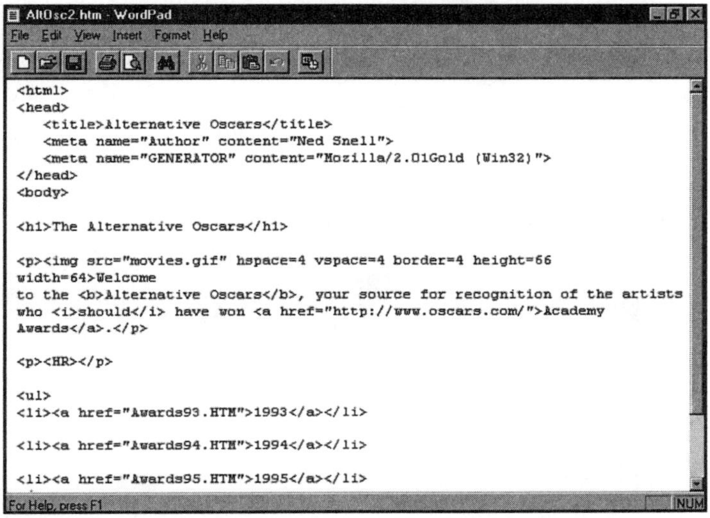

Figure 9.6.
An HTML file in WordPad.

```
AltOsc2.htm - WordPad
File  Edit  View  Insert  Format  Help

<html>
<head>
    <title>Alternative Oscars</title>
    <meta name="Author" content="Ned Snell">
    <meta name="GENERATOR" content="Mozilla/2.01Gold (Win32)">
</head>
<body>

<h1>The Alternative Oscars</h1>

<p><img src="movies.gif" hspace=4 vspace=4 border=4 height=66
width=64>Welcome
to the <b>Alternative Oscars</b>, your source for recognition of the artists
who <i>should</i> have won <a href="http://www.oscars.com/">Academy
Awards</a>.</p>

<p><HR></p>

<ul>
<li><a href="Awards93.HTM">1993</a></li>

<li><a href="Awards94.HTM">1994</a></li>

<li><a href="Awards95.HTM">1995</a></li>
```

Although Notepad and WordPad can be used to edit HTML, neither knows anything about HTML, so neither gives you any help. That's what makes actual non-WYSIWYG HTML source editors handy accessories to Netscape Gold.

Although an HTML editor produces and edits simple text files like Notepad can, it also offers menus and toolbar buttons to make entering tags more convenient and more accurate. For example, in a typical HTML editor, you might apply the tags for bold character formatting simply by highlighting text and then clicking a B button on the toolbar. Instead of seeing the text turn bold (as you would in the Netscape Editor), you'll see the bold tags (,) appear around the text.

Tags entered with another HTML editor appear in the Gold Editor in full WYSIWYG fashion, unless they're tags the Editor doesn't support (table tags, for example). Unsupported tags show up in the Editor as tag icons; their actions show up properly in the browser.

There are many HTML editing utilities for Windows, including commercial, shareware, and freeware examples you can find on the Web. (See Chapter 17, "Developing Your Authoring Skills.") The CD-ROM bundled with this book includes several such editors, including HotDog and Microsoft's Internet Assistant suite.

HotDog

The general-purpose HTML editor, HotDog, is a shareware application that makes an excellent companion to Gold because it's good at doing things the Gold Editor won't, especially forms (see Chapter 12, "Creating Interactive Forms and Image Maps") and tables (see Chapter 10, "Building Tables"). In HotDog, you can define Netscape

Navigator as a viewer for HTML files; after you do so, clicking HotDog's Preview button opens Navigator to display the file you're editing in HotDog.

When you open HotDog to create a new file, it instantly supplies the required structure tags for you. (See Figures 9.7 and 9.8.) But as a Gold user, you'll typically create documents in the Netscape Editor (to take advantage of Gold's WYSIWYG capability as you work), switch to HotDog for the extras, and then switch back to Gold to fine-tune. (You can make switching easy by defining HotDog as your default HTML editor, as described later under the Task section titled "Setting Up an HTML Editor.")

Figure 9.7.
A new HTML file in HotDog.

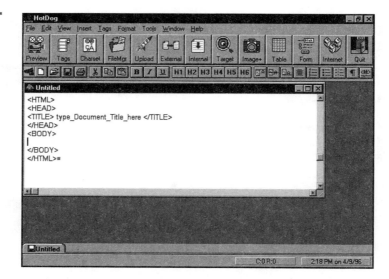

Figure 9.8.
A file created in the Editor as seen in HotDog.

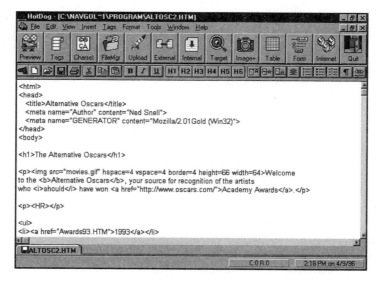

Microsoft Internet Assistant

The CD-ROM includes Microsoft's Internet Assistant add-ins to its Office application suite: Word 95, Excel 95, and PowerPoint 95. Internet Assistant adds to these applications all of the tools of a basic WYSIWYG HTML editor.

For other word processing, spreadsheet, or presentation file formats, there are other HTML utilities similar to Internet Assistant. URLs for learning about or downloading other HTML converters appear in Chapter 17.

When you edit an HTML document in an Internet Assistant-equipped copy of Word, Excel, or PowerPoint, new toolbar buttons appear (see Figure 9.9) for such functions as inserting images or creating links. Internet Assistant offers a rudimentary WYSIWYG capability, displaying the actual tag for any tags it cannot properly interpret. It also displays inline images as icons, rather than showing them as a browser would.

Using Internet Assistant, you can save an existing Word file, for example, as HTML to convert it from Word to Web. Internet Assistant converts the Word page formatting into HTML tags by making some educated guesses. For example, a large, bold heading near the top of a Word document might be converted into an HTML level 1 heading.

After creating or converting a file with Internet Assistant, you'll still want to tune it in the Netscape Editor; for example, you'll need the Editor (or HotDog) to add anything based on a Netscape extension, such as a background.

Internet Assistant also turns Word, Excel, or PowerPoint into bona fide Web browsers. The immediate application of this capability is that you can instantly switch from editing an HTML document to a browser view to see how your document might appear on the Web. (In reality, the document's appearance will vary with the browser.) You can also use the Office application with Internet Assistant as an everyday Web browser. However, if I may be so presumptuous as to make a value judgment, using Word, Excel, or PowerPoint as a Web browser is, y'know, goofy. Office is for writing, counting, and presenting; Navigator is for browsing.

Figure 9.9.

Enhanced by Internet Assistant, Word's toolbar and menus change when you edit an HTML document.

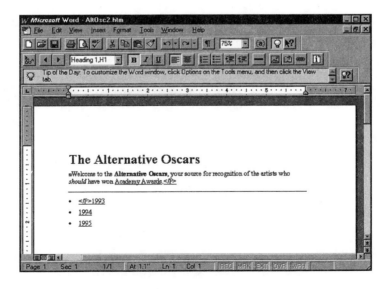

NOTE: Internet Assistant for Word 95 includes facilities for publishing pages on the Web not as HTML documents but as native Word documents. To view such pages, readers must have Word or a free Word viewer that Microsoft offers over the Web.

Publishing non-HTML documents on the Web has some advantages, especially because it allows much more elaborate and specific document formatting than is possible under HTML. However, what you can gain in formatting you lose in compatibility. A Web document published as a Word file is inaccessible to the millions of non-PC users, PC users who don't use Windows, and Windows users who don't run Word or Microsoft's Word viewer utility. An HTML document, on the other hand, is available to anyone and everyone.

 # Setting Up an HTML Editor

To make editing HTML source convenient, configure an HTML source editor in the General tab of the Editor Preferences. (See Figure 9.10.) The program you define opens automatically when you choose **V**iew | **E**dit Document Source in the Gold Editor.

1. Open the Editor Preferences by choosing **O**ptions | **E**ditor Preferences. (This same choice works from within the Browser or the Editor.)

2. Under External editors, in the box for **H**TML source, enter the path and filename for your editing application (or browse for one). You can use any program you like: HotDog, Word (with Internet Assistant), WordPad, another HTML editor, and so on.

3. Click OK.

Figure 9.10.
Configuring an HTML source editor in the Editor Preferences, General tab.

Workshop Wrap-Up

Coding HTML is no great challenge. In fact, the beauty of HTML is that coding simple stuff—such as text paragraphs, links, and inline images—is actually simple, whereas coding more complex elements builds naturally upon the skills required for the easy stuff.

As a Gold author, you won't spend much time coding the simple stuff, because the Editor offers buttons and menus for all of it. Instead, you'll lay out most of your document in the Editor and then use Insert Tag or an HTML editor to code the rest. In the next eight chapters of this book, you'll do just that.

Next Steps

Now...

- ❏ To code interactive, on-screen forms or inline images that contain multiple links, see Chapter 12, "Creating Interactive Forms and Image Maps."
- ❏ To code attractively formatted tables in your page, see Chapter 10, "Building Tables."
- ❏ To create a page fractured into separate, independently operating "frames," see Chapter 11, "Making Frames."
- ❏ To work with sample pages that showcase all of the techniques described in Chapters 9 through 13, see Chapter 14, "Real-Life Examples II."
- ❏ To begin learning how to add unique functions to your document with JavaScript, see Chapter 13, "Using JavaScript."

Q&A

Q: I noticed in the HTML source code example (Figure 9.2) that the lines of code in the header were indented. What does indenting do?

A: Nothing. The indenting of blocks of HTML code has no effect on the display of the page. Authors (and the Editor) indent portions of code to make the structure of the file easier to identify when a human reads it. Browsers don't care; they pay no attention to indents in HTML source code. So do whatever works best for you.

Q: I've also noticed that tags are sometimes typed in uppercase letters (<TITLE>) and other times lowercase (<title>). Does it matter which I use?

A: As a rule, type your tags in uppercase letters. You are not required to do so; browsers will correctly interpret the tags if they appear in lowercase. In fact, as you can see in Figure 9.2, the Editor itself does not bother to use uppercase tags.

Uppercase is the accepted convention, and using uppercase tags may help you easily distinguish tags from content text in your document (unless, of course, your page content is in uppercase, too). If you add your own uppercase tags in a document otherwise created by the Editor, you can also easily distinguish your own coding from the Editor's, which may be helpful to you when trying to locate the source of a problem.

Q: I've looked at the source for some pages on the Web, and I've seen lines of text preceded by a <!- tag. The text doesn't appear to be part of the header, but it appears nowhere in the browser view of the page. *Que pasa, mi amigo*?

A: Any text preceded by <!- is a *comment*, a note inserted in the file to explain something to anyone who might read the HTML source. Comments are inserted in all types of program code, including HTML, by programmers to help others (or the programmer him/herself) understand the code when reading it. Comments have no effect on the display or actions of the document, and the text within comments is hidden when the browser displays the document. (If you want to add comments to your HTML source file, you can do so with Insert Tag or with an HTML editor. Just precede your comment with <!-, type anything you want and then wrap up with a </!-.)

The HTML source example in this chapter, shown in Figure 9.2, contains no comments because it was created by the Editor, which does not automatically insert any comments. But you will see comments in other HTML source files you view. When you use the Editor to view a file containing comments, they appear as tag icons. When you view the file in the browser, the comments simply don't show.

TEN

Building Tables

No—despite the title, this chapter is not about woodworking.

But it might as well be. In HTML, as in carpentry, a table is a pretty simple project. And although a basic, functional table—whether wood or Web—is a snap, you can apply optional tools and some extra elbow grease to expand the project from a particle-board coffee table to a work of art—a Chippendale or Louis XIV. (That's the end of the metaphor; I swear I won't resume it in Chapter 11, "Making Frames.")

This chapter shows basic tables made easy, and then describes the many ways you can upgrade your table with optional tags and attributes.

In this chapter, you

- ❏ Build a basic HTML table and position it in your Web page
- ❏ Use Gold 3's Insert Table feature
- ❏ Learn how to create and customize table borders, headings, and captions
- ❏ Discover advanced formatting options such as table alignment, text alignment, and blank or empty table cells
- ❏ Learn how to use Gold 3's new table background color feature
- ❏ Learn how to use HotDog (from the CD-ROM) to build and edit tables
- ❏ Learn about the drawbacks to using tables, and how you can get the effect of an HTML table without using one

Tasks in this chapter:

- ❏ Composing a Table in HTML
- ❏ Using Gold 3's Create Table Dialog

NOTE: The two versions of Gold released so far (versions 2 and 3) differ in their handling of tables. Version 3 includes a rudimentary Create Table dialog, and version 3 can display tables in correct WYSIWYG form in the Editor. Version 2, on the other hand, has no table creation features, and cannot display WYSIWYG tables in the Editor; in version 2, you must view tables in the Browser. If you use version 2, you must write your tables in HTML code in an HTML source editor. And even if you use version 3, you might want to write tables in HTML instead of using the Create Table dialog. (To learn why, see the Task "Using Gold 3's Create Table Dialog" later in this chapter.)

Table-building in HTML requires multiple lines of HTML code, and Netscape Gold's Insert | HTML Tag function inserts only one line at a time—which makes it a labor-intensive choice for building HTML tables.

The best approach for coding tables is to write them in an HTML source editor and to check your work by viewing the tables in the Netscape Browser (or in the Editor, if you use Gold 3). For maximum convenience, compose and format the rest of your page in the Netscape Editor first, leaving out the table. Then choose **V**iew | **E**dit Document Source to open the page file in an HTML editor, and insert your table code.

For more about HTML source editing, see Chapter 9, "Editing HTML Source Code."

About Tables

A table—regardless of the medium in which it appears—is chunks of information arranged in rows and columns. The box made by the intersection of a table and a row is called a *cell*; cells contain the table content, or *data* (when's the last time you heard *that* dated term, outside of *Star Trek*?). To create a table in any medium, you make rows and columns to form a grid of cells, and insert data within each cell.

And in fact, a simple HTML table requires a little less effort than that. To create a bare-bones HTML table, you need to define only the rows and the data for each cell in the row. The number of columns is determined automatically by the number of data entries you make in each row. For example, if your HTML table definition has four rows and each row has three pieces of data in it, a table of four rows and three columns results.

Although rows, columns, and data are the minimum requirements for any table, a fully fleshed-out table contains more elements. It might have column or row headings and

Because browsers automatically derive the number of columns from the number of data entries supplied for each row, you must take special steps when you want an empty, or blank, cell, as described later in this chapter.

a title above the table or caption below. (Both titles and captions are called *captions* in HTML table code.)

NOTE: The HTML tags used to create tables are part of the proposed HTML 3 specification and the Netscape extensions. Tables you publish in your Web pages can be viewed only by visitors whose browsers support HTML 3 (or, in some cases, browsers that support Netscape extensions but not support HTML 3).

The most recent versions (in fact, the two most recent versions) of all three of the major graphical browsers—Navigator, Internet Explorer, and Mosaic—support HTML 3 and display tables. However, if you're concerned about whether your tables will be visible to everyone, consider presenting your tabular material in one of the alternatives to tables. (See the Q&A section at the end of this chapter.)

An HTML table is created with a block of code—call it a *table definition*—inserted in the body of the document file. A table definition begins with <TABLE> and ends with </TABLE>; together, the tags tell browsers that everything between them is the table definition.

At its most basic, a table definition includes nothing but lines of code that either start a new row or supply data for the cells in the row. The number of columns is determined automatically by the number of data entries in each row. (You must make the same number of cell entries in each row.)

The precise formatting of your tables is controlled to a great extent by the browser displaying it. The height and width of cells is calculated automatically based on the number of columns and the length of the cell content. The width of a column is determined by the width necessary to contain the longest cell data in the column. When the data in a cell is long or when a table has many columns, the cell content may be wrapped automatically to allow the table to fit within the window. Although all of this formatting happens automatically, you can apply optional HTML coding to override various aspects of the automatic formatting and precisely control the appearance of your table.

The three essential HTML tags used to build a table are

<TABLE>...</TABLE>	Surrounds the whole table definition
<TR>...</TR>	Starts and ends a row, surrounding the <TD> lines for the row
<TD>...</TD>	Surrounds the cell data for one cell within a row

You learn how to apply these tags in the following task.

Composing a Table in HTML

In this task, I'll add a table to the document shown in Figure 10.1. To position the table where I want it on the page (just under the horizontal line), I'll locate the <HR> (horizontal rule) code in the body of the HTML source file and insert my table code immediately following it.

Figure 10.1.

The document into which the table will be inserted.

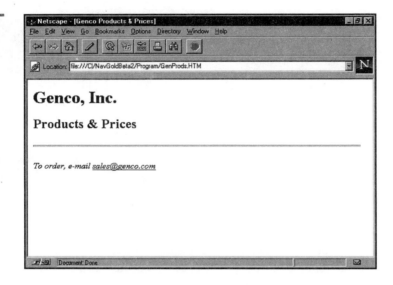

To help you understand how the table definition corresponds to the table it creates, I'll show you first the content of the table I will make:

```
L110    Home Scalpel    Sharp, EZ-Kleen   $44.95
P125    Glucose Tester  Pain-Free         $28.99
D652    Bandage Kit     Long stick        $8.95
```

To create the table:

1. Open the document file in your HTML source editor.

2. In the body of the HTML file, position the edit cursor at the spot where you want to your table to go (between the code for what the table will follow on the page and what it will precede).

3. Begin the table definition on a new line with the <TABLE> tag, as shown:

You may indent your table definition, as shown. Indenting the code has no effect on the table's appearance, but it makes the table definition easier to see within the body code.

```
<html>
<head>
   <title>Genco Products &amp; Prices</title>
</head>
<body>
<h1>Genco, Inc.</h1>
```

```
<h2>Products &amp; Prices</h2>
<p>
<hr>
     <TABLE>
</p>
<address>To order, e-mail <a
href="mailto:sales@genco.com">sales@genco.com</a></address>
</body>
</html>
```

4. Start a new row of the table by entering a table row (<TR>) tag.

5. On the line following <TR>, enter a table data (<TD>) tag, followed by the data for the first cell, a single blank space, and the close table data tag </TD>.

6. On subsequent lines, repeat step 5, entering the data and tags for the second and third rows.

7. Close off the first row with the close table row tag, </TR>. You have created one whole row of the table and indicated that the table has four columns (by entering four <TD> lines). So far, the table definition looks like this:

```
<TABLE>
    <TR>
       <TD>L110 </TD>
       <TD>Home Scalpel </TD>
       <TD>Sharp, EZ-Kleen </TD>
       <TD>$44.95 </TD>
    </TR>
```

In the table data (<TD>) lines, observe that a space is typed between the cell content and the closing tag (</TD>). The space improves the spacing of the content within the cell. Adding more than one space has no additional effect.

Tables usually contain only text. But you can insert links or images in a table by entering the link or image tags (<A HREF> or <IMG SRC>, respectively) between the <TD>...</TD> tags, as if they were cell text.

8. Repeat steps 4 through 7 for the remaining two rows in the table:

```
<tr>
    <td>P125 </td>
    <td>Glucose Tester </td>
    <td>Pain-free </td>
    <td>$28.99 </td>
</tr>
<tr>
    <td>D652 </td>
    <td>Bandage Kit </td>
    <td>Long stick </td>
    <td>$8.95 </td>
</tr>
```

9. On the line following the </TR> tag that closes off the last row, close off the table definition with the close table tag </TABLE>.

The finished table definition appears in the HTML file as it does in Figure 10.2, and the resulting table appears in the browser as shown in Figure 10.3.

In Figure 10.3, observe that there are no gridlines around the table or cells. Gridlines, called *borders* in HTML, are a formatting option, described in the section titled "Formatting Tables," later in this chapter.

Figure 10.2.
The completed table definition in the HTML source file.

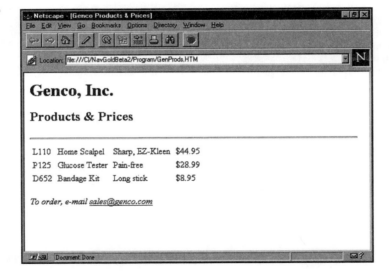

```
HotDog - [C:\NAVGOL~1\PROGRAM\GENPRODS.HTM]
File  Edit  View  Insert  Tags  Format  Tools  Window  Help
<body>
<h1>Genco, Inc.</h1>
<h2>Products &amp; Prices</h2>
<p>
<hr>
   <table>
      <tr>
         <td>L110 </td>
         <td>Home Scalpel </td>
         <td>Sharp, EZ-Kleen </td>
         <td>$44.95 </td>
      </tr>
      <tr>
         <td>P125 </td>
         <td>Glucose Tester </td>
         <td>Pain-free </td>
         <td>$28.99 </td>
      </tr>
      <tr>
         <td>D652 </td>
         <td>Bandage Kit </td>
         <td>Long stick </td>
         <td>$8.95 </td>
      </tr>
   </table>
<p>
<address>To order, e-mail <a href="mailto:sales@genco.com">sales@genco.com</a></address>
```

Figure 10.3.
The finished page, con table, in the Netscape browser.

```
Netscape - [Genco Products & Prices]
File  Edit  View  Go  Bookmarks  Options  Directory  Window  Help
Location: file:///C|/NavGoldBeta2/Program/GenProds.HTM
```

Genco, Inc.

Products & Prices

L110	Home Scalpel	Sharp, EZ-Kleen	$44.95
P125	Glucose Tester	Pain-free	$28.99
D652	Bandage Kit	Long stick	$8.95

To order, e-mail sales@genco.com

```
Document: Done
```

Formatting Tables

Most of the ways you can alter the appearance of a table involve adding attributes within the table tag (<TABLE>) or table data tag (<TD>). A few options, such as adding a caption, require inserting new, optional tags in or around the table definition.

Adding a Border

Borders, in the context of HTML tables, are the lines around the whole table and between each cell (see Figure 10.4), the complete set of gridlines that contains and delineates a table.

Adding a basic, default border to your table is as easy as adding the word BORDER to your <TABLE> tag:

```
<TABLE BORDER>
```

The results are shown in Figure 10.4.

Figure 10.4.
A default border (created by <TABLE BORDER>) around the table shown in Figure 10.3.

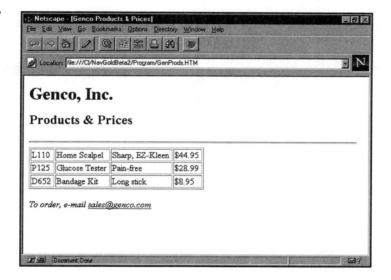

Customizing Borders

To modify the appearance of the border, HTML 3 offers three additional attributes to BORDER. Each attribute is inserted in the <TABLE> tag following the BORDER attribute.

Following the BORDER attribute with an equals sign (=) and a number sets the width (in pixels) of a beveled border around the outside of the table (the border lines between cells are unaffected). For example:

```
<TABLE BORDER=6>
```

puts a beveled border six pixels wide around the table. (See Figure 10.5.)

You can combine the =, CELLSPACING, and CELLPADDING attributes to create unique looks for your table border.

The CELLSPACING= attribute sets the width (in pixels) of the entire border, including the border surrounding the table and the lines between cells. For example:

```
<TABLE BORDER CELLSPACING=6>
```

puts a plain border three pixels wide around the table and between each cell. (See Figure 10.5.)

The CELLPADDING= attribute sets the space between the border lines and the cell content. Increasing the value of CELLPADDING creates more open space surrounding the text in the cell. For example:

```
<TABLE BORDER CELLPADDING=7>
```

puts an extra seven pixels of space between the content of each cell and the border surrounding it. (See Figure 10.5.)

Figure 10.5.
Tables using BORDER *attributes* =, CELLSPACING=, *and* CELLPADDING=.

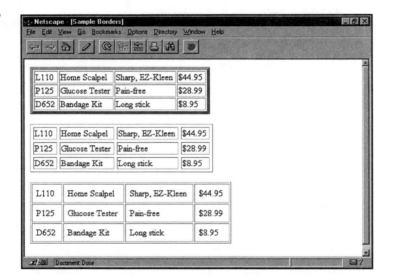

Adding Column or Row Headings

Use the table heading (<TH>) tag in place of any <TD> tag to create column or row headings. In a cell defined with the <TH> tag, browsers typically display the content centered in the cell and more bold than regular table data, to make it stand out as a heading should.

❏ To create row headings (see Figure 10.6), use the <TH> tag in place of the <TD> tag in the first column of each row.

❏ To create column headings (see Figure 10.6), use <TH> tags in place of <TD> tags for the whole first row.

In the sample code, note that I've added the line <TD> </TD> to the first row. This code creates an empty cell in the upper-left corner. (See Figure 10.6.) See the section titled "Making Blank and Empty Cells."

Observe in the following code that a new first row has been added to the table definition to add column headings. Each cell in that new row is defined with <TH>. Note also that a new first cell has been added to the other rows and is tagged <TH>. These new entries form the row headings. The result of the edited table definition appears in Figure 10.6.

```
<tr>
    <TD> </TD>
    <TH>Product # </td>
    <TH>Name </td>
    <TH>Features </td>
    <TH>Price </td>
</tr>
<tr>
    <TH>Sale! </TH>
    <td>L110 </td>
    <td>Home Scalpel </td>
    <td>Sharp, EZ-Kleen </td>
    <td>$44.95 </td>
</tr>
<tr>
    <TH>Last Chance! </TH>
    <td>P125 </td>
    <td>Glucose Tester </td>
    <td>Pain-free </td>
    <td>$28.99 </td>
</tr>
<tr>
    <TH>Try One! </TH>
    <td>D652 </td>
    <td>Bandage Kit </td>
    <td>Long stick </td>
    <td>$8.95 </td>
</tr>
```

Figure 10.6.

Row and column headings added with the table heading (<TH>) tag.

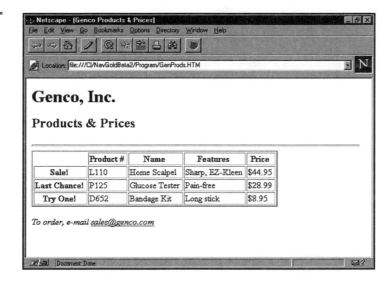

Adding a Caption

A *caption* is a title for the table, which you surround with `<CAPTION>...</CAPTION>` in the table definition. You can specify that the title appear directly above the table, or directly below the table (like a true caption). You cannot, however, do both; browsers recognize only one `<CAPTION>` line within a single table definition.

To place the caption above the table, you include the attribute `ALIGN="TOP"` following `<CAPTION`. To place the caption below the table, use `ALIGN="BOTTOM"`, as shown in the sample code and in Figure 10.7.

The `<CAPTION>...</CAPTION>` block should always immediately follow the `<TABLE>` tag, regardless of whether you want the caption displayed above or below the table. For example:

```
<TABLE>
    <CAPTION ALIGN="BOTTOM">Prices and Features Subject to Change</CAPTION>
```

Actually, the text provided for `CAPTION` needn't be an actual title or caption. It can be any text you want displayed directly above or below the table.

Figure 10.7.
The table with a bottom caption.

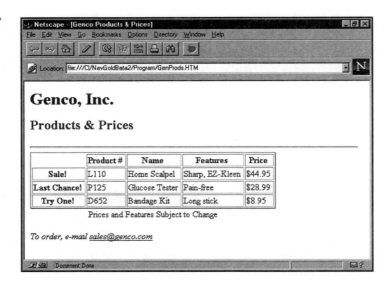

Customizing Table Width, Height, and Alignment

By default, browsers make a table just wide enough and high enough to hold the cell contents. (See the section titled "About Tables," earlier in this chapter.) If the table contents would make the table too wide for the window, the browser would automatically wrap cell contents to make the table fit. However, you can customize the width and height of the table, and its alignment (left, center, right) on the page.

The height and width are controlled by attributes to <TABLE>, HEIGHT= and WIDTH=, which can be used together or separately. With either attribute, you can express table height or table width as one of the following:

❏ A percentage of the total window height or width (WIDTH="80%")

❏ A number of screen pixels (HEIGHT="400")

Observe that the value following HEIGHT= or WIDTH= automatically refers to a number of pixels unless followed by the percent (%) sign. For example:

<TABLE HEIGHT="25%"> makes the table 25% the height of the window.

<TABLE WIDTH="300"> makes the table 300-pixels wide.

<TABLE HEIGHT="200" WIDTH="75%"> makes the table 200 pixels high and 75% as wide as the window.

By default, tables are aligned along the left side of the page. (See Figure 10.8.) You can use the <DIV> tag, along with the ALIGN="CENTER" or ALIGN="RIGHT" attribute, to center or right-align a table on the page. Observe that the <DIV> tags go outside of the table definition; that is, the <DIV> tag (including the attribute for alignment) goes before the table definition, and the close tag (</DIV>) goes after the table.

> If a table stretches across the entire window, any alignment attributes applied to it are irrelevant; left, center and right all look the same.

For example, this code centers the table on the page:

```
<DIV ALIGN="CENTER">
   <TABLE>
      table definition goes here
   </TABLE>
</DIV>
```

Figure 10.8.
Table alignment.

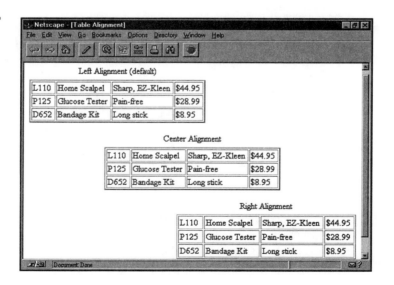

Customizing Cell Width and Height

As discussed in the preceding section, the HEIGHT= and WIDTH= attributes can appear within a <TABLE> tag to control the height and width of a table. However, you can insert the same attributes in a <TD> or <TH> tag to control the height or width of a cell.

Because browsers automatically even up rows and columns so that the table always forms a nice, straight grid, you need only apply the WIDTH= or HEIGHT= attribute to one cell to affect all cells in the column or row, respectively. In other words, a single instance of the WIDTH= attribute affects all cells in the same column; one use of HEIGHT= affects all cells in the same row.

For example, the <TH HEIGHT… line in the example below increases the height of the row of column headings to 40 pixels. (See Figure 10.9.) The <TH WIDTH… lines change the width of the columns.

```
<TR>
    <TD> </TD>
    <TH HEIGHT="40">Product # </td>
    <TH WIDTH="18%">Name </td>
    <TH>Features </td>
    <TH WIDTH="8%">Price </td>
</tr>
```

NOTE: Any time you use a percent value with the WIDTH attribute for one column but not for all others, the table automatically stretches across the entire width of the window (unless you have also used in the <TABLE> tag a width less than 100% or used WIDTH values for all cells that together don't add up to 100%).

Notice in Figure 10.9 that the table now stretches across the whole window, even though it didn't in earlier figures (before WIDTH was added), and the WIDTH measurements entered, plus the default width of the other columns, would not have appeared to add up to 100%.

When you use a percent value for one column but don't also supply a WIDTH for *every* column, the browser sets the column widths you specified and then widens or narrows the other columns (beginning with the column farthest to the right) so that the table fits exactly in the window.

After entering a percent value for the width of a column, browse the table and then adjust other widths as necessary to achieve the effect you desire. You might find that to get what you want, you'll have to specify the width of every column, not just one.

Figure 10.9.
Tables using cell WIDTH *and* HEIGHT *controls.*

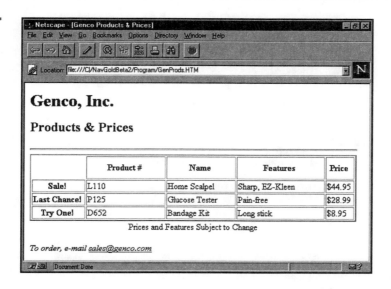

Aligning Text

By default, content in cells created by <TD> is left-aligned within the cell. (Content in table headings created by <TH> is centered.) By using the ALIGN attribute, you can center or right-align text within the cell.

You may apply this horizontal text alignment to a specific cell or to a whole row at a time. For example, to right-align the data in every cell in a row, add ALIGN="CENTER" or ALIGN="RIGHT" to the table row <TR> tag:

```
<TR ALIGN="RIGHT">
```

To right-align just the data in one cell, apply the attribute to a <TD> tag:

```
<TD ALIGN="RIGHT">
```

In addition to aligning text horizontally, you can align it vertically within the cell by using the VALIGN= attribute and options "TOP" (text aligns at the top of the cell), "CENTER" (text aligns at the vertical center), and "BOTTOM" (text aligns at the bottom of the cell).

For example, the following code vertically aligns the column headings of my table at the tops of their cells and also horizontally centers all entries in the Product # column. (Figure 10.10 shows the result.)

```
<TR VALIGN="TOP">
   <TD> </TD>
   <TH HEIGHT="40">Product # </td>
   <TH>Name </td>
```

```
    <TH>Features </td>
    <TH>Price </td>
</tr>
<tr>
    <TH>Sale! </TH>
    <td ALIGN="CENTER">L110 </td>
    <td>Home Scalpel </td>
    <td>Sharp, EZ-Kleen </td>
    <td>$44.95 </td>
</tr>
<tr>
    <TH>Last Chance! </TH>
    <td ALIGN="CENTER">P125 </td>
    <td>Glucose Tester </td>
    <td>Pain-free </td>
    <td>$28.99 </td>
</tr>
<tr>
    <TH>Try One! </TH>
    <td ALIGN="CENTER">D652 </td>
    <td>Bandage Kit </td>
    <td>Long stick </td>
    <td>$8.95 </td>
</tr>
</table>
```

Figure 10.10.
Using the ALIGN *attribute to control text alignment within table cells.*

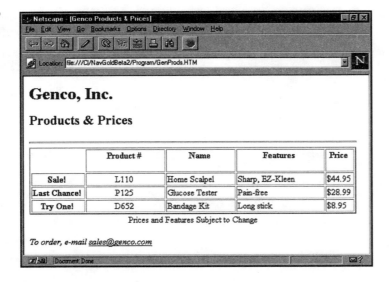

Making Blank and Empty Cells

By now, you've certainly noticed that the upper-left cell of the table shown in Figure 10.10 is missing. This effect is called a *blank cell* and is created simply by making a cell entry of a single space:

```
<TD> </TD>
```

A blank cell contains no data and has no borders. Suppose you wanted the effect of a blank cell, but wanted to keep the borders around it. You would create an *empty cell*, a cell entry of the code for a non-breaking space ( ). Here is an example:

```
<TD> </TD>
```

The following table definition contains not only the upper-left blank cell but also a new column with the heading Qty?. After the top row, all cell entries for the new column are empty cells, as shown. (The results appear in Figure 10.11.)

```
<TR VALIGN="TOP">
<TD> </TD>
<TH HEIGHT="40">Product # </td>
<TH>Name </td>
<TH>Features </td>
<TH>Price </td>
<TH>Qty?</TH>
</tr>
<tr>
<TH>Sale! </TH>
<td ALIGN="CENTER">L110 </td>
<td>Home Scalpel </td>
<td>Sharp, EZ-Kleen </td>
<td>$44.95 </td>
<TD> </TD>
</tr>
<tr>
<TH>Last Chance! </TH>
<td ALIGN="CENTER">P125 </td>
<td>Glucose Tester </td>
<td>Pain-free </td>
<td>$28.99 </td>
<TD> </TD>
</tr>
<tr>
<TH>Try One! </TH>
<td ALIGN="CENTER">D652 </td>
<td>Bandage Kit </td>
<td>Long stick </td>
<td>$8.95 </td>
<TD> </TD>
</tr>
</table>
```

Choosing Table Colors

The BGCOLOR attribute for changing cell background colors is a new extension added for version 3 of Navigator and Navigator Gold. In earlier versions of Navigator, and in other browsers, the BGCOLOR attribute has no effect.

You can select the color of the text in any cell and the color of the cell background. To change text colors, select the desired table text and click the Font Color button as described in Chapter 4, "Composing, Editing, and Formatting Text."

To change the background color of the cells in a table, add the BGCOLOR attribute and the correct color hex value code (see Colors by name and Hex Value in Appendix B) to any of the following tags:

<TABLE> To select the color of the whole table

<TR> To select the background color of a row

<TD> To select the background color of a cell

<TH> To select the background color of a heading

Figure 10.11.
*A table with a blank cell
and an empty cell.*

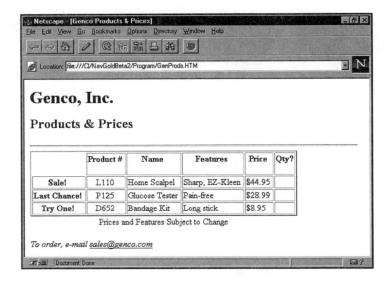

For example, to make the background color of all cells in a table blue:

```
<TABLE BGCOLOR=#0000FF>
```

To make the background color of a row red:

```
<TR BGCOLOR=#FF0000>
```

NOTE: If you choose to use BGCOLOR, keep the following in mind:

❑ You must change the text color (using the Font Color button on the
toolbar) in the cells to contrast properly with the chosen background
color.

❑ At this writing, only Navigator 3 and Navigator Gold 3 support table cell
background colors. But earlier versions of Navigator, and many other
extension-supporting browsers (including most that support tables),
support text colors. That means that many visitors will see your selected
text colors, but not the background color. To ensure that your text
remains readable even if the background color does not appear, you

must choose a text color that contrasts with the background but will still be readable in the absence of a background color. For example, if you choose a dark background and a very light text color, the text will contrast nicely in browsers that support background colors, but may seem to blend into the page color in browsers that don't support table background colors.

TASK

Using Gold 3's Create Table Dialog

Yes, Netscape Navigator Gold 3 (the second release of Gold) has a Create Table dialog, unlike its predecessor, Gold 2. Also unlike its predecessor, Gold 3's Editor displays tables properly, in true WYSIWYG format.

So why, you ask, did I spend the last umpteen pages describing how to code tables in HTML? Why didn't I just describe the Create Table dialog in the first place? Why must I make you an HTML martyr?

Well, Gold 3's Create Table dialog is not necessarily a big help in table creation. First, to really understand what each element in the dialog does, you must already understand the actions of the HTML tags described earlier in this chapter.

At this writing, Gold 3 and its Create Table feature are still under development, so they may have improved by the time you try them. Give 'em a whirl.

More importantly, there are a number of idiosyncracies in Gold 3's table support that may force you to play with the HTML code after using the Create table dialog. For example, if you use Create Table to create two tables together, with no intervening text or images between them, you cannot insert text or images between them in the Editor. You must edit the HTML file, and insert your desired content between the </TABLE> tag of the first table and the <TABLE> tag of the second. (See Gold 3's Help for more about the Do's and Don'ts of tables.)

Those caveats aside, the Create Table dialog can be a handy accessory when your needs are simple and your time is short.

To create a table with the Create Table dialog in Gold 3's Editor:

1. Create and format your document (except for any tables). This will help prevent problems Gold may experience when tables are positioned together and content must be inserted between them, or when tables appear at the beginning or end of a file.

2. Position the edit cursor at the spot in the document where you want a table, and choose **I**nsert, **T**able. The Create Table dialog opens, like the one shown in Figure 10.12.

Figure 10.12.
*The Create Table dialog
in Gold 3.*

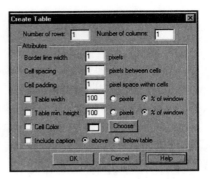

3. Complete the dialog as desired. To learn how each element in the dialog affects the table, see the preceding sections of this chapter.

4. After you complete the Create Table dialog, an empty table appears in your document. Create the cell contents by clicking in a cell, and then typing. You may customize the appearance of cell contents using the editing features described in the next section.

Editing a Table in Gold 3

You can edit existing tables in Gold 3 three ways:

Table Properties: Position the cursor within the table and choose **P**roperties | **T**able. The Table dialog opens (see Figure 10.13), which features the same settings as the Create Table dialog. Change settings as desired, and click OK.

Row/Cell Properties: Position the cursor within a cell, and choose **P**roperties | **R**ow to change row properties, or **P**roperties | **C**ell to change cell properties. In the Row dialog (see Figure 10.14), you can change the horizontal or vertical alignment of text in the cell, or choose a background color for the row. In the Cell dialog (see Figure 10.15), you can change the horizontal or vertical alignment of text in the cell, make the cell contents a Heading, and choose other formatting options described earlier in this chapter.

Figure 10.13.
Editing Table properties in Gold 3.

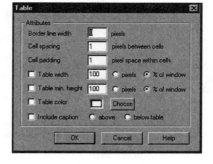

Figure 10.14.
Editing Row properties in Gold 3.

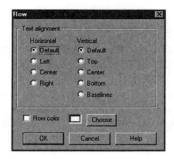

Insert/Delete: Using choices on the Insert menu, you can insert not just a table, but also a row, column or cell. Using choices on the Properties menu, you can delete a row, column or cell.

Figure 10.15.
Editing Cell properties in Gold 3.

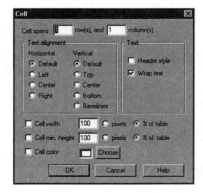

Using HotDog for Easy Tables

HotDog 2.5 includes a set of dialogs for quickly generating a table definition. Although they're not a part of Gold, they are more full featured than Gold 3's Create Table dialog.

To use the dialogs, position the edit cursor in the file where you want to insert the table and click the Table button on HotDog's toolbar.

By highlighting any HTML table definition— even one you wrote yourself—from <TABLE> through </TABLE> and then pressing the Table button, you may edit the table or change its formatting in HotDog's Create Table dialog.

Using HotDog's dialog, you can build a table that includes a caption and headings, and formatting options such as alignment, height/width, and cell padding. More important, the Sample Table window allows you to drag the table's gridlines around to change row size and column width.

When you finish creating a table in the Create Table dialog, click OK to insert the finished code into the HTML file. Then view the finished file and table in the Netscape Browser.

Workshop Wrap-Up

A simple table is a simple deal. If you're at all comfortable with writing HTML code, then tables—even fancy ones—are among the things that offer the greatest page bang for your effort buck. If you're not yet accustomed to composing HTML, then getting used to HTML and your editor is the toughest part of tables. Fortunately, tables have a growth curve. You can start out with simple tables and then work your way up to the fancy stuff as you gain confidence.

If you're really intimidated by tables, you can always use HotDog's Table button. But you'll probably find tables simple enough without HotDog. If you do use HotDog, you might still want to edit the code HotDog writes, applying a few optional tags or attributes to give the table your own stamp or accommodate an unusual data requirement.

Next Steps

Now...

❏ To learn how to fracture your page into lovely frames, see Chapter 11, "Making Frames."

❏ To learn about adding scripted routines to your page, see Chapter 13, "Using JavaScript."

❏ To publish your page, see Chapter 15, "Publishing Web Documents."

Q&A

Q: I have stuff I want to put in a table, but I really don't want my table seen only by the HTML 3 world. Are there other options?

A: There are several ways you can create the effect of a table without limiting its appearance to HTML 3-compatible browsers. First, you can simply type your table into the page (in the Netscape Editor), using spaces to align the columns, and apply the Formatted paragraph property to it. This instructs browsers to display the material in a monospaced font and to properly display all extra spaces. (See Chapter 4, "Composing, Editing, and Formatting Text.") You won't get borders or fancy formatting, but virtually everyone—including folks without HTML 3 browsers and even those with text-only browsers—will see your table.

Alternatively, consider putting your table in a GIF file. Some image editors enable you to type text, dress it up, and save it as an image or as part of an image. (Another way to do this is to create your table in a word processor or spreadsheet, and then use a screen-capture program to crop out the table and save it as an image.) If your table is fairly simple, presenting it as a GIF image is a good way to put it out to virtually all graphical browser users. If you want to, you can provide a link as an alternative representation (see Chapter 5, "Linking Everywhere, Anywhere") to the table image. This link can open an HTML file or simple text file containing a text-only version of the table for nongraphical browsers.

Q: Can I put a table inside a table?

A: Certainly, and you can achieve some interesting effects by using a different border for the table inside, the "nested" table. You can even nest tables within tables within tables.

To nest a table, you create the main, or parent, table definition. Then you add the entire table definition of the nested table as a cell entry (<TD> line) in the parent table. For example:

```
<TABLE>
  <TR>
  <TD>A cell in the parent table</TD>
  <TD>
      <TABLE>
         <TR>
         <TD>A cell in the nested table</TD>
             rest of nested table definition
      </TABLE>
  </TD>
  rest of parent table definition
</TABLE>
```

Q: In some of my cells, I have lots of text, which the browser wraps when displaying the table. But in other cells with very little text, the text wraps, too—even when it really doesn't need to. Can I fix this?

A: Add the NOWRAP attribute to the table data (<TD>) or table heading (<TH>) line for the cell whose text you don't want to wrap. For example:

```
<TD NOWRAP>This text will not be wrapped in the cell.</TD>
```

ELEVEN

Making Frames

Frames are simultaneously the best and worst thing to happen to the Web lately. If you've hit a frame-based document in your browsing, you know that they're cool. They make your display look like the control panel of a jet fighter—so many different, independent chunks of information stimulating your brain at once. It's like picture-in-picture on a new TV, for people with eyes so info-hungry that just one program—or one page—at a time provides inadequate sensory input. Of course, frames also greatly expand the author's ability to offer a variety of document navigation scenarios to visitors.

For all that excitement, frames make us pay. Most significantly, because frames are a recently introduced Netscape extension, most browsers still do not support them. Even the previous release of Netscape Navigator (release 1.2) does not support them, just as many browsers that support the other extensions do not support frames. Frames also generally slow down initial access to a document (because the browser must download multiple files), and when poorly designed, frames force visitors to do a lot of scrolling simply to read the contents of a single page.

The moral? Before cramming your document into frames, ask yourself three questions: "Are frames appropriate for the content I'm presenting?" "Can each portion of my content be effectively presented within the frame size I'm planning?" and "Do the advantages of frames presentation justify leaving behind the many Web surfers who can't see frames?" (You can fudge this last question. See the section titled "Accommodating the Frame-Intolerant," later in this chapter.)

In this chapter, you

- ❏ Discover the frame definition document, an HTML file that creates frames
- ❏ Learn about properly formatting content files for frames
- ❏ Create frame documents, from the basic to the complex
- ❏ Learn how to provide an alternative version for visitors whose browsers cannot display frame-based documents

Tasks in this chapter:

- ❏ Building a Simple, Two-Frame Document
- ❏ Building a Complex Frame Document

If the answer to all three questions is Yes, push ahead with frames. You'll find making them fun.

> # NOTE:
> The tags used to create frames are Netscape extensions to HTML. Frame-based documents are entirely inaccessible to visitors whose browsers do not support Netscape's frames extensions. (Some browsers that support other extensions do not support frames.) To make your material accessible to those who can't see frames documents, you must supply an alternative version of it that is not frame-based; see the section titled "Accommodating the Frame-Intolerant," later in this chapter.
>
> This chapter assumes you have seen and used frame-based documents on the Web. If not, familiarize yourself with them before attempting to create your own.
>
> The default home page at Netscape:
>
> `http://home.netscape.com/`
>
> is a frames document. You can learn more about frames by exploring the home page, and by clicking About our New Design, which appears in the bottom-right frame of the Netscape home page.
>
> If you access Netscape's home page to learn about frames and the page does not appear to be divided into frames, scroll to the bottom of the page and click the button labeled SHOW FRAMES.

When publishing and publicizing your frame-based document, take care to direct visitors to the frame definition document, not one of the files that appears within a frame. See Chapter 15.

In the frame definition document, you can insert a message to be displayed only to visitors who can't see links. See the section titled "Accommodating the Frame-Intolerant," later in this chapter.

What Does It Take to Make a Frame Document?

In a frame-based document, the content of each frame is contained within a separate HTML document. (See Figure 11.1.) The multiple documents are tied together by yet another HTML file, the *frame definition document*, which also contains the code dictating the number and size of the frames.

The Frame Definition Document

The frame definition document supplies no content to the page; it merely specifies how the page is to be split up, and which HTML document is to be displayed in each frame. In Figure 11.1, the URL shown in the Location box is the URL of the frame definition document; that's the URL a visitor accesses to open the document. The frame definition document then takes care of accessing the page within each frame.

Creating a frame-based document requires creating the various HTML documents that will appear within the frames, composing the frame definition document to define the number, size, and other aspects of the frames, and tying a specific file to each frame.

Figure 11.1.
A frame-based document.

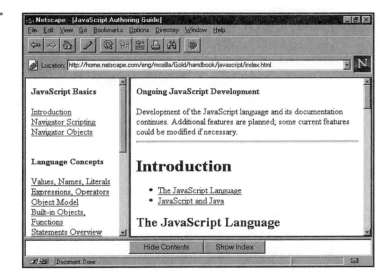

Rows and Columns

Within the frame definition document, you break up the page into frames by applying either of two attributes (or both together):

❏ The ROWS attribute splits the page into horizontal rows.

❏ The COLS attribute splits the page into vertical columns.

❏ Used together (see the Task section titled "Building a Complex Frame Document," later in this chapter), ROWS and COLS split the page into any combination of rows and columns.

The ROWS or COLS attribute is always followed by an equals sign (=) and a measurement, in quotes. It is the measurement that determines the relative size and number of frames on the page. The measurement is expressed in one of three ways:

❏ A number value: Creates a row (or column) the given number of pixels high (or wide)

❏ A percentage: Creates a row (or column) the given percentage of the total height (or width) of the browser window

❏ An asterisk: Creates a row (or column) whose size is determined automatically by the space left over after other frames are created

Avoid using a number of pixels as a measurement, since the number of pixels available in a window varies with the browser platform.

The number of measurement entries between the quotes determines the number of frames on the page. For example:

`<FRAMESET ROWS="40%,60%">` — Creates two rows: the first (top row) 40% of the height of the window and the second (bottom) 60% of the height of the window.

`<FRAMESET COLS="200,*">` — Creates two columns: the first (left) column 200 pixels wide and the second (right) column taking up the rest of the window.

`<FRAMESET COLS="*,20%,50%">` — Creates three columns: the first (left) column filling the space left by the other columns, the second (middle) column 20% of the width of the window, and the third (right) column 50% of the window.

`<FRAMESET ROWS="*,*,*,*">` — Creates four rows of equal size. (When multiple asterisks are used, each is given the same value.)

The Frame Content

The content of each frame is supplied by a separate HTML file, which you compose like any other Web document. However, when composing files that will appear in frames, you must try to account for the size and shape of the frame in which the file will appear.

Browsers help adjust content for frames: They automatically wrap text to fit within a frame and also automatically shorten horizontal lines. Alignment properties are also preserved in a frame; for example, if your text is centered in the page when you compose it, the browser centers it within the frame when displaying it. However, browsers cannot adjust the positions or spacing of images (or images used as rules or bullets); images often make framing difficult.

Because frames are not created in the Editor, you may create your content files in the Editor, but you must use an HTML source editor to compose the frame definition document. After composing all your files, you'll want to browse the frame definition document and adjust the frame definition document and/or the formatting of the content files, to make the frames fit nicely.

Browsers automatically add scrollbars to a frame when the contents exceed the frame size. But a frame document showing a collection of fragmentary files and scrollbars is unappealing, and visitors tire quickly of excessive scrolling, especially horizontal scrolling to read wide text. Whenever practical, make the content fit the frame—or vice versa.

Building a Simple, Two-Frame Document

1. Using the medium of your choice (such as Netscape Editor or HotDog), compose the content documents that will appear in the frames. Be sure to organize and format them, if possible, in a way that will minimize the need for visitors to scroll them in their frames.

2. In an HTML source editor, create a new HTML file, including the required structure tags and the title for your frames document, as shown here:

> If you're unfamiliar with HTML source files and editors, see Chapter 9, "Editing HTML Source Code."

```
<HTML>
<HEAD>
<TITLE>Frames Demo</TITLE>
</HEAD>
    <BODY>
    </BODY>
</HTML>
```

3. Replace the <BODY> tags with <FRAMESET> tags, as shown. (Note that in a frame definition document, the <FRAMESET> block replaces the <BODY> block, and you may not include a <BODY> block elsewhere in the file.)

```
<HTML>
<HEAD>
<TITLE>Frames Demo</TITLE>
</HEAD>
    <FRAMESET>
    </FRAMESET>
</HTML>
```

The <FRAMESET> tags enclose the entire definition. All further coding is inserted between these tags.

> You may indent your frame definition, as shown. Indenting the code has no effect on the page's appearance, but it makes the frame definition easier to see within the file.

4. My frame document will be split into two columns, and not into any rows. So in the <FRAMESET> tag, I add the COLS attribute. I want the first column to be narrow (30% of the window), and the second column to take up the remainder of the window.

```
<FRAMESET COLS="30%,*">
</FRAMESET>
```

> In the <FRAMESET> tag in the example, COLS="*,70%" or COLS="30%,70%" would have the same effect as the entry shown.

5. Having defined the frames, I define their content by adding the <FRAME SRC> tag and the filenames of the content files (in quotes). In the columns on the page, the files will appear in the same order (left to right) in which they appear in the <FRAMESET> block (top to bottom). In the example, MULTI.HTM will appear in the first (left) column.

```
<FRAMESET COLS="30%,*">
    <FRAME SRC="MULTI.HTM">
    <FRAME SRC="DESCRIP.HTM">
</FRAMESET>
```

The finished frame document appears in Figure 11.2. Here's the complete code of the frame definition document:

```
<HTML>
<HEAD>
    <TITLE>Frames Demo</TITLE>
</HEAD>
    <FRAMESET COLS="30%,*">
        <FRAME SRC="MULTI.HTM">
        <FRAME SRC="DESCRIP.HTM">
    </FRAMESET>
</HTML>
```

Figure 11.2.
The final page.

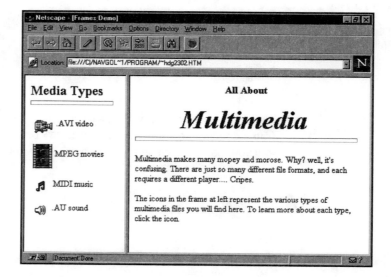

Observe that a single change to the attributes in the <FRAMESET> block dramatically alters the resulting page. Suppose, for example, I wanted rows instead of columns. Besides reformatting my source documents so that they conformed better to wide rows than narrow columns, I'd need to do nothing to the frame definition document but change the COLS attribute to ROWS, as shown:

```
<FRAMESET ROWS="30%,*">
    <FRAME SRC="MULTI.HTM">
    <FRAME SRC="DESCRIP.HTM">
</FRAMESET>
```

The files referenced in the <FRAME SRC> tags will appear in rows from top to bottom, in the order listed. In other words, MULTI.HTM will appear in the top row because it appears in the first <FRAME SRC> tag, while DESCRIP.HTM appears in the second (bottom) row.

The result of the ROWS variation appears in Figure 11.3.

Figure 11.3.
A ROWS variation of the page shown in Figure 11.2.

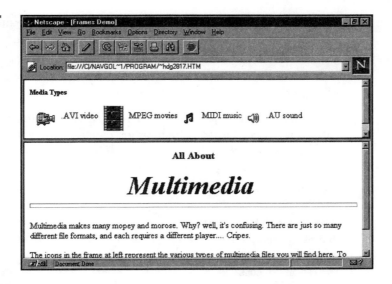

 # Building a Complex Frame Document

Although the examples shown in Figure 11.2 and 11.3 are legitimate frames documents, they have certain limitations:

❑ They involve only rows or columns, not both within the same page.

❑ If you execute a link in either frame, the file the link points to replaces the file in the frame containing the link. Often in frames documents, you want visitors to click a link in one frame to open a file in another frame.

The following two sections show how to modify your frame definition document and the links within the content files to build a leading-edge frames document.

To Use Both Rows and Columns

Creating a document like the one in Figure 11.4, which has both rows and columns, requires nesting multiple framesets, each with its own ROWS and COLS attributes.

To begin, you must first determine which frameset—a frameset for ROWS or one for COLS—comes first, or which frameset is the parent frameset within which the next frameset is nested. You decide this based on the configuration of the page you want to create:

❑ If any row in the page will extend all the way across the window (without being broken up into columns), the parent frameset defines the rows (ROWS).

❏ If any column in the page in the page will extend the entire window height, top to bottom (without being broken up into rows), the parent frameset defines the columns (COLS).

❏ If all rows are broken into columns and all columns are broken into rows, the parent frameset defines columns (COLS).

For example, in the page shown in Figure 11.4, the bottom row stretches across the entire window. So the parent frameset will define the rows of the page. The page has two rows (the bottom row and the top row, which is broken into columns), at a 75/25 split. So here's the parent frameset:

```
<FRAMESET ROWS="75%,*">
</FRAMESET>
```

Next, I have to break that top row into two columns (at a 30/70 ratio). I accomplish that by inserting a new frameset within the parent frameset, as shown:

```
<FRAMESET ROWS="75%,*">
   <FRAMESET COLS"30%,*")
   </FRAMESET>
</FRAMESET>
```

Finally, I add the <FRAME SRC> tags to each frameset to call document files into the three frames:

```
<FRAMESET ROWS="75%,*")
   <FRAMESET COLS"30%,*")
       <FRAME SRC="MULTI.HTM">
       <FRAME SRC="DESCRIP.HTM">
   </FRAMESET>
   <FRAME SRC="DEFINI.HTM">
</FRAMESET>
```

Figure 11.4.
The complex document.

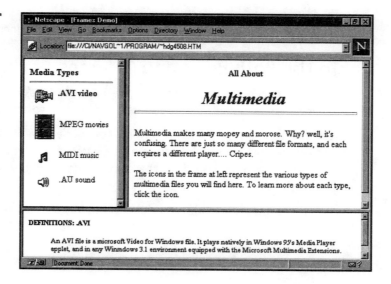

To Specify the Frame a Linked Document Opens In

If you code your frame definition documents as shown up to this point in the chapter, a link appearing in any of the documents will open its corresponding file in the same frame that held the link. If you want a link in one frame to open a new document in another frame, you need to do two things:

- ❏ In the <FRAME SRC> lines of the frameset, you must give each frame a name.
- ❏ In the links within the content files, you must reference the name of the frame in which the linked file will open.

Using the page shown in Figure 11.4 as a starting point, I'll name the frames. The NAME= attribute is added to the <FRAME SRC> tag after the filename (and a blank space). It doesn't matter what you call the frames, as long as you give each a unique name. The frame names do not appear on the page; just in the source code.

```
<FRAMESET ROWS="75%,*")
    <FRAMESET COLS"30%,*")
        <FRAME SRC="MULTI.HTM" NAME="Icons">
        <FRAME SRC="DESCRIP.HTM" NAME="Text">
    </FRAMESET>
    <FRAME SRC="DEFINI.HTM" NAME="Definitions">
</FRAMESET>
```

Within the content files, I edit the links in order to add the name of the frame in which the linked files should open. This is done by adding the attribute TARGET= and the frame name (in quotes) to the link, following the filename. For example:

```
<A HREF="avidef.htm" TARGET="Definitions"></a>
```

Although adding the TARGET attribute is easy enough in an HTML source editor, you can add TARGET attributes in the Netscape Editor.

When entering the filename in the Link Properties dialog (see Figure 11.5), place a double quote mark (") following the filename, and leave off the closing quote mark following the frame name after TARGET. The Editor automatically places quotes around the entire string you enter in this field. If you quote it as shown, your entry comes out correctly in the HTML source, with quotes around the filename and the frame name.

When the link shown in Figure 11.5 is executed, the file AVIDEF.HTM opens in the frame named Definitions (the bottom frame), replacing DEFINI.HTM.

Now suppose you wanted every link in the MULTI.HTM file to open its file in the Text frame. When all links are to open in the same frame, you can save time by using the <BASE TARGET> tag in the content file's header. All links in a file containing a

If you omit the TARGET attribute from any link, that link will open its file in the same frame that contains the link.

`<BASE TARGET>` tag open their files in the frame named by `<BASE TARGET>`; you do not need to add any TARGET attributes to the link tags. For example:

```
<HTML>
<HEAD>
    <TITLE>
    <BASE TARGET="Text">
</HEAD>
    <BODY>
page definition goes here
    </BODY>
</HTML>
```

All links in the sample content file will open their files in the Text frame.

Figure 11.5.
Adding a TARGET
*attribute to a link in the
Editor.*

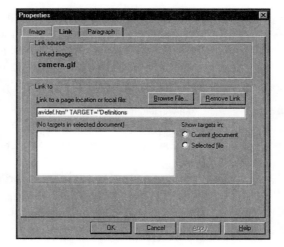

Accommodating the Frame-Intolerant

As mentioned earlier in this chapter (twice, in fact, so you wouldn't miss it), frame-based documents cannot be displayed by browsers that don't support Netscape's frames extensions.

In most other cases, extensions don't prevent whole pages from appearing—at worst, a portion of a page (such as a table) doesn't show up, or the page layout or character formatting reverts to the browser's defaults. But frames are *evil*—they render the whole page *terra incognita* to frame-intolerant browsers, which show nothing of a frames document but a sad, empty page (sniff!).

What can you do about it, short of denying yourself frames as an authoring tool? In your frame definition document, you can add the `<NOFRAME>...</NOFRAME>` tag to display a message or a link to the no-frames world. In the example below, I've added a `<NOFRAME>` message containing a link that leads to a no-frames version of my document.

```
<FRAMESET ROWS="75%,*")
    <FRAMESET COLS"30%,*")
        <FRAME SRC="MULTI.HTM">
        <FRAME SRC="DESCRIP.HTM">
    </FRAMESET>
    <FRAME SRC="DEFINI.HTM">
<NOFRAME>This document uses frames. If your browser does not support frames,
please view our <A HREF="framefree.HTM">no frames version.</A></NOFRAME>
    </FRAMESET>
</FRAMESET>
```

You'll need a nonframe-supporting browser, such as Microsoft's Internet Explorer, to check your work when you use `<NOFRAME>`, because its effects don't show up in Navigator Gold.

When the frame definition document is browsed, the content within `<NOFRAME>` does not appear at all in frame-supporting browsers—even you won't see it in Netscape's Browser window. Only when the browser does not support frames does the `<NOFRAME>` content appear, as shown in Figure 11.6.

Figure 11.6.

The `<NOFRAME>` message, as seen through Microsoft Internet Explorer, which does not support frames.

NOTE: The Windows 95 version of Microsoft's Internet Explorer (see Figure 11.6), at this writing, is release 2.0, which does not support frames. However, at the time this book went to press, a new version, Internet Explorer 3.0, was in its early testing cycle. According to Microsoft's Web page, Internet Explorer 3.0 will support frames in its final release.

All too frequently, Web authors use `<NOFRAME>` to inform frame-impaired visitors that they're out of luck. Messages like "Sorry, this document must be viewed with

Netscape Navigator 2.0 (or 3.0)" almost always mean frames lie ahead. This approach needlessly abandons a large percentage of the Web population.

Alternatively, you can supply a link to a no-frames version of your document, as I do in the example. Creating the no-frames version is a no-brainer: just copy and rename the content files, and adapt their formatting and links so that they look and act properly as a multipage, nonframe document. In the <NOFRAME> block of the frame definition document, supply a link to the top page of your frame-free version.

Pages created with the Page Wizard (see Chapter 2) or with Netscape's templates (see Chapter 3) automatically include the Netscape Now! button and link.

Instead of supplying a no-frames version (or in addition to it), you can apply for Netscape Now!, a program in which Netscape Communications Corp. grants you the right to put the Netscape Now! button on your page. The Netscape Now! button is the link source for a link to a page at Netscape Communications. This page leads visitors through a series of forms and selections to download a version of Netscape for their system. (They'll need version 2.0 or higher to see frames.)

Through the program, you can add the Netscape Now! button to your <NOFRAME> block, so visitors who find themselves locked out of your frame-based document can hop over to Netscape, pick up a copy of Navigator 3.0, and return to see your page.

Should you use the button? On the one hand, you help your visitors acquire the software they need to use your page. On the other hand, you're spending your time and server dollars to supply free advertising to a multimillion-dollar company. It's up to you.

About FrameGang

The CD-ROM at the back of this book includes a program called FrameGang, which makes creating frame definition documents a snap. The program requires that you understand the basics of coding frames yourself, but it still makes framing simpler by automatically supplying some of the code, and by adjusting the measurements in the <FRAMESET> lines when you drag frame borders on the screen.

Workshop Wrap-Up

Frames are an exercise in careful choices and organization. Most important among the choices is choosing whether to use frames at all. Once committed to using frames, always try to supply a useful <NOFRAME> message and an alternative for the frameless.

Next Steps

Now...

❏ To learn how to script interactive routines for your pages, see Chapter 12, "Creating Interactive Forms and Image Maps."

❏ To add programmed functions to your Web pages, see Chapter 13, "Using JavaScript."

❏ To see some frames documents in action, see Chapter 14, "Real-Life Examples II."

Q&A

Q: Sometimes, Netscape adds scrollbars to my frames when they're not really necessary. What can I do about that?

A: By default, browsers add scrollbars whenever a file's contents appear to exceed the frame. You may be able to eliminate the problem by adjusting the formatting of the content file, or the size of the frame it appears in, so that the contents sits comfortably in the frame.

If you're confident that scrollbars are unnecessary, but they still show up, you can prevent them from displaying by adding the attribute SCROLLING="NO" to the <FRAME SRC> line for the frame—for example:

```
<FRAME SRC="sample.htm" SCROLLING="NO">
```

By the way, you can force browsers to display scrollbars on a frame, even when the browser considers them unnecessary, by adding SCROLLING="YES" to the <FRAME SRC> line.

Q: Can a link that appears within a frame open a new file not in a frame, but filling the entire window (replacing the frames)?

A: Instead of a frame name, use "TOP" as the value for the TARGET attribute in the link. (See the section titled "To Specify the Frame a Linked Document Opens In," earlier in this chapter.) When the link is executed, the file it opens fills the browser window, replacing the frame definition document. Clicking the Back button restores the frames document.

Q: Will frames support among browsers catch up?

A: Netscape has proposed its frames tags for inclusion in HTML 3, and it's likely they'll wind up there. But a final HTML 3 specification is still a few years off, and by the time it shows up, most leading graphical browsers will have already added frames support; they *must* do so, to keep up with Navigator. Look for frames support to be a key ingredient of any major graphical browser release for the next year or so.

Small players among the graphical fold and the text-only browsers are pushed further behind the curve by frames, and that's unfortunate. But, frankly, users of such products have been surfing on borrowed time for a few years. The Web has become a *de facto* graphical environment, one whose evolution is largely an echo of Navigator's feature set. Sooner or later, everyone's going to have to go graphical (and go extensions) or drop out. *C'est la Web*.

TWELVE

Creating Interactive Forms and Image Maps

In one sense, any old HTML document is *interactive*, in that it lets you jump around to other URLs and anchors. You click, it responds. That's interactivity.

But there's another level of interactivity possible, one that is not directly supported within the confines of HTML code. A *script* is a program that accepts input of some kind from the visitor to a page, does something with that input, and spits back a result. The interaction can be as simple as collecting a user's name and address and adding them to a mailing list, or it can be as elaborate as showing the visitor a monthly mortgage payment calculated from a home price and interest rate the visitor enters.

HTML cannot support such functions on its own. To provide interactive functions to visitors, your document must call a script program residing on the client or server. HTML is smart enough to collect input from the visitor and to pass it on to the script program, and HTML can display what the script produces, provided the script formats its output with HTML codes. But the actual processing of the visitor's input is the exclusive province of script programs.

Today, there are two principle methods for scripting interactive functions in Web pages: the Common Gateway Interface (CGI) and JavaScript. The latter you'll discover in Chapter 13, "Using JavaScript." Here, you'll learn about the two most important applications of CGI scripting, forms and image maps.

About CGI Scripting

A book this size devoted entirely to CGI scripting would be too short. And at that, reading such a book might not be the most effective use of your time. The need to know CGI scripting is evaporating, as JavaScript and other approaches to scripting gain in popularity.

For now, though, CGI scripts are the best way to enable forms and image maps in your document. But before you can consider scripting, you have to know a few things about CGI.

CGI programs run, not in the browser, but on the server. (There is one exception to this rule, which you'll discover in the discussion of image maps later in this chapter.) The rules and preferred programming languages for scripting vary with the server type and platform. Most Web servers today are UNIX-based and work best with scripts written in either of the well known, popular UNIX shell languages: Bourne shell or Perl shell. Windows-based servers, on the other hand, are configured for Visual Basic scripts. As a result, it's impossible for this book to offer sample script code that will work on any server. The HTML code shown here that defines the way a form or image map appears in the document will work fine in Netscape Gold, but the scripts shown are for Bourne and Perl, which your server might or might not support.

Even if your server does support scripting, there's no guarantee that your server supplier will permit you to use scripts. The greater interaction between visitors and the server that scripts enable is a potential security risk for the server. Before building a document that uses CGI scripts, talk to your server supplier or system administrator to find out whether, and how, you may use scripts. Then work closely with the system administrator on the testing and implementation of any script you write.

In the remainder of this chapter, you'll learn how to create documents for the two most common script-based activities: forms and image maps. But as you learn about these, remember two very important points:

❏ There is much more to scripting than can be covered here. If you really want to get into CGI scripting, you'll need some UNIX programming classes and/or advanced programming texts.

❏ Although UNIX-based CGI scripting using Bourne or Perl shell programs is the most widely supported, and therefore preferred, way to script forms and image maps, CGI will probably slip away in coming years to JavaScript. You still need CGI today, because JavaScript is not yet widely supported. But if you want to learn a script programming skill with a future, learn JavaScript. (See Chapter 13, "Using JavaScript.")

To learn about CGI scripting in detail, see either of the following Sams.net titles (choose depending on whether you have two weeks to spare or three):

Teach Yourself Web Publishing with HTML in 14 Days (by Laura Lemay)

Teach Yourself CGI Scripting with Perl 5 in 21 Days (by Eric Herrman)

Creating Interactive Forms

As a surfer, you've seen forms. For example, when you enter a search term for a directory (such as Yahoo), you're using a form. Search forms like Yahoo's work like this:

1. Following instructions embedded in the HTML file, the browser takes the search term that you've entered and passes it to Yahoo's server, along with the filename and location of a script for processing that input.

2. The server starts the designated script program and provides your search term as an *input* variable to the program.

3. When the script program finishes, it produces *output*—a listing of hits on your search—plus instructions on how to display the output in an HTML document.

4. The server sends the output back to the browser to be displayed.

How Forms Are Made

Because of the problems associated with server variability and complexity of writing CGI scripts, the forms section of this chapter focuses primarily on step 1, creating the on-screen form.

There are two parts to making an interactive form:

1. Using special HTML tags, you create the visible form that appears in your Web page. The form definition includes names for each separate piece of information (input) the form collects and a pointer to the CGI script that will process that input.

2. Then you write a CGI script that accepts the form input, submits it to the server, processes it, and returns it in a particular format.

About GET and POST

When you build a form, you must specify one of two values in the METHOD attribute of the FORM tag: GET or POST. Both of these values indicate that the entries visitors make in the form should be submitted as input to a specified script. But how they present that input differs.

For most forms, POST is the preferred value because it directs the server to pass the input directly to the script as standard input. GET, on the other hand, is put into a special environment variable and then submitted to the script. The use of an environment variable allows programmers to more specifically define how the input is to be treated by the script, which opens up a range of advanced processing capabilities. But for ordinary forms processing, POST is simpler and better.

About Submit Buttons

One of the HTML tags used for forms, when used with the SUBMIT attribute, creates an onscreen button labeled "Submit." (Look ahead to Figure 12.2.) For example, the line below creates a Submit button.

```
<INPUT TYPE="Submit">
```

The Submit button is optional if your form is designed to send only one input value to the server; pressing Enter automatically submits the form. However, it's good practice to add a Submit button for every form.

The Submit button is what your visitors must click in order to confirm that they have finished making entries in a form. When a visitor clicks the button, the browser sends all input in the forms to the designated script for processing.

By default, the label text on the button reads "Submit." By adding the VALUE attribute to the tag, you can label the button anything you want. (It still does the job of a Submit button.) For example, the line

```
<INPUT TYPE="Submit" VALUE="Send Answers">
```

Creates a Submit button labeled Send Answers.

NOTE: Forms coding requires multiple lines of HTML code, and Netscape Gold's Insert Tag function inserts only one line at a time—which makes it a labor-intensive choice for building forms. Also, the Gold Editor cannot display forms in WYSIWYG form; you must view your document in the Netscape Browser to see your forms.

The best approach for coding forms is to write them in an HTML source editor and to check your work by viewing them in the Netscape browser. For maximum convenience, compose and format the rest of your page in the Netscape editor first, leaving out the forms. Then choose **V**iew I **E**dit Document Source to open the page file in an HTML editor, and insert your form's code.

For more about HTML source editing, see Chapter 9, "Editing HTML Source Code."

Scripting a Form

To begin, compose your document, leaving out the form. For this task, I've created a page for collecting visitors' e-mail addresses. (See Figure 12.1.) Here's the source code:

```
<HTML>
  <HEAD>
    <TITLE>Address Form</TITLE>
  </HEAD>
  <BODY>
    <H2>Tell Us Your Address</H2>
  </BODY>
</HTML>
```

Figure 12.1.

The sample document, sans form.

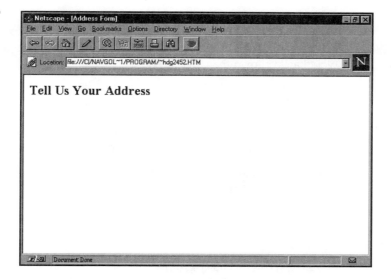

To Build the Form Definition

The form definition goes in the body of the document, surrounded by the tags <FORM> and </FORM>. The form definition includes not only the tags that create form fields but also any text associated with those fields.

In the <FORM> tag, you enter an attribute for input METHOD (GET or POST), plus the ACTION attribute. The ACTION attribute points to the filename (in quotes) or the script program used to process the form input.

Observe that in order to properly point to the CGI-BIN directory, I must use a double-period (..) to move upward in the hierarchy on my server. See Chapter 5.

My form definition uses POST as the input METHOD, and my input is to be processed by a script I'll call MAILPOST.CGI. Also, my server requires that all CGI scripts be stored in the CGI-BIN directory.

Here's the form definition so far:

```
<FORM METHOD="POST" ACTION="../CGI-BIN /MAILPOST.CGI">
</FORM>
```

There are several values for the TYPE attribute of <INPUT> and two alternatives to <INPUT>, each of which creates a different type of input field: a text box, a radio button, and so on. See the section titled "Form Input Types" later in this chapter.

Having defined the input method and the name of the script file, all I need to do is create the onscreen input field and give it a name so that the script will know what the value refers to. Input fields are created with the <INPUT> tag and two attributes, TYPE and NAME. TYPE identifies (in quotes) the type of input field to use; for example, TEXT is used below to create a one-line text field. The value entered in quotes following NAME= is the name you assign to the value the visitor enters.

```
<FORM METHOD="POST" ACTION="../CGI-BIN /MAILPOST.CGI">
<INPUT TYPE="TEXT" NAME="VisitorAddress" SIZE="40">
</FORM>
```

Now I want to label the form field, to tell the visitor what to enter. I can enter text adjacent to the input field and assign it paragraph or character properties, just as I would anywhere in the HTML body.

```
<FORM METHOD="POST" ACTION="../CGI-BIN /MAILPOST.CGI">
Tell us your <b>E-mail Address</b><INPUT TYPE="TEXT" NAME="VisitorAddress">
</FORM>
```

Following the "TEXT" value for the TYPE attribute, I could have added the SIZE attribute and a value (for example, SIZE="20") to set the length (in characters) of the text field.

Finally, I'll add a Submit button inside the </FORM> tag. Note that I've also added a <P> tag before the button, just to add a little extra space.

Here's the complete document file, including the Submit button. The final onscreen form appears in Figure 12.2.

```
<HTML>
  <HEAD>
    <TITLE>Address Form</TITLE>
  </HEAD>
  <BODY>
    <H2>Tell Us Your Address</H2>
    <FORM METHOD="POST" ACTION="../CGI-BIN /MAILPOST.CGI">
      Tell us your <b>E-mail Address</b><INPUT TYPE="TEXT"
      ↪NAME="VisitorAddress">
      <P>
      <INPUT TYPE="Submit">
      </P>
    </FORM>
</BODY>
</HTML>
```

To Write the Script

Again, this book is not really about CGI scripting—and in fact, you might choose to use JavaScript (see Chapter 13, "Using JavaScript) or Visual Basic (if the server supports it) to process your form.

Figure 12.2.
The final form.

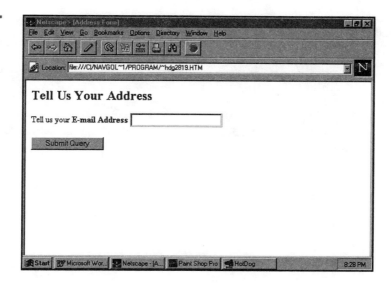

But for illustration, here's the simple MAILPOST.CGI script. What happens in this script is this: First, note that lines beginning with echo are meant to send information back to the browser. The first line describes the type of data (according to the MIME specification) that's being sent to the browser, so the browser knows how to treat it (in this case, as an HTML file).

As you can see, later lines define an entire HTML file to be displayed in the browser. Within the body of that file, notice the two lines beginning with echo. The first displays the line Thanks! You told us your address is, and the second displays the VisitorAddress value, which was the value the visitor entered in the form. Near the end of the file, a link back to the original form page appears, so after viewing the script output visitors can return.

The EOF at the end of the file stands for End of File. Figure 12.13 shows the output from a visitor's queries.

```
echo Content-type: text/html
echo
   cat << EOF
   <HTML>
     <HEAD>
        <TITLE>Your Address</TITLE>
     </HEAD>
     <BODY>
         EOF
         echo "Thanks! You told us your address is "
echo $WWW_VisitorAddress
         fi
         cat << EOF
   </P>
   <P><A HREF="../www/Address.html">Return to previous page</A><P>
```

```
        </BODY>
        </HTML>
EOF
```

Figure 12.3.
*The output from a
visitor's entries in
the form shown in
Figure 12.2.*

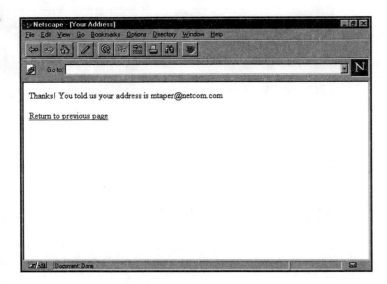

Figure 12.3.
*The output from a
visitor's entries in
the form shown in
Figure 12.2.*

Form Input Types and Formatting

The example shown earlier uses a text input field (TYPE="TEXT"), which creates an on-screen box into which the visitor types an entry.

However, there are two other values you may enter in TYPE: RADIO and CHECKBOX. Each creates a different type of form field. These values are useful when there are only a few possible entries for a form, so a text box is unnecessary.

Radio Buttons (<INPUT TYPE="RADIO">)

The RADIO type is used to create a list of items from which a visitor chooses only one by clicking its radio button. When the Submit button is pressed, a predetermined value for the selected radio button is sent as input to the script. Observe in the example below that the lines are formatted as an ordered list (<OL>).

Each item in a list of radio buttons is created by a separate <INPUT> line. All of the radio buttons in the list use the same name, but a different value. For example:

```
<OL>
<LI><INPUT TYPE="RADIO" NAME="Character" VALUE="Vito">Vito
<LI><INPUT TYPE="RADIO" NAME="Character" VALUE="Michael">Michael
<LI><INPUT TYPE="RADIO" NAME="Character" VALUE="Fredo">Fredo
</OL>
```

Observe that the lines are identical, except for the VALUE value and the text at the end of the line (outside the tag), which provides the onscreen label. This form definition appears within the page shown in Figure 12.4. When a visitor clicks a radio button and then the Submit button, the VALUE of the radio button selected is sent to the server as the input for Character.

Figure 12.4.
Radio buttons.

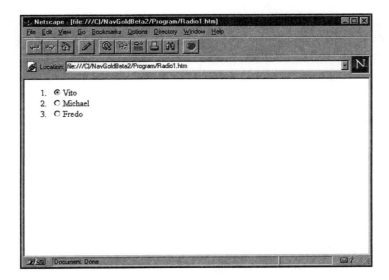

Checkboxes (<INPUT TYPE="CHECKBOX">)

The CHECKBOX type is similar to RADIO, except that it allows the visitor to make more than one selection from the list. Each selection is submitted as input for a different NAME. (See Figure 12.5.) For example:

```
<UL>
<LI><INPUT TYPE="CHECKBOX" NAME="Vito">Vito
<LI><INPUT TYPE="CHECKBOX" NAME="Michael">Michael
<LI><INPUT TYPE="CHECKBOX" NAME="Fredo">Fredo
</UL>
```

This form definition appears within the page shown in Figure 12.4. When a visitor clicks a radio button and then the Submit button, the value of the radio button selected is sent to the server as the input for Character.

Selections and Text Areas

Instead of using an INPUT TYPE attribute to determine your formatting, you can use either of two optional alternatives to the INPUT tag: SELECT or TEXTAREA.

The SELECT and TEXTAREA tags replace <INPUT>; in other words, you can use them just as you would the <INPUT> tag, including the NAME and VALUE attributes. But they each create a different type of form.

Figure 12.5.
Checkboxes.

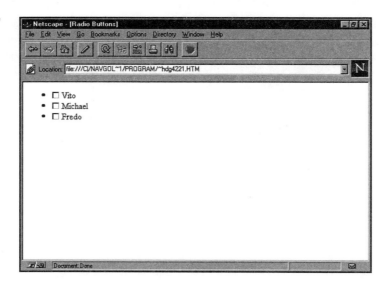

<SELECT> creates a drop-down list of choices. You code each choice with an <OPTION> tag within a SELECT block. For example:

```
<SELECT NAME="TVshow">
<OPTION>Friends
<OPTION>Seinfeld
<OPTION SELECT>Hee-Haw
<OPTION>The Simpsons
<OPTION>NBC Nightly News
</SELECT>
```

Note that one <OPTION> tag includes the SELECT attribute. This is the choice that will be preselected as the default when the visitor first sees the form. When the user makes a selection from the form described by the example, the selection option will be submitted to the script as a value for TVShow.

The form is shown in Figure 12.6.

<TEXTAREA> also replaces <INPUT> and produces a text box in which a visitor can make a long text entry. <TEXTAREA> is especially useful for collecting comments from visitors to your page.

The size and behavior of the text box is determined by a long list of attributes. These include

❑ ROWS="*value*" The number of rows in the text box

❑ COLS="*value*" The number of columns in the text box

❑ WRAP="OFF" Shuts off automatic text wrapping in the box

Figure 12.6.
A SELECT list.

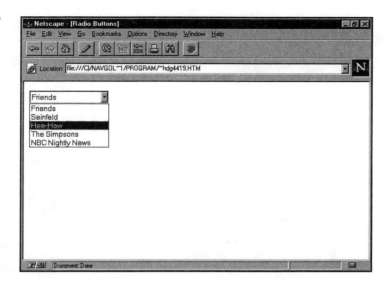

For example:

```
<TEXTAREA NAME="Comments" ROWS="10" COLS="50">
</TEXTAREA>
```

This produces a text box like the one shown in Figure 12.7. When the visitor types an entry and clicks the Submit button, the entry will be submitted to the script as a value for Comments.

Figure 12.7.
A TEXTAREA box.

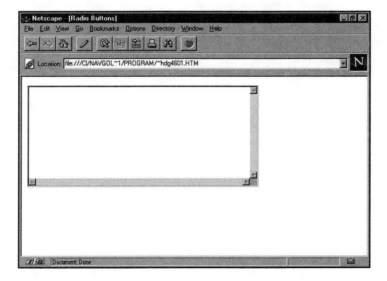

Building a Form in HotDog

The HotDog HTML source editor included on the CD-ROM at the back of this book includes an easy-to-use forms dialog. (See Figure 12.8.) By making selections in the dialog, you can quickly and easily produce the HTML entries for good-looking forms.

Note that HotDog produces the onscreen form only; you must code the script to process the form separately.

Figure 12.8.
Creating forms in HotDog.

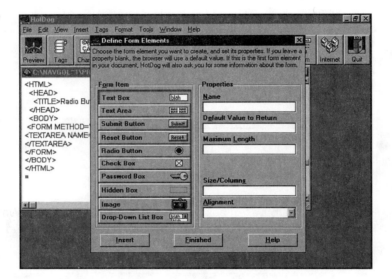

Creating Image Maps

You know from Chapter 6, "Working with Graphics," that an image file can serve as a link source; clicking the image activates the link. By creating an image map script, different areas within one image can activate different links.

Image maps are used for fancy jobs, such as maps; click a country, and a link opens a document about it. But they have more mundane uses, as well. For example, the button bars that appear at the top and bottom of every page at Netscape's home are image maps. The whole bar is one big GIF file, but the image map assigns a separate URL to each button.

Server Side Versus Client Side

An image map can be written to reside on the server and be processed by a server-based, image-mapping CGI program, or it can be coded into the HTML file itself, to be run by the browser, or *client*.

From an authoring standpoint, client-side image maps have great advantages: You needn't store an extra map file on the server, and you needn't deal with the fact that server-side image maps are CGI scripts and must therefore accommodate the CGI peculiarities of the server. Unfortunately, client-side image maps work only if the browser understands the relatively recent Netscape extensions for client-side maps. Right now, that's just Netscape 2/3 and Netscape Gold.

Eventually, though, client-side image maps will probably become the norm because they're simpler to use and will be standardized across all browsers (when browser support catches up).

Choosing an Image and Regions

Regardless of which type of image map you choose to use, the essential steps in image mapping are

❏ Selecting an appropriate image

❏ Deciding in what way the image will be divided up into different regions for different URLs

❏ Determining the coordinates of each region

You can use any GIF image for an image map, but highly geometrical images work best. You can use photos, or other images that aren't characterized by clearly defined shapes, by arbitrarily defining regions within them; but visitors might find using such image maps confusing.

For example, consider the Windmill image (W6.GIF) shown in Figure 12.9. This image is a good choice for mapping, because it is divided naturally into identifiable shapes that visitors will naturally assume contain different links.

I want this image map to call three different URLs. I'll use the top two blades of the windmills (both rectangles) as two regions. For my other two regions, I'll use the circle that forms the hub of the windmill and the polygon making up the windmill house.

Figure 12.9.

A GIF image for an image map.

The image editor Paintshop Pro is included on the CD-ROM at the back of this book.

Having selected my regions, I need to find out what their coordinates are within the graphic. If I open the image within an editor like PaintShop Pro (see Figure 12.10), and move the mouse to any spot within the graphic, I can see the exact x,y coordinates of that point in the center of the status bar. Using this technique, I can discover the exact coordinates for each corner in each region. The corners define the region.

Figure 12.10.
Determining region coordinates in PaintShop Pro.

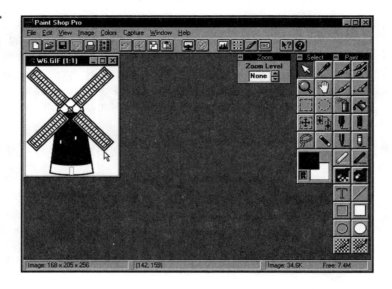

You needn't be pixel-perfect when noting the coordinates of your regions. Getting in the ballpark—within two or three pixels of a precise corner, for example—is usually good enough, unless the region is so small that precision is critical.

For example, the regions in the image shown in Figure 12.9 can be described as follows. Note that, for rectangles, you typically need enter only two corners: the upper left and lower right. (Because it's a rectangle, the other two points are easily calculated by the mapping program.) However, because these rectangles are at an angle, I might get inaccurate results unless I enter every corner. For a circle, I list the coordinates of the center point and then the length of the radius (in pixels). For the polygon, I must note every corner.

Left blade: `3,19 18,5 78,64 60,76`

Right blade: `139,4 158,17 99,75 84,58`

Circle hub: `80,80 24`

Polygon house: `56,87 104,87 124,197 44,198`

These shape names, coordinates, and the URLs to which I want each region to point are all I need to know to create my image map.

Creating a Client-Side Image Map

Client-side image maps work only in a small selection of browsers. See the section titled "Server Side Versus Client Side" earlier in this chapter.

To add a client-side image map to your HTML document:

1. Start with the `<MAP>` tag, which informs browsers that what follows is an image map. The `<MAP>` tag contains a NAME attribute and a name you assign to your image map (any name you like):

   ```
   <MAP NAME="MyMap">
   ```

As long as you put it in the body of the HTML file, it doesn't matter where you insert your image map definition, or where it is in relation to the <IMG SRC> line that embeds the image.

2. Next, define each region and its associated URL with the AREA tag. The AREA tag contains a SHAPE attribute in which you enter a value for the type of shape (CIRCLE, RECT, POLY), followed by a COORDS attribute in which you enter the coordinates (in quotes), followed by the link (<HREF> tag). Each set of coordinates is separated by a space. Here are the <AREA> lines for my image map, plus the <MAP> tag and closing </MAP> tag. This is the entire map definition for MyMap.

```
<AREA SHAPE="RECT" COORDS="3,19 18,5 78,64 60,76" HREF="leftblade.htm">
<AREA SHAPE="RECT" COORDS="139,4 158,17 99,75 84,58 HREF="rightblade.htm">
<AREA SHAPE="CIRCLE" COORDS="80,80 24 HREF="hub.htm">
<AREA SHAPE="POLY" COORDS="56,87 104,87 124,197 44,198 HREF="house.htm">
```

3. The <IMG SRC> tag that embeds the inline image does not appear within the map definition. It appears in the body of the HTML file wherever you want it to appear (or rather, wherever you want the image to appear on the page), just as if it were not an image map, but a regular inline image. To connect the image to its image map, you add the USEMAP attribute, using as a value the NAME you gave the image map in the <MAP> tag:

```
<IMG SRC="W6.GIF" USEMAP="MyMap">
```

Creating a Server-Side Image Map

The concepts behind server-side image maps are analogous to those used in client-side maps, but the execution is different. Most importantly, the image map file defining the regions of the image is contained not in the HTML file, but in a separate map file you must upload to the server.

Your first step in creating a server-side image map is to find out which of the popular CGI image map programs is running on your server, and where the program is located in the directory structure. Most servers use one of two CGI image map programs:

❏ Imagemap, used on NCSA HTTPd servers

❏ HTImage, used on w3c httpd servers

Each of these programs requires slightly different coding in the map file and in your HTML document.

To create the map file, you list each region, one line at a time, including in the line for each region the name of the shape, the coordinates, and the URL to which the region will point.

For Imagemap, you list the shape, the URL, and then the coordinates, as shown:

```
rectangle /leftblade.htm 3,19 18,5 78,64 60,76
rectangle /rightblade.htm 139,4 158,17 99,75 84,58
circle /hub.htm 80,80 24
polygon /house.htm 56,87 104,87 124,197 44,198
```

For HTImage, you list the shape, then the coordinates, then the URL. Each set of coordinates must be placed in parentheses (observe that the circle radius does not go in parentheses):

```
rectangle (3,19) (18,5) (78,64) (60,76) /leftblade.htm
rectangle (139,4) (158,17) (99,75) (84,58) /rightblade.htm
circle (80,80) 24 /hub.htm
polygon (56,87) (104,87) 124,197 44,198 /house.htm
```

Save your file with the extension .MAP and upload it to the server. Your system administrator must tell you which directory to use.

In the examples shown, the paths assume the image map program is stored in the directory CGI-BIN, and the image map file is stored in a MAPS directory within CGI-BIN.

Finally, in your HTML document, you build a link that uses the image as a link source and also identifies the server program and the map file. Also, in the IMG SRC tag that identifies the image file, add the attribute ISMAP to indicate that this is the image to use for the image map.

For example, for the Imagemap program:

```
<A HREF="../cgi-bin/htimage/maps/MyMap.map">
<IMG SRC="W6.GIF" ISMAP>
</A>
```

And for HTImage:

```
<A HREF="../cgi-bin/imagemap/maps/MyMap.map">
<IMG SRC="W6.GIF" ISMAP>
</A>
```

Using the CD-ROM to Help with Image Maps

Two programs on the CD-ROM help you generate server-side map files for Imagemap or HTImage servers:

❑ Web HotSpots

❑ MapEdit (see Figure 12.11)

In either of these programs, you can open the GIF file you will use for your image map and then select regions with a mouse and enter the URL for each region. The program automatically generates a map file, coordinates and all, for the specified server type. This capability is no substitute for knowing how to code image maps, but it's a great time saver.

Figure 12.11.

MapEdit, a program for conveniently generating image maps.

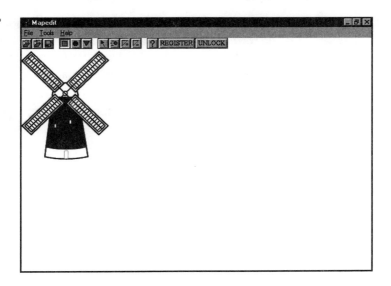

Workshop Wrap-Up

If you're willing (and able!) to face the world of CGI, you can do a lot with forms and image maps. Other authoring techniques are flashier, but none is more powerful. In fact, forms and image maps are prestige items of a sort—if you use them, visitors in the know consider you a pro.

However, once support for client-side image maps and client-side JavaScript (for forms) proliferates, *everybody* will use image maps and forms, and these features will lose their *caché*. So don't wait. Get into CGI, and be cool today.

Next Steps

Now...

- ❏ To learn about JavaScript, see Chapter 13, "Using JavaScript."
- ❏ To explore some sample documents using forms, image maps, and other techniques from Part III, see Chapter 14, "Real-Life Examples II."

Q&A

Q: In a frames document, can I create a form in one frame whose output appears in another?

A: Yes—in fact, that's exactly what the Page Wizard does (see Chapter 2, "Making the Page Wizard Do the Work"). Every time a user submits a form in the bottom frame (which offers forms for creating parts of a page), a script processes the input, and the preview page in the upper-right frame reflects the change.

To specify the frame in which the output from a form script should appear, include the TARGET attribute and the name of the desired frame in the <FORM> tag following the script filename, as shown:

```
<FORM METHOD="POST" ACTION="../CGI-BIN/SAMPLE.CGI TARGET="TopFrame">
```

Of course, for this to work, you must have named your frames. For more about frames, see Chapter 11, "Making Frames."

Q: What about image maps? Can a link in an image map in one frame open a file in another?

A: Same deal as forms (almost). In the AREA tag, follow the URL with the TARGET attribute and frame name.

```
<AREA SHAPE="CIRCLE" COORDS="35,10" 20 HREF="topframe.htm"
TARGET="TopFrame">
```

THIRTEEN

Using JavaScript

Not long ago, Netscape Communications introduced a proprietary scripting language for the then upcoming Navigator 2.0. This language, called LiveScript, allowed the embedding of small programs in an HTML document to control various actions related to a Web page. The language was a scaled-down version of the powerful Java programming language, developed by Sun Microsystems for Internet and World Wide Web programming.

The idea—but not the implementation—was great. Because LiveScript was proprietary, it didn't catch on. Unlike most of the current Netscape extensions, the proprietary nature of LiveScript meant that it was unlikely to ever be supported by other Web browsers. Pages that took advantage of LiveScript were definitely in the category of "Netscape Navigator Only" pages and, it seemed, would be so for a long time.

Then, suddenly, LiveScript was no more, and in its place a new scripting language called JavaScript appeared. In reality, the two languages are basically identical—like a Ford Escort and a Mercury Tracer, two different nameplates for the same chassis. But JavaScript is backed and supported not only by Netscape, but also by Sun Microsystems, America Online, Apple Computers, Borland International, MacroMedia, Paper Software, Silicon Graphics, the Santa Cruz Operation, and Toshiba Corporation, just to mention a few of the companies that stand behind the endorsement of JavaScript as the new, open Internet scripting language standard.

With this critical mass of Web movers and shakers behind it, JavaScript is emerging as a *de facto* standard for general-purpose Web programming. If you want to learn one way to build functions into your Web page, JavaScript is the name to know.

> # NOTE:
> Although JavaScript is expected to gain wide acceptance, it's understood today only by the various flavors of Netscape Navigator 2.0 and above. For the time being, you must accept that your JavaScript-coded functions are available only to users of Navigator 2.0 and higher. If you want a function to be available to a wider audience, you might need to use a CGI script. (See Chapter 12, "Creating Interactive Forms and Image Maps.")
>
> JavaScript is an emerging language, and it's still changing and growing rapidly. To keep up with JavaScript specification and any new features, you'll want to visit the JavaScript reference information at Netscape often. See the section titled "Learning More About JavaScript," near the end of this chapter.

Introducing JavaScript

According to a press release issued by Netscape Communications, "JavaScript is an easy-to-use, object-scripting language designed for creating live online applications that link together objects and resources on both clients and servers. JavaScript is designed for use by HTML page authors and enterprise application developers to dynamically script the behavior of objects running on either a client or server." So there.

What Is JavaScript, Really?

To learn about the other common scripting language, CGI, see Chapter 12.

Put into simple English, Netscape enables you, when you use JavaScript, to add functionality to your Web pages, which in the past would have demanded access to complex CGI-based programs on a Web server. In many ways, JavaScript is a lot like Visual Basic—the user-friendly programming language developed by Microsoft—in that people with little or no programming knowledge can use JavaScript (with study, patience, practice, and a positive attitude). These novices can quickly and easily create complex Web-based applications without having to deal with all the background complexities such activities involve.

What makes JavaScript so different, however, is the unique way in which it integrates itself with the World Wide Web. Instead of being stored as a separate file—like a CGI script—JavaScript code is included as part of a standard HTML document, just like any other HTML tags and elements. In fact, you can type your JavaScript code directly into a document in the Netscape Editor. (See the section titled "Using JavaScript in the Netscape Editor," later in this chapter.)

In addition, unlike CGI scripts, which run on a Web server, JavaScript scripts are run by the Web browser itself. Thus, they are portable across any Web browser that includes JavaScript support, regardless of the computer type or operating system.

Why Would I Want to Use JavaScript?

A server-side version of JavaScript will soon emerge to replace the Perl and Bourne shell CGI scripts (see Chapter 12), making JavaScript both the server and the client scripting language.

The answer to this question depends, to a certain extent, on exactly what capabilities are eventually included as part of the JavaScript language. It is likely, however, that scripts written using JavaScript will eventually be able to control all aspects of a Web page or Web form, and to communicate directly with plug-ins displayed on a Web page and with compiled Java applets.

In fact, Paper Software—the developers of the WebFX VRML Plug-in—is working on such technology for future versions of WebFX. By using these capabilities, you will eventually be able to create fully interactive 3-D virtual worlds on the World Wide Web that can be modified and controlled by Java applets.

Don't confuse JavaScript with Java, a more complex, more powerful language for creating Web-based applications called *applets*. JavaScript is based on Java but is another animal.

Apart from such futuristic possibilities, what JavaScript enables you to do now is perform many simple (and not so simple) programming tasks at the Web browser (or client end) of the system, instead of relying on CGI scripts at the Web server end. In addition, JavaScript enables you to control with far greater efficiency the validation of information entered by users on forms and other data-entry screens. And finally, when integrated with frames, JavaScript brings a wide variety of new document presentation options to the Web publishing domain.

Ease of Use

Unlike Java, JavaScript is designed for nonprogrammers. As such, it is relatively easy to use and is far less pedantic about details such as the declaration of variable types. In addition, you do not need to preprocess, or *compile*, JavaScript code before it can be used—something you need to do with many other programming languages, including Java.

Increasing Server Efficiency

As more people flood the Web, popular Web sites are being pushed to the limit of their current processing capabilities. As a result, Web operators are continually looking for ways to reduce the processing requirements for their systems—to ward off the need for expensive computer upgrades. This was one of the main reasons for the development of client side image maps like those discussed in Chapter 12.

With the introduction of JavaScript, some exciting new performance options are now available to Web publishers. For example, say you have created a form that people use to enter their billing details for your online ordering system. When this form is submitted, the first thing your CGI script needs to do with it is validate the information provided to make sure that all the appropriate fields have been filled out correctly. You need to check that a name and address have been entered, that a billing method has been selected, that credit card details have been completed—and the list goes on.

But what happens if your CGI script discovers that some information is missing? You would need to alert the user that there are problems with the submission and then ask him to edit the details and resubmit the completed form. This entire process is very resource-intensive. First, the Web server needs to allocate a dedicated resource to perform all the validation and checks, and second, when there are errors, two additional data transmissions must be handled by the server—one to alert the user of errors and one to receive the updated information.

On the other hand, by moving all the validation and checking procedures to the Web browser—through the use of JavaScript—you remove the need for any additional transactions, because only one "valid" transaction will ever be transmitted back to the server. And, in addition, because the Web server does not need to perform any validations of its own, there is a considerable reduction in the amount of server hardware and processor resources required to submit a complex form.

JavaScript and Web Service Providers

With an increasing number of Web service providers severely limiting the availability of CGI script support for security reasons, JavaScript offers an excellent method of regaining much of the missing CGI functionality. It moves tasks that would previously have been performed by a server side CGI script onto the Web browser.

Most Web service providers usually furnish some form of basic CGI script, which can take a form submitted by a user and perform basic processing operations such as saving it to disk or mailing it to the site's owner. When it comes to more complex forms, however, in the past the only alternatives were to find another service provider or set up your own Web server. But now, with JavaScript, this no longer is the case.

By using a Web service provider's basic form-processing CGI scripts with JavaScript routines buried in the Web page itself, there are very few form-based activities that cannot be duplicated on even the most restrictive and security-conscious Web service provider's site. In addition, after the full integration of Java, JavaScript, and plug-ins has been achieved, you will be able to do things on a Web page that would never have been considered possible previously with even the most capable CGI script.

Submitting Forms Without CGI

To learn about CGI forms, see Chapter 12.

The ACTION attribute of the <FORM> tag has traditionally been associated with a CGI script located on a Web server. But, in fact, any URL can be assigned to the ACTION attribute. Doing so, however, has little value unless the resource associated with the URL can process the contents of the form in some way.

That having been said, there is one type of URL—apart from a CGI script—that can process the results of a form in a meaningful way—mailto. For example, if you included the following <FORM> tag on a page, clicking the SUBMIT button would e-mail the contents of the form to my e-mail address:

```
<FORM METHOD="POST" ACTION="mailto:wtatters@world.net">
```

To make use of the ACTION attribute with mailto, the visitor's browser must be configured to open an e-mail client in response to a mailto link. (See Chapter 5.)

In the past, however, using such an ACTION could be relied upon only when the contents of the form were not vital, because there was no way to validate the information. But by using JavaScript, you can now validate the data before it is e-mailed and even perform basic calculations or other processing.

The javascript: Protocol

To complement the use of the mailto: protocol within the ACTION attribute, a new URL and protocol specifically for JavaScript has also been introduced. This new URL takes the following form:

```
javascript:function()
```

where function() can be replaced by any of the functions and methods you will learn about later in this chapter. This new URL can be used in place of any of the previously discussed URLs: inside <FORM> tags, <A> tags, and even inside the <AREA> tag of a client-side image map.

The <SCRIPT> Tag

You don't need to use the <SCRIPT> tag when you enter your JavaScript code directly in the Netscape Editor. See the section titled "Using JavaScript in the Netscape Editor," later in this chapter.

To accommodate the inclusion of JavaScript programs in a normal HTML document, Netscape has proposed the introduction of a new <SCRIPT> tag. By placing a <SCRIPT> tag in a document, you tell the browser to treat any lines of text following the tag as script—rather than as content for the Web page. This action then continues until a corresponding </SCRIPT> tag is encountered, at which point the Web browser reverts to its usual mode of operation—treating text as Web content.

In general, you need not use the LANGUAGE attribute. Navigator 2.0, the only browser that supports JavaScript, assumes the language is JavaScript if no LANGUAGE is specified.

When used in a document, a script tag may include an optional LANGUAGE attribute to declare the scripting language to be used. Currently, the two possible values for this attribute are LANGUAGE="LiveScript" and LANGUAGE="JavaScript".

The Structure of a JavaScript Script

When you include any JavaScript code in an HTML document, apart from using the <SCRIPT> tag, you should also follow a few other conventions:

As a rule, the <SCRIPT> tag should be placed inside the <HEAD> and </HEAD> tags at the start of your document and not inside the <BODY> tags. This is not a hard and fast requirement (as you will learn later), but it is a standard you should adopt whenever possible. Basically, because the code for your scripts is not to be displayed on the Web page itself it should not be included in the <BODY> section, but instead in the <HEAD> section with all the other control and information tags such as <TITLE> and <META>.

Because Web browsers that are not JavaScript-aware will attempt to treat your JavaScript code as part of the contents of your Web page, it is important to surround your entire JavaScript code with a <![--] comment tag [--]>. Doing this will ensure that non-JavaScript–aware browsers can at least display your page correctly, if not make it work properly.

Unlike HTML, which uses the <![--] comment tag [--]>, comments inside JavaScript code use the // symbol. Any line of JavaScript code that starts with this symbol will be treated as a comment and ignored.

When you enter JavaScript in the Netscape Editor, no comment tags are entered automatically. You may enter them with the Editor's Insert Tag function or in an HTML source editor. (See Chapter 9.)

Taking these three points into consideration, the basic structure for including JavaScript code inside an HTML document looks like this:

```
<HEAD>
<TITLE>Test script</TITLE>
<SCRIPT>
<![--] Use the start of a comment tag to hide the JavaScript code
  Your JavaScript code goes here
// close the comment tag on the line immediately before the </SCRIPT> tag [--
]!>
</SCRIPT>
</HEAD>
<BODY>
   Your Web document goes here
</BODY>
</HTML>
```

The SRC Attribute

Besides the LANGUAGE attribute, the <SCRIPT> tag can also include an SRC attribute. Doing this allows a JavaScript script stored in a separate file to be included as part of the current Web page. This is a handy option if you have several Web pages that all use the same JavaScript code and you don't want to type the scripts separately into each page.

You must follow certain procedures when using the SRC attribute in the Netscape Editor.

When used like this, the `<SCRIPT>` tag takes the following form:

```
<SCRIPT SRC="http://script.js">
```

In this form, *script* can be any relative or absolute pathname (see Chapter 5, "Linking Everywhere, Anywhere"), and .js is the file extension for a JavaScript file, a simple text file containing just the JavaScript code (and not including the `<SCRIPT>` tag).

Using JavaScript in the Netscape Editor

Observing a few important differences, you may enter JavaScript code directly into the Netscape Editor, just as you would (well, almost) in any HTML source editor. (See Chapter 9, "Editing HTML Source Code.") The code itself is visible when you view the page in the Editor (see Figure 13.1); when you view the document in the Netscape Browser, the proper effects of the script appear instead.

CAUTION:
It is the recommendation of this book that you not, as a rule, enter your JavaScript code in the Editor. Using an HTML source editor is the recommended approach, and all examples in this chapter are presented as they should be coded in an HTML source editor, not in the Netscape Editor.

Why not use the Netscape Editor for JavaScript?

❏ The Editor provides you with no way to enter the script in the header, rather than the body, of the document. As you'll learn throughout this chapter, entering the script in the header is almost always the way to go.

❏ The Editor provides no mechanism through which to use attributes to the `<SCRIPT>` tag. To use attributes, you must enter your script in the Editor, then open the file in an HTML source editor to add the attributes.

❏ The JavaScript support in the Editor is rather clumsily implemented. This will probably be remedied in a later version of Gold (after version 2.01), so it's important for you to know, generally, how to use JavaScript in the Editor. But for now, do your JavaScript work in an HTML source editor, until Netscape does a better job.

To enter JavaScript code in the Editor, you must observe two important differences from entering the code in an HTML source editor:

❏ To identify your code as JavaScript, you must assign it the Character property JavaScript client (see Figure 13.2). Observe that there are two Character properties for JavaScript: Client and Server. For scripts in your Web pages, always use Client. Server is for scripting server-side JavaScript functions, which are not covered in this book.

❏ Do not enter <SCRIPT> tags in the Editor. Enter only the code itself—the lines between <SCRIPT> and </SCRIPT>. The <SCRIPT> tags are added automatically by the Editor. You won't see them in the Editor, just as you never see any HTML tag in the Editor. But if you enter JavaScript code in the Editor, then view the HTML source (see Figure 13.3), you'll see that the <SCRIPT> tags have been added.

Figure 13.1.
Entering a simple JavaScript in the Editor.

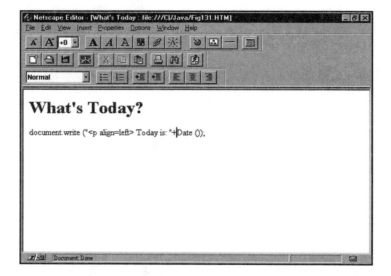

Figure 13.2.
Assigning the JavaScript Client Character property to the script code.

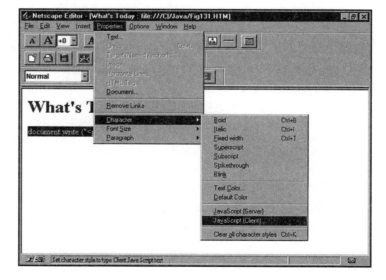

Figure 13.3.
The HTML source for the document shown in Figures 13.1 and 13.2, showing that the <SCRIPT> tags were added automatically.

Figure 13.4.
The document shown in Figures 13.1–13.3, viewed through the browser to show the script's effects.

Basic JavaScript Commands

At its heart, JavaScript uses an object-oriented approach to computer programming. This basically means that all the elements on a Web page are treated as objects that are grouped together to form a completed structure.

Using this structure, all the elements of a single Web page are said to be contained within a base object container called window. Inside the window *object* are a set of smaller containers (or objects) that hold information about the various elements of a Web browser page. These are some of the main objects:

location   Inside the `location` object is information about the location of the current Web document, including its URL and separate components such as the protocol, domain name, path, and port.

history   The `history` object holds a record of all the sites a Web browser has visited during the current session, and it also gives you access to built-in functions that enable you to change the contents of the current window.

document   The `document` object contains the complete details of the current Web document. This includes all the forms, form elements, links, and anchors. In addition, it provides many types of functions that enable you to programmatically alter the contents of items such as textboxes, radio buttons, and other form elements.

Properties and Methods

Within each object container, there are two main types of resources you can access.

The first type are called properties. Properties are basically variables that hold a value associated with the object you are interested in. For example, within the `document` object, there is a property called `title` that contains the title of the current document as described by the `<TITLE>` tag.

In JavaScript, you could obtain the value of this property by using the statement `document.title`. The first part of the statement tells JavaScript which object you want to work with, and the second part—following the dot—represents the physical property itself.

Netscape's online documentation covers in detail all the properties and methods associated with each object. See the section titled "Learning More about JavaScript," later in this chapter.

In addition to properties, most objects also have special functions associated with them called methods. Methods are basically programming commands that are directly related to a particular object. For example, the `document` object has a method associated with it that enables you to write text directly onto a Web page. This method takes the following form:

```
document.write( "Hello world") ;
```

As was the case for properties, you describe a method by first declaring the object it is associated with, followed by a dot, and then indicating the method itself. In this example, the method must be assigned a value by including the relevant information inside the parentheses () that follow the method name. It is important to realize, however, that the parentheses must be included even if no values are assigned to the method, as is the case for the `toString()` method of the `location` object. This method is used to convert the current document's URL into a form suitable for use with other methods such as `document.write()`.

All examples in this chapter are presented as you should code them in an HTML source editor, not in the Netscape Editor.

By combining these methods and the `document.title` property mentioned previously into an HTML document like the following one, you would produce the results shown in Figure 13.5.

```
<HTML>
<HEAD>
<TITLE>Test JavaScript</TITLE>
<SCRIPT LANGUAGE="JavaScript">
document.write( document.title + "<BR>" ) ;
document.write( location.toString() ) ;
</SCRIPT>
</HEAD>
</HTML>
```

Figure 13.5.
The results of your first JavaScript script.

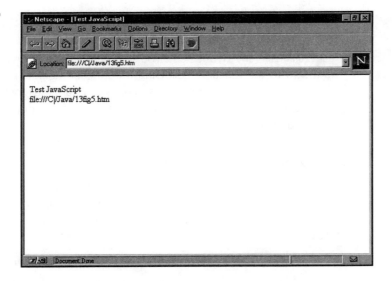

CAUTION:

Method, property, function, and variable names are all *case-specific;* you must capitalize them *exactly* as shown. For example, `Location.toSTRing()` will not work in place of `location.toString()`.

Events and JavaScript

Although implementing methods such as `document.write()` to create Web pages might have some use, the real power behind JavaScript lies in its capability to respond to events generated by a Web page.

Events are actions that occur on a Web page, normally when a user interacts with the page in some way. For example, when a person enters a value into a textbox on a form or clicks a submit button, a series of events are triggered inside the Web browser, all of which can be intercepted by JavaScript programs, usually in the form of functions.

Functions

JavaScript includes built-in objects and functions that perform mathematical operations, string manipulation, and date and time calculations. See Netscape's online JavaScript documentation.

Functions are very similar to methods. The difference, however, is that whereas methods are associated with a specific object, functions are stand-alone routines that operate outside the bounds of an object. To define a function for the current Web page, you would write something like this:

```
<SCRIPT LANGUAGE="JavaScript">

function functionName( operands ) {
   The actions to be performed by your function go here
}
</SCRIPT>
```

functionName is any unique name you choose, and operands is a list of any values you want sent to the function. Following the function definition and inside the set of braces, { }, you include the list of instructions you want the function to perform. These could be a set of calculations, validation tests for a form, or just about anything else you can think of.

Assigning Functions to Events

After you have your functions defined, the next thing you need to do is assign them to the various events you want trapped. You do this by assigning what are called event handlers to the various elements of a Web page or form. Currently, you can set the following event handlers:

onFocus	Whenever a user enters a specified field
onBlur	Whenever a user leaves a specified field
onSelect	Whenever a user selects the contents of a specified field
onChange	Whenever a user changes the contents of a specified field
onClick	Whenever a user clicks a specified button
onMouseOver	Whenever a user places the mouse cursor over a specified field
onSubmit	Whenever a user submits a specified form
onLoad	Whenever a Web page is loaded or reloaded
onUnload	Whenever the current Web page is changed

To specify functions that should be associated with any of these events, all you need to do is include the appropriate event handler as an attribute of the field you want to control. For example, take a standard form with a couple of text fields and a submit button as shown here:

```
<FORM METHOD="POST" SRC="../cgi-bin/form">
<INPUT TYPE="TEXT" NAME="username">
<INPUT TYPE="TEXT" NAME="emailAddress">
<INPUT TYPE="SUBMIT">
</FORM>
```

By adding onSubmit="return checkform(this)" to the <FORM> tag, the function called checkform() will be run before Navigator 2.0 submits the form. In checkform(), you can do any checks you want and, if there are any problems, halt the form submission and ask the user to fix them. The this parameter, inside the parentheses (()), is used to tell the checkform() function which form object is associated with the <FORM> tag.

In addition, you can do checking field by field, by including either onChange or onBlur event handlers in each <INPUT> tag. Because the onBlur handler is called each time a person leaves a field, it is ideal for input validation.

You can also include onClick events in buttons like the submit button which will be activated whenever the user clicks the specified button. For example, <INPUT TYPE="SUMBIT" onClick="processclick()"> would launch a function called processclick() whenever the submit button was clicked.

JavaScript introduces a new <INPUT> type called button, which simply places a button on the Web page.

Variables

In addition to properties, JavaScript also enables you to assign or retrieve values from what are called variables. A variable is basically a user-defined container that can hold a number, some text, or an object. But unlike most high-level languages that force you to limit the contents of each variable to a specific type, in JavaScript variables are said to be loosely typed language. This means that you don't need to specify the type of information a variable contains when the variable is created. In fact, the same variable can be assigned to data of different types depending on your requirements.

To declare a variable for a JavaScript program, you would write this:

```
var variablename = value ;
```

Variable names (and function names) can consist of the letters a through z, the numbers 0 through 9, and the underscore (_) symbol. But names cannot start with a number.

In this form, *variablename* is any unique name you choose. The equals (=) sign following the *variablename* is called an assignment operator. It tells JavaScript to assign whatever is on the right side of the = sign—*value*—as the contents of the variable. This *value* can be a text string, a number, a property, the results of a function, an array, a date, or even another variable. Here's an example:

```
var name = "Ned Snell" ;
var age = 34 ;
```

If a variable is inside a function, you can access the contents of the variable only from inside the function. If the variable is inside a <SCRIPT> block but not in a function, you can access the contents of the variable anywhere in the page.

```
var title = document.title ;
var documenturl = location.toString() ;
var myarray = new Array(10);
var todaysdate = new Date();
var myname = anothername ;
```

Operators and Expressions

After a variable has been defined, you can work with its contents, or alter them, by using what are called operators. Table 13.1 lists some of the more popular operators provided by JavaScript and includes an example that demonstrates the use of each. (As before, for a full list of all the supported operators, refer to the online JavaScript documentation.)

NOTE: The examples shown in the second column of Table 13.1 are called expressions. Basically, an *expression* is any valid set of variables, operators, and expressions that evaluate to a single value. For example, b + c evaluates to a single value, which is assigned to a.

Table 13.1. JavaScript operators and expressions.

Operator	Example	Description
+	a = b + c	Add variables b and c, and assign the result to variable a.
-	a = b - c	Subtract the value of variable c from variable b, and assign the result to variable a.
*	a = b * c	Multiply variable b by variable c, and assign the result to variable a.
/	a = b / c	Divide variable b by variable c, and assign the result to variable a.
%	a = b % c	Obtain the modulus of variable b when it is divided by variable c, and assign the result to variable a. (Note: modulus is a function that returns the remainder.)
++	a = ++b	Increment variable b by 1, and assign the result to variable a.
[--]	a = [--]b	Decrement variable b by 1, and assign the result to variable a.

The + and += operators can be used with string variables and numeric variables. When they're used with strings, the result of a = "text" + " and more" is a variable containing "text and more".

There is also a special set of operators that combine the assignment function (=) and an operator into a single function. Such operators are called assignment operators. Table 13.2 lists the assignment operators provided by JavaScript.

Table 13.2. JavaScript assignment operators.

Assignment Operator	Example	Description
+=	a += b	This is equivalent to the statement a = a + b.
-=	a -= b	This is equivalent to the statement a = a - b.
*=	a *= b	This is equivalent to the statement a = a * b.
/=	a /= b	This is equivalent to the statement a = a / b.
/=	a %= b	This is equivalent to the statement a = a % b.

JavaScript Programming

To tie together all the event handlers, methods, parameters, functions, variables, and operators, JavaScript includes a simple set of programming statements that are similar to those provided by Java and the old BASIC programming language.

If you have any programming experience at all, spending a few minutes browsing through the list of supported statements discussed in Netscape Communication's online documentation will set you well on your way toward creating your first JavaScript programs. But for those of you who don't have the experience, the following section includes a quick crash course on basic programming.

What Is a Program?

Regardless of what language you use, a program is simply a set of instructions that describe to a computer some action, or group of actions, you want it to perform. In the most basic case, this set of instructions starts at the beginning of a list of code and works through each instruction in the list one at a time, until it reaches the end:

```
<SCRIPT LANGUAGE="JavaScript">
// start of program - NOTE: lines that start with '//' are treated as comments
document.write( "step one") ;
document.write( "step two") ;
// end of program
</SCRIPT>
```

It is rare, however, that you will ever want a program to proceed straight through a list of steps—especially in JavaScript—because it would be easier to write the messages on the screen using HTML than to code them by using JavaScript. For this reason, most programming languages include a basic set of instructions that enable you to control the flow of the instructions.

The `if` Statement

The first such instruction is called the `if` statement. Basically, it enables you to perform tests inside program code to determine which parts of the program should be run under any given situation. For example, assume that you have a Web form that asks whether a person is male or female. In such cases, you might want to respond to the person using a gender-specific response, based on the indicated sex:

```
if ( form.theSex.value == "male" ) {
    document.write("Thank you for your response, Sir" ) ;
}
if ( form.theSex.value == "female") {
    document.write("Thank you for your response, Madam" ) ;
}
```

If this piece of code were run and the property `form.theSex.value` had been assigned a value of `"male"`, the first `document.write()` method would have been called. If it had been assigned a value of `"female"`, the second statement would have been displayed.

The block of code next to the `if` statement performs comparison between the property `form.theSex.value` and the word `"male"`. This comparison is controlled by what are called comparison operators. In this case, a test for equivalence was performed as signified by the `==` symbol. Table 13.3 lists the comparison operators currently recognized by JavaScript.

Table 13.3. JavaScript comparison operators.

Operator	Operator Description	Notes
==	Equal	a == b: tests to see if a equals b
!=	Not equal	a != b: tests to see if a does not equal b
<	Less than	a < b: tests to see if a is less than b
<=	Less than or equal to	a <= b: test to see if a is less than or equal to b
>=	Greater than or equal to	a >= b: tests to see if a is greater than or equal to b
>	Greater than	a > b: tests to see is a is greater that b

The `if...else` Statement

The preceding example could have also been written in a slightly different way by using a different version of the `if` statement that incorporates an `else` statement:

```
if ( form.theSex.value == "male" ) {
   document.write("Thank you for your response, Sir" ) ;
}
else {
   document.write("Thank you for your response, Madam" ) ;
}
```

In this example, because there is no need for a second `if` test—because a person can be only male or female—the `else` statement was used to tell the program to display the second message if the first test failed.

Looping Statements

On occasion, you will want a group of statements to run multiple times rather than just once. Two looping statements are supported by JavaScript to carry out this task. The first kind of statement, called a `for` loop, is ideal for situations in which you want a group of instructions to occur a specified number of times. And the second kind, the `while` loop, is better suited to situations in which the number of loops required is to be determined by an outside source.

`for` Loops

The basic structure of a `for` loop looks like this:

```
for (var count = 1; count <= 10; ++count ) {
   your statements go here
}
```

In this example, a variable called `count` is declared and set to a value of 1. Then a test is made to see whether the value of `count` is less than or equal to 10. If it is, all the statements inside the braces, `{}`, following the `for` statement are executed once. Then, the value of `count` is incremented by 1 by the statement `++count`, and the `count <= 10` test is performed again. If the result is still true, all the instructions inside the braces are executed again. This process then proceeds until the value of `count` is greater than 10, at which stage the `for` loop ends.

`while` Loops

The basic structure of a `while` loop looks like this:

```
while ( contition ) {
   your statements go here
}
```

Unlike the `for` loop, which has a built-in increment mechanism, the only test required for a `while` loop is a true result from the condition test following the `while` statement. This test could be an equivalence test, as in `a == b`, or any of the other tests mentioned previously in the `if` statement.

As long as this condition tests true, the statements inside the braces following the `while` loop will continue to run forever—or at least until you close your Web browser.

CAUTION: When using `while` loops, avoid creating endless loops, or *infinite loops*. If you do create an endless loop, you must shut down the browser to kill it.

Creating Random Link Generators

A random link generator is basically a link that takes you to different locations every time you click it. In the past, the only way to implement such a link was through the use of a CGI; but with JavaScript, all the previous server side processing can now be performed by the Web browser itself.

An inline `<SCRIPT>` tag is one that is embedded in the `<BODY>` section of an HTML document rather than in the `<HEAD>` section, as is the more common practice.

In the sections that follow, you will learn how to create three different random-link generators. The first uses an inline `<SCRIPT>` tag and a single function, the second uses event handlers, and the third examines the use of arrays within a script.

Because the JavaScript code for this generator will be incorporated in a standard HTML document, open the text editor or HTML editor you normally use for designing Web pages and create a new file called `random.html`.

In this new file, create a basic document framework like the following one. You should recognize all the elements of this document from previous chapters, including the `<A>...</A>` tag combinations on the third-from-last line. If you were to run this document as it is, you would see a result like the one shown in Figure 13.6.

```
<HTML>
<HEAD>
<TITLE>Random Link Generator</TITLE>
</HEAD>
<BODY>
<H1>My random link generator</H1>
Click <A HREF="dummy.html">here</A> to visit a randomly selected site
from my list of favorites.
</BODY>
```

Figure 13.6.
Clicking the link loads a document called dummy.html.

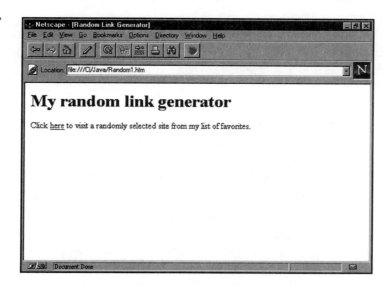

Now it's time to add some JavaScript code to turn the link into a random link generator. First, add a <SCRIPT> tag to the <HEAD> section immediately after the <TITLE> tag block:

```
<TITLE>Random Link Generator</TITLE>
<SCRIPT LANGUAGE="JavaScript">
<!-- the contents of the script need to be hidden from other browsers
  the JavaScript code goes here.
// End of script -->
</SCRIPT>
</HEAD>
```

The next step involves adding the code that generates the random links, based on a list of your favorite sites. Inside the <SCRIPT> tag—and comment tag—you will create a function called picklink(). So you first define the framework for a function like this:

```
function picklink() {
  your JavaScript code goes here.
}
```

And finally, here's the code that actually makes the picklink() function work:

```
function picklink() {

var linknumber = 4 ;
var linktext = "nolink.html" ;

var randomnumber = Math.random() ;
var linkselect = Math.round( (linknumber-1) * randomnumber) + 1 ;

if ( linkselect == 1 )
   { linktext="http://www.netscape.com/" }
if ( linkselect == 2 )
   { linktext="http://www.webcom.com/taketwo/" }
```

```
if ( linkselect == 3 )
    { linktext="http://java.sun.com/" }
if ( linkselect == 4 )
    { linktext="http://www.realaudio.com/" }

document.write('<A HREF="' + linktext + '">here.</A>') ;

}
```

To help you understand what this code is doing, I'll examine it section by section. The first two lines following the function definition declare some work variables for the function: `linknumber` tells the function how many links it has to choose from when selecting a random link, and `linktext` is a work variable used to hold the value of the URL for the selected random link.

The next line—`var randomnumber = Math.random() ;`—declares a variable called `randomnumber` and assigns a randomly selected decimal value between 0 and 1 to it by calling a special built-in function named `Math.random()`. The next line then takes the `randomnumber` variable and uses it to create a second number called `linkselect`, which will contain an *integer* number between 1 and the value set in `linknumber`. (An integer number is any whole number that does not contain any decimals. 1, 2, and 10 are integers, 1.3, 2.356, and 10.9999 are called *decimal* or *floating point* numbers.)

NOTE: The `Math.random()` function is still under development as this book goes to press. If it does not make the final release of 2.0, you will need to use the replacement `random()` function shown below. This function is based loosely on one developed by Bob Jamison.

(`rjamison@gothamcity.jsc.nasa.gov`):

```
function random() {
    var curdate = new Date()
    var work = curdate.getTime() + curdate.getDate()
    return ( (work * 29 + 1) % 1024 ) / 1024
}
```

Simply add this function before the `// End of script [--]>` line and replace the `Math.random()` statement with `random()`.

The set of `if` statements that follows then checks the randomly selected value assigned to `linkselect` and, when a match is found, assigns a URL to the variable `linktext`. You can add any number of URLs you like here, but remember that you need to alter the value of `linknumber` so that it reflects how many links you have defined.

After you have a URL assigned to `linktext`, the final step in the process is to create the physical link by using a `document.write()` method. You do this by writing this line:

```
document.write('<A HREF="' + linktext + '">here.</A>') ;
```

The value inside the parentheses takes advantage of JavaScript's capability to add strings of text together. In this case, `'<A HREF="'`, the value of `linktext` and `'">here.</A>'` are added together to create a properly formed link tag.

With the function definition complete, all that now remains to be done is to replace the original `<A HREF=` tag from the basic framework with the new link created by `picklink()`. This can be done in various ways, but the simplest method is by embedding a call to `picklink()` inside the body of your document, as shown here:

```
Click <SCRIPT LANGUAGE="JavaScript">picklink()</SCRIPT>
 to visit a randomly selected site from my list of favorites.
```

Here is the completed HTML document:

```
<HTML>
<HEAD>
<TITLE>Random Link Generator</TITLE>
<SCRIPT LANGUAGE="JavaScript">
<!-- the contents of the script need to be hidden from other browsers
function picklink() {
var linknumber = 4 ;
var linktext = "nolink.html" ;
var randomnumber = Math.random() ;
var linkselect = Math.round( (linknumber-1) * randomnumber) + 1 ;
// Add as many links as you want here
if ( linkselect == 1 )
    { linktext="http://www.netscape.com/" }
if ( linkselect == 2 )
    { linktext="http://www.webcom.com/taketwo/" }
if ( linkselect == 3 )
    { linktext="http://java.sun.com/" }
if ( linkselect == 4 )
    { linktext="http://www.realaudio.com/" }
// Remember to alter linknumber so it reflects the number of links you define
document.write('<A HREF="' + linktext + '">here</A>') ;
}
// End of script -->
</SCRIPT>
<BODY>
<H1>My random link generator</H1>
Click <SCRIPT LANGUAGE="JavaScript">picklink()</SCRIPT>
 to visit a randomly selected site from my list of favorites.
</BODY>
```

To Create a Random Link Generator Using an Event Handler

Besides being bad style-wise, using inline `<SCRIPT>` tags can cause unpredictable problems when images are displayed on a page. To avoid such difficulties, the safest way to work with scripts is by using them only in the `<HEAD>` block, when at all practical.

But this situation poses a problem for your random link generator, which needs to alter the value of a link each time it is used. If you can't include `<SCRIPT>` tags in the `<BODY>` of a document, how can the link be randomly selected?

Whenever you click a link, a button, or any form element, Navigator 2.0 generates an event signal that can be trapped by one of the event handlers. By taking advantage of this fact, and the fact that each link in a document is actually stored as an object that can be referenced by JavaScript, you will find it surprisingly easy to alter your existing script to avoid the need for an inline <SCRIPT> tag.

First, look at the changes that need to be made in the body of the document to accommodate the use of an event handler. In this part of the task, the inline <SCRIPT> tag is replaced by a normal <A> tag as shown here:

```
Click <A HREF="dummy.html">here</A> To visit a randomly selected site
from my list of favorites.
```

After this is done, you need to associate an onClick event handler with the link by including the handler as an attribute of the <A> tag. When onClick is used as an attribute, the value assigned to it must represent a valid JavaScript instruction or function call. For this task, you want to call the picklink() function created previously and make the URL it selects overwrite the default URL defined in the <A> tag as HREF="dummy.html".

The **this** statement tells JavaScript to reference an object without having to know its name or location. In the example, **this** points to the link object and **this.href** indicates the **href** property. By assigning a new value to **this.href**, you change the destination URL.

This job is easy to do because each link is actually stored as an object of type link, and the link type contains the same properties as the location object. As a result, all you need to do is assign a new value to the HREF property of the link, in the onClick event handler, as shown here:

```
Click <A HREF="dummy.html" onClick="this.href=picklink()">here</A>
 To visit a randomly selected site from my list of favorites.
```

With the onClick handler set up, all you need to alter in the picklink() function is the document.write() method. Because you are no longer physically writing anything onto the Web page, the document.write() function needs to be removed. But in its place, you need some way for the value of linkselect to be sent back to the this.href property.

You achieve this by using the return statement, which sends a value back from a function call, as shown here:

```
return linkselect ;
```

In the picklink() function, you need to replace

If you get error messages when using the built-in Math.random() function, you may need to use the replacement random() function discussed earlier in this chapter.

```
document.write('<A HREF="' + linktext + '">here</A>')
```

with this new statement.

If you examine the completed text for this new HTML document, you will notice that there is very little difference between it at the preceding task, except for the removal of the inline <SCRIPT> tag and the replacement of document.write() with a return statement:

```
<HTML>
<HEAD>
<TITLE>Random Link Generator with events</TITLE>
<SCRIPT LANGUAGE="JavaScript">
<!-- the contents of the script need to be hidden from other browsers
function picklink() {
var linknumber = 4 ;
var linktext = "nolink.html" ;
var randomnumber = Math.random() ;
var linkselect = Math.round( (linknumber-1) * randomnumber) + 1 ;
if ( linkselect == 1 )
    { linktext="http://www.netscape.com/" }
if ( linkselect == 2 )
    { linktext="http://www.webcom.com/taketwo/" }
if ( linkselect == 3 )
    { linktext="http://java.sun.com/" }
if ( linkselect == 4 )
    { linktext="http://www.realaudio.com/" }
return linktext;
}
// End of script -->
</SCRIPT>
<BODY>
<H1>My random link generator</H1>
Click <A HREF="dummy.html" onClick="this.href=picklink()">here</A>
 to visit a randomly selected site from my list of favorites.
</BODY>
```

To Create a Random Link Generator Using an Array

The only problem with the preceding example is the need to keep adding additional `if` tests for each new link you want to include in your random list of favorites. To get around this difficulty, and to streamline the appearance of the script considerably, JavaScript provides a mechanism that enables you to create lists of variables—or what are called arrays.

Arrays in JavaScript work differently from arrays in other languages. The arrays in this example are technically objects, but JavaScript enables you to treat them like arrays. Refer to Netscape's JavaScript documentation for more about arrays.

An array is a list of variables that are all referenced by the same variable name. For example, an array called `mylinks[]` could be used to contain a list of all the links used by the `picklink()` function. The value of each link in the list is then referenced by the placement of a numeric value inside the square `[]` brackets: The first variable can be found with `mylinks[1]`, the second with `mylinks[2]`, and so on.

To take advantage of the possibilities offered by arrays, you first need to create a small function known as a constructor method. This function is needed because arrays are really objects. The online JavaScript documentation listed in the preceding Note provides additional information about how such a constructor should look. The `MakeArray()` constructor is based on a function created by Brenden Eich—the programmer at Netscape Communications responsible for the creation of JavaScript. Here is the `MakeArray()` function:

```
function MakeArray(n) {
// Initial concept Brenden Eich - Netscape Communications
   this.length = n;
   for (var i = 1; i <= n; i++)
       { this[i] = 0 }
   return this
   }
```

You need to include this function in your JavaScript code whenever you want to use arrays in a program. After the `MakeArray()` function has been defined, you can create the `mylinks[]` array discussed previously by writing

```
mylinks = new MakeArray( value )
```

in which *value* is the number of elements to be declared in the array.

You can then fill the `mylinks[]` array with values by simply assigning them as you would any other variable. Here's an example of an array with five elements with a URL assigned to each:

```
<SCRIPT LANGUAGE="JavaScript">
<!-- the contents of the script need to be hidden from other browsers

mylinks = new MakeArray( 5 ) ;

mylinks[1] = "http://www.netscape.com/" ;
mylinks[2] = "http://www.webcom.com/taketwo/" ;
mylinks[3] = "http://java.sun.com/" ;
mylinks[4] = "http://www.realaudio.com/" ;
mylinks[5] = "http://www.worlds.com/" ;
```

Now that you have a list of URLs defined, you'll modify the original `picklink()` function so that it selects a link by choosing from those included in the array, instead of by using `if` tests. Here is the new code:

```
function picklink() {
   linknumber = mylinks[0] ;
   randomnumber = Math.random() ;
   linkselect = Math.round( (linknumber-1) * randomnumber ) + 1 ;
   return mylinks[ linkselect ] ;
}
```

The first change you need to make deals with the value assigned to `linknumber`. In the previous examples, you set this value manually, but now you need to set it to the number of elements in the `mylink[]` array. You do this by using the value stored automatically by the `MakeArray()` constructor in `mylinks[0]`. This element contains the number of elements in the array.

You should also have noticed that all the `if` tests from the earlier task have been removed, and a single `return mylinks[ linkselect ]` statement has been put in their place. This statement causes the value assigned to the element referenced by `mylinks`

[linkselect] to be returned, linkselect being a random number between 1 and the value of linknumber.

It is important to note that you can consolidate the picklink() function even further by removing all the work variables and simply performing all the math inside the return statement, as shown here:

```
function picklink() {
    return mylinks[ ( Math.round( ( mylinks[0] - 1) * Math.random() ) + 1 ) ] ;
}
```

Finally, incorporate all these changes into the document created in the earlier task, remembering to include the MakeArray() constructor function. If you are a little lost at this stage, you can use the following completed HTML document as a guide:

To add new links to your list, simply increase the *value* assigned by new MakeArray (*value*), and add the new links to the list following the array elements already defined.

```
<HTML>
<HEAD>

<TITLE>Random Link Generator with an Array</TITLE>

<SCRIPT LANGUAGE="JavaScript">
<!-- the contents of the script need to be hidden from other browsers

mylinks = new MakeArray( 5 );

mylinks[1] = "http://www.netscape.com/" ;
mylinks[2] = "http://www.webcom.com/taketwo/" ;
mylinks[3] = "http://java.sun.com/" ;
mylinks[4] = "http://www.realaudio.com/" ;
mylinks[5] = "http://www.worlds.com/" ;

function picklink() {
    return mylinks[ ( Math.round( ( mylinks[0] - 1) * Math.random() ) + 1 ) ] ;
}

function MakeArray( n ) {
// Initial concept Brenden Eich - Netscape Communications
    this.length = n;
    for (var i = 1; i <= n; i++)
        { this[i] = 0 }
    return this ;
    }

// End of script -->
</SCRIPT>

<BODY>
<H1>My random link generator</H1>
Click <A HREF="dummy.html" onClick="this.href=picklink()">here</A>
 to visit a randomly selected site from my list of favorites.
</BODY>
```

Creating a Web Tour Guide

One of the more interesting possibilities offered by JavaScript is introduced through its capability to programmatically control the contents of a frame or frames. In the following task, you will learn how to use this capability to create a Web tour guide like the one shown in Figure 13.7.

The top frame of Figure 13.7 contains a set of buttons that enable people to take a guided tour of the World Wide Web by clicking the displayed navigation buttons. Whenever a navigation button is clicked, a new Web page is displayed in the frame at the bottom of the screen. At the same time, a description of the page currently being viewed is constantly displayed in the textbox on the right of the screen, with a second textbox below it showing the next destination on the tour.

To Create the Tour Frameset

Before examining the JavaScript code, you need to create a frameset document to describe the layout of the frames. Name this document `tourframe.html` and add the following HTML code to it:

```
<HTML>
<HEAD>
<TITLE>Web Tours Unlimited</TITLE>
</HEAD>
<FRAMESET ROWS="20%, *">
<FRAME SRC="tourscript.html" NAME="tourtop">
<FRAME SRC="tourstart.html" NAME="tourbottom">
</FRAMESET>
```

To Create the `tourstart.html` Document

When the Web tour first starts, the frameset needs to display a default page in the bottom frame. Create another new document and name it `tourstart.html`. In this document, include the following text:

```
<HTML>
<HEAD>
<TITLE>Web Tours Unlimited</TITLE>
</HEAD>
<BODY>
<P><I>This tour is best viewed by first turning off your Web browser's
Toolbar and Location or Document URL line. </I></P>
Click start to begin the tour...
</BODY>
```

NOTE: If you had not wanted to display any information in the bottom frame, you could have made use of a special protocol in the `<FRAME>` tag called `about:blank`. In this case the frame definition would have looked like this:

```
<FRAME SRC="about:blank" NAME="tourbottom">
```

This tells Navigator 2.0 to display a blank page.

To Create the Form Details

The top frame of the frameset contains the `tourscript.html` document that looks after all the magic that makes the Web Tour work. Before looking at the JavaScript itself, you'll create the table and form layout. To start, enter this basic HTML structural code:

```
<HTML>
<HEAD>
<TITLE> Web Tours Unlimited</TITLE>
</HEAD>
<BODY
BACKGROUND="http://home.netscape.com/assist/net_sites/bg/paper/peach_paper.gif"
BGCOLOR="PINK" >
```

Next, you need to define the `<FORM>` tag and `<TABLE>` definition that holds all the buttons and fields for the tour navigator. The table consists of five columns on two rows, and on the top row the first cell spans four columns. In addition, the form is assigned the name `tourform` by using the NAME attribute. Here is the basic structure for such a table:

```
<FORM NAME="tourform">
<TABLE WIDTH="100%" BORDER="3">
```

```
<TR> <!-- Start of row one -->
  <TD ALIGN="CENTER" COLSPAN=4> <BR> </TD>
  <TD ALIGN="RIGHT"> <BR> </TD>
</TR>
<TR ALIGN="CENTER">  <!-- Start of row two -->
  <TD WIDTH="10%"> <BR> </TD>
  <TD WIDTH="10%"> <BR> </TD>
  <TD WIDTH="10%"> <BR> </TD>
  <TD WIDTH="10%"> <BR> </TD>
  <TD ALIGN="RIGHT" WIDTH="*"> <BR> </TR>
</TABLE>
</FORM>
</BODY>
```

After you have defined and tested this basic layout—remembering to test it within the frameset as well— you are ready to add the buttons and other elements of the form, as shown here:

```
<FORM NAME="tourform">
<TABLE WIDTH="100%" BORDER="3">
<TR> <!-- Start of row one -->
  <TD ALIGN="CENTER"COLSPAN=4> <FONT SIZE=5>Web Tours Unlimited</FONT> </TD>
  <TD ALIGN="RIGHT">Current Page:
  <INPUT TYPE="text" NAME="currenturl" VALUE="Start Tour" SIZE=35></TD>
</TR>
<TR ALIGN="CENTER">  <!-- Start of row two -->
  <TD WIDTH="10%"><INPUT TYPE="button" VALUE="  Start  " onClick="firstlink()">
  </TD>
  <TD WIDTH="10%"><INPUT TYPE="button" VALUE="Previous" onClick="prevlink()">
  </TD>
  <TD WIDTH="10%"><INPUT TYPE="button" VALUE="  Next   " onClick="nextlink()">
  </TD>
  <TD WIDTH="10%"><INPUT TYPE="button" VALUE="  Last   " onClick="lastlink()">
  </TD>
  <TD ALIGN="RIGHT" WIDTH="*">Next Page:
  <INPUT TYPE="text" NAME="nexturl" VALUE="Start Tour" SIZE=35>
  </TR>
</TABLE>
</FORM>
</BODY>
```

At this stage, the only difference between this form and any of the other forms you have encountered previously is the addition of onClick handlers for each of the buttons. The button labeled Start calls a function named firstlink(). The one labeled Previous calls the prevlink() function. The nextlink() function is assigned to the button labeled Next. And finally, the button labeled Last calls the function lastlink().

To Write the Script

With the <FORM> and <TABLE> blocks defined and tested, we'll return to the <HEAD> block and the <SCRIPT> definition. The first part of the script is very similar to the random links script in the earlier section called "To Create a Random Link Generator Using an Event Handler." An array called mylinks[] is first defined with five elements;

but this time, an additional array called `mylinksnote[]` is also declared with five elements, as shown here:

```
<SCRIPT LANGUAGE="JavaScript">
<!-- the contents of the script need to be hidden from other browsers
mylinks = new MakeArray(5);
mylinksnote = new MakeArray(5);
```

After the two arrays have been declared, they are loaded with a URL and corresponding description like the ones shown next. You can include your own links or use these for now. In addition, you can include extra links by increasing the *value* assigned in the new MakeArray(*value*) statement.

```
mylinks[1] = "http://www.netscape.com/" ;
mylinksnote[1] = "Netscape Communications" ;
mylinks[2] = "http://www.webcom.com/taketwo/" ;
mylinksnote[2] = "Take TWO home Page" ;
mylinks[3] = "http://www.worlds.net/" ;
mylinksnote[3] = "Worlds Inc: The home of Alpha World" ;
mylinks[4] = "http://java.sun.com/" ;
mylinksnote[4] = "The Java Home Page" ;
mylinks[5] = "http://www.realaudio.com/" ;
mylinksnote[5] = "RealAudio Home Page" ;
```

Finally, after all the URLs and descriptions have been defined, you need to declare a global work variable called `currentlink`. This variable will be used to keep track of the current location of the Web tour. You declare this variable by writing this:

```
var currentlink = 0;
```

To Create the Navigation Functions

When you click any of the navigation buttons, its `onclick` handler calls a corresponding function.

The first of these functions is `firstlink()`. When `firstlink()` is called, the value of `currentlink` is set to 1, and a function named `updatepage()` is called. The code for the `firstlink()` function is as follows:

```
function firstlink() {
   currentlink = 1;
   updatepage() ;
}
```

As you will learn soon, `updatepage()` is what looks after the loading of each new page into the bottom form. It also ensures that the correct notes are displayed in the Current Page and Next Page fields.

When the `prevlink()` function is called, the value of `currentlink` is decremented by one and a check is made to see whether the start of the tour has been reached. If this is the case, an alert message is displayed; otherwise, the `updatepage()` function is called to display the previous page of the tour.

The code required to perform these functions is shown here:

```
function prevlink() {
   if ( --currentlink < 1 ) {
```

```
        currentlink = 1 ;
        alert("Already at start of tour")
        }
    else {
        updatepage() ;
    }
}
```

When the `nextlink()` function is called, the value of `currentlink` is incremented by one, and a check is made to see whether the end of the tour has been reached. If this is the case, an alert message is displayed; otherwise, the `updatepage()` function is called to display the next page of the tour.

The code required to perform these functions is shown here:

```
function nextlink() {
    if ( ++currentlink > mylinks[0] ) {
        currentlink = mylinks[0] ;
        alert("The tour is over")
    }
    else {
        updatepage() ;
    }
}
```

When the `lastlink()` function is called, the value of `currentlink` is set equal to the value of `mylinks[0]`, and then the `updatepage()` function is called to display the last page of the tour.

The code required to perform these functions is shown here:

```
function lastlink() {
    currentlink = mylinks[0] ;
    updatepage() ;
}
```

To Use the `updatepage()` Function

As mentioned previously, the `updatepage()` function actually looks after the task of updating the contents of the bottom frame. It does this by setting the `location` property of the bottom frame. The location property contains the URL of the current document, displayed in either a frame or a main Web browser window. By altering the contents of this property, a new URL can be assigned to a frame or Web browser window. Doing so causes a new Web document to be loaded in place of the current one.

The `location` property of a frame can be addressed by the statement `parent.frames[0].location`, which indicates the `location` property of the first frame of the current Web window, and `parent.frames[1].location` the `location` property of second frame. Alternatively, you can also address a frame using the name assigned to it using the NAME attribute of its `<FRAME>` tag, which in the case of the bottom frame in this example is `tourbottom`. As a result, the bottom frame's `location` property can also be addressed by using `parent.tourbottom.location`.

Therefore, to change the contents of the bottom frame to the URL pointed to by `mylinks[ currentlink ]`, you need to do only this:

```
function updatepage() {
   parent.tourbottom.location = mylinks[ currentlink ] ;
```

or alternatively this:

```
function updatepage() {
   parent.frames[1].location = mylinks[ currentlink ] ;
```

The `updatepage()` function also updates the contents of the `currenturl` and `nexturl` text fields by explicitly addressing them. You can access the contents of any field in a form by using the following:

```
document.forms[0].fieldname.value
```

where *fieldname* is replaced by the name of the field as defined by the forms `<INPUT>` tags, and `forms[0]` is the first form of the current Web document. As a result, the contents of the `currenturl` and `nexturl` text fields can be found by using `document.forms[0].currenturl.value` and `document.forms[0].nexturl.value`, respectively.

Alternatively, you can make use of the name assigned to the form by its NAME attribute, as discussed previously. In this case, you could use `document.tourform.currenturl.value` and `document.tourform.nexturl.value`.

Using this information, the code required to maintain the correct values for the `currenturl` and `nexturl` text fields is shown here:

```
   document.tourform.currenturl.value = mylinksnote[ currentlink] ;
   if (currentlink == mylinks[ 0 ] {
     document.tourform.nexturl.value = "Tour End"
     }
   else {
     document.tourform.nexturl.value = mylinksnote[ currentlink + 1 ]
   }
```

The Completed `tourscript.html` Document

To complete this part of the task, listed after the Note is the full text of the `tourscript.html` document, with the `MakeArray()` function added to permit the creation of `mylinks[]` and `mylinksnote[]`:

NOTE: If you want to experiment with the Web Tour but don't want to key in all the code yourself, you can find an operation version at http://www.webcom.com/taketwo/samstyn.shtml. In addition, you will find another version of the Web Tour that is completely automated and moves from site to site without any user intervention.

```
<HTML>
<HEAD>
<SCRIPT LANGUAGE="JavaScript">
<!-- the contents of the script need to be hidden from other browsers
mylinks = new MakeArray(5);
mylinksnote = new MakeArray(5);
mylinks[1] = "http://www.netscape.com/" ;
mylinksnote[1] = "Netscape Communications" ;
mylinks[2] = "http://www.webcom.com/taketwo/" ;
mylinksnote[2] = "Take TWO home Page" ;
mylinks[3] = "http://www.worlds.net/" ;
mylinksnote[3] = "Worlds Inc: The home of Alpha World" ;
mylinks[4] = "http://java.sun.com/" ;
mylinksnote[4] = "The Java Home Page" ;
mylinks[5] = "http://www.realaudio.com/" ;
mylinksnote[5] = "RealAudio Home Page" ;
var currentlink = 0;
// Functions start here ----------------------------------------
function firstlink() {
   currentlink = 1;
   updatepage() ;
}
function prevlink() {
  if ( --currentlink < 1 ) {
     currentlink = 1 ;
     alert("Already at start of tour")
  }
  else {
     updatepage() ;
  }
}
function nextlink() {
   if ( ++currentlink > mylinks[0] ) {
      currentlink = mylinks[0] ;
      alert("The tour is over")
   }
   else {
      updatepage() ;
   }
}
function lastlink() {
   currentlink = mylinks[0] ;
   updatepage() ;
}
function updatepage() {
   parent.tourbottom.location = mylinks[ currentlink ] ;
   document.tourform.currenturl.value = mylinksnote[ currentlink] ;
   if (currentlink == mylinks[ 0 ] ) {
      document.tourform.nexturl.value = "Tour End"
```

```
    }
    else {
        document.tourform.nexturl.value = mylinksnote[ currentlink + 1 ]
    }
}
function MakeArray( n ) {
// Initial concept Brenden Eich - Netscape Communications
    this.length = n;
    for (var i = 1; i <= n; i++)
        { this[i] = 0 }
    return this ;
    }
// End of script -->
</SCRIPT>

<BODY
 BACKGROUND="http://home.netscape.com/assist/net_sites/bg/paper/
peach_paper.gif"
 BGCOLOR="PINK"
>
<FORM NAME="tourform">
<TABLE WIDTH="100%" BORDER="3">
<TR> <!-- start of row one -->
  <TD ALIGN="CENTER"COLSPAN=4>
  <FONT SIZE=5>Web Tours Unlimited</FONT>
  </TD>
  <TD ALIGN="RIGHT">Current Page:
  <INPUT TYPE="text" NAME="currenturl" VALUE="Start Tour" SIZE=35>
  </TD>
</TR> <!-- start of row two -->
<TR ALIGN="CENTER">
  <TD WIDTH="10%"><INPUT TYPE="button" VALUE=" Start    " onClick="firstlink()">
  </TD>
  <TD WIDTH="10%"><INPUT TYPE="button" VALUE="Previous" onClick="prevlink()">
  </TD>
  <TD WIDTH="10%"><INPUT TYPE="button" VALUE="  Next  " onClick="nextlink()">
  </TD>
  <TD WIDTH="10%"><INPUT TYPE="button" VALUE="  Last   " onClick="lastlink()">
  </TD>
  <TD ALIGN="RIGHT" WIDTH="*">Next Page:
  <INPUT TYPE="text" NAME="nexturl" VALUE="Start Tour" SIZE=35>
  </TR>
</TABLE>
</FORM>
</BODY>
```

Learning More About JavaScript

The list of statements, functions, and options included in this chapter represents only part of the potential offered by JavaScript. And in fact, many new statements and functions are being added as JavaScript evolves.

For this reason, I cannot overemphasize the importance of the JavaScript authoring guide and other resources provided by Netscape Communications. (See Figures 13.8 and 13.9.) I realize that this document has been mentioned previously, but currently, it is the only full documentation for the JavaScript language.

You can find the JavaScript Authoring guide at

`http://home.netscape.com/eng/mozilla/Gold/handbook/javascript/index.html`

You can also find a great directory of JavaScript-related resources at Netscape at

`http://home.netscape.com/comprod/products/navigator/version_2.0/script/`
`index.html`

Figure 13.8.

The JavaScript authoring guide, a great way to keep up with JavaScript.

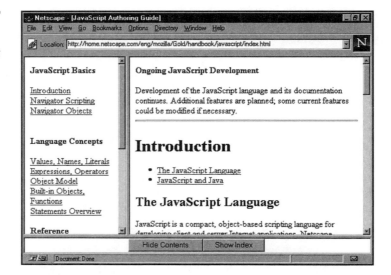

Figure 13.9.

The JavaScript resources list at Netscape, a directory of great ways to learn more.

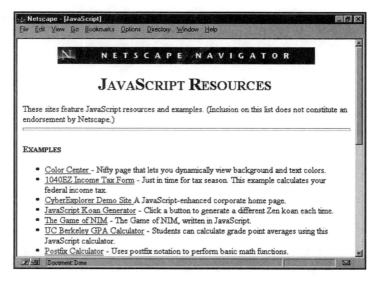

Workshop Wrap-Up

JavaScript offers you a way to include simple programs or scripts within a Web page without having to deal with the many difficulties associated with programming in high-level languages such as Java or C++. While JavaScript is clearly simpler than those languages, it is perhaps not the "novice" language Netscape wants it to be. Non-programmers will find that using JavaScript effectively require a little study, and some practice.

Still, ambition always demands effort. And JavaScript functions are for ambitious Web authors, those who want their pages not to simple look pretty, but to sing, dance, and take names.

Next Steps

Now...

- ❏ To explore some example Web documents that exploit all of the techniques covered in Part III of this book, see Chapter 14, "Real-Life Examples II."
- ❏ To learn how to publish your page (and scripts!), see Chapter 15, "Publishing Web Documents."

Q&A

Q: If JavaScript is being proposed as an Internet standard, does that mean it will run on any Web browser?

A: Yes and no. If and when it is approved as an Internet standard, it will then be up to Web browser developers to integrate support for JavaScript into their browsers.

FOURTEEN

Real-Life Examples II

This chapter describes a variety of sample Web pages created entirely in Netscape Navigator Gold, with authoring techniques introduced in Part III (Chapters 9 through 14). The examples include

Example 1. An online store (using forms and tables)

Example 2. An online brochure/bulletin board (using frames and image maps)

Example 3. An online calculator (using JavaScript)

Example 1: Sharon's Shirts

Document Title: Sharon's Handmade Camp Shirts

Files: Page files SHARON1.HTM (Figure 14.1) and ORDERF.HTM (Figure 14.2), and image BLUEBAR.GIF.

Description: An online store. Row headings on the table are links to fact sheets and photos about the products. A link in the paragraph leads to an order form (ORDERF.HTM), in which the visitor selects a product and then clicks the Submit button to open a second, secure form for collecting payment and shipping information.

Techniques Applied:

Tables. (See Chapter 10, "Building Tables.") The table is center-aligned and features a border, an empty cell, row and column headings, links embedded as cell data, and custom colors for the column headings (see Chapter 4, "Composing, Editing and Formatting Text") that correspond to the colors they describe. (See the HTML source code for SHARON1.HTM.)

Font sizing. (See Chapter 4.) The word Sharon's has a +5 font size value. Extra non-breaking spaces have been added between to and Sharon's to make the spacing more attractive.

Inline image. (See Chapter 6, "Working with Graphics.") The image BLUEBAR.GIF is used as a horizontal line.

Forms. (See Chapter 12, Creating Interactive Forms and Image Maps.") A link in SHARON1.HTM opens ORDERF.HTM (see Figure 14.2), which features a form using radio buttons, a Select list, and a Submit button with a custom label.

Figure 14.1.
Sharon1.HTM.

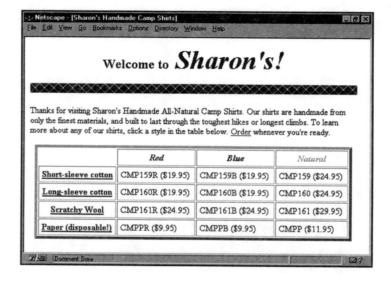

Figure 14.2.
Orderf.HTM.

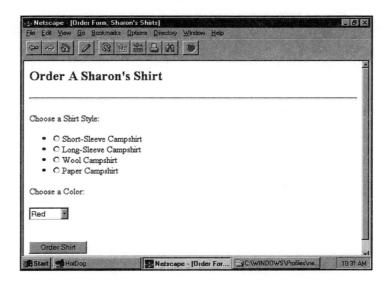

Listing 14.1. SHARON1.HTM (Figure 14.1).

```
<html>
<head>
    <title>Sharon's Handmade Camp Shirts</title>
    <meta name="GENERATOR" content="Mozilla/2.01Gold (Win32)">
</head>
<body>
<h2 align=center>Welcome to  <i><font SIZE=+4>Sharon's!</font></i></h2>
<IMG SRC="java/bluebar.gif">
<p>Thanks for visiting Sharon's Handmade All-Natural Camp Shirts. Our shirts
are handmade from only the finest materials, and built to last through
the toughest hikes or longest climbs. To learn more about any of our shirts,
click a style in the table below. <a href="orderf.htm">Order</a>
whenever you're ready.
<p>
<DIV ALIGN="CENTER">
<table BORDER=5 CELLPADDING=5>
<tr>
<th> </th>
<th><i><font COLOR="#FF0000">Red</font></i></th>
<th><i><font COLOR="#0000FF">Blue</font></i></th>
<th><i><font COLOR="#FFFF80">Natural</font></i></th>
</tr>
<tr>
<th><a href="ssleeve.htm">Short-sleeve cotton</a></th>
<td>
CMP159R ($19.95)
</td>
<td>
CMP159B  ($19.95)
</td>
<td>
```

continued

Listing 14.1. continued

```
CMP159   ($24.95)
</td>
</tr>
<tr>
<th><a href="lsleeve.htm">Long-sleeve cotton</a></th>
<td>
CMP160R  ($19.95)
</td>
<td>
CMP160B  ($19.95)
</td>
<td>
CMP160   ($24.95)
</td>
</tr>
<tr>
<th><a href="wool.htm">Scratchy Wool</a></th>
<td>
CMP161R ($24.95)
</td>
<td>
CMP161B  ($24.95)
</td>
<td>
CMP161   ($29.95)
</td>
</tr>
<tr>
<th><a href="paper.htm">Paper (disposable!)</a></th>
<td>
CMPPR   ($9.95)
</td>
<td>
CMPPB   ($9.95)
</td>
<td>
CMPP ($11.95)
</td>
</tr>
</table>
</div>
</body>
</html>
```

Listing 14.2. ORDERF.HTM (Figure 14.2).

```
<HTML>
<HEAD>
<TITLE>Order Form, Sharon's Shirts</TITLE>
</HEAD>
<BODY>
<h2>Order A Sharon's Shirt</h2>
<hr>
<FORM METHOD=POST ACTION="/CGI-BIN/ORDER.CGI">
Choose a Shirt Style:
<ul>
```

```
<li><INPUT NAME="Shirt Style" TYPE="RADIO" VALUE="Short">Short-Sleeve Campshirt
<li><INPUT NAME="Shirt Style" TYPE="RADIO" VALUE="Long">Long-Sleeve Campshirt
<li><INPUT NAME="Shirt Style" TYPE="RADIO" VALUE="Wool">Wool Campshirt
<li><INPUT NAME="Shirt Style" TYPE="RADIO" VALUE="Paper">Paper Campshirt
</ul>
<P>Choose a Color:<p>
<SELECT NAME="Color">
<option>Red
<option>Blue
<option>Natural
</select><BR>
<p>
<INPUT TYPE="Submit" VALUE="Order Shirt">
</FORM>
</BODY>
</HTML>
```

Example 2: Rocks Is Us

Document Title: Rocks Is Us.

Files (see Figure 14.3)**:** Frame definition document ROCKUS.HTM, content files BUTTONS.HTM and ROCKS.HTM, image file BUTTONS.GIF.

Description: An online brochure and bulletin board, presented in a frames document. An image map in the top frame allows visitors to click a graphical button to open various documents and activities in the bottom frame.

Techniques Applied:

Frames. (See Chapter 11, "Making Frames.") The frame definition document (ROCKUS.HTM) includes a <NOFRAME> block to accommodate browsers that don't support frames, SCROLLING="NO" to prevent scrollbars from appearing in a frame—named frames so that links can designate which frame to open a file in.

Client-side image map. (See Chapter 12.) The BUTTONS.HTM content document includes a client-side image map based on the button bar BUTTONS.GIF. The regions are defined as rectangles that loosely conform to each apparent button in the image. BASE TARGET is used to make all links in the map open their files in the frame named Main (bottom frame), so the button bar is always displayed.

Image properties. (See Chapter 6.) The image BUTTONS.GIF is centered in the BUTTONS.HTM content document.

Inline images. (See Chapter 6.) The button bar BUTTONS.GIF is an inline image in the BUTTONS.HTM document, and inline image stands in for a rule in the ROCKS.HTM content document.

Blinking text. (See Chapter 4.) In ROCKS.HTM, the word AWESOME blinks.

Figure 14.3.
Rocks-Is-Us.

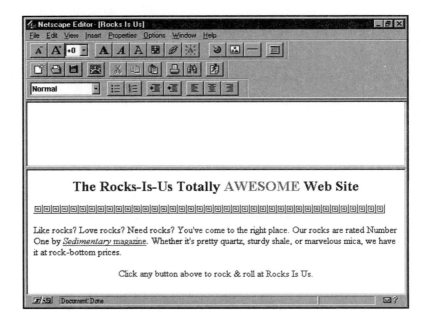

Listing 14.3. Frame definition document ROCKUS.HTM.

```
<HTML>
<HEAD>
<TITLE>Rocks Is Us</TITLE>
</HEAD>
<FRAMESET ROWS="35%,*">
<FRAME SRC="buttons.HTM" NAME="Buttons">
<FRAME SRC="rocks.htm" NAME="Main" SCROLLING="NO">
<NOFRAME>Sorry! This document requires a browser that can display frames, such
as Netscape Navigator. If your browser displays this message, it does not
support frames. Enjoy our <A HREF="rocksno.htm"> no-frames version</A> instead.
</FRAMESET>
</HTML>
```

Listing 14.4. Content document BUTTONS.HTM.

```
<HTML>
<HEAD>
<TITLE>My Buttons</TITLE>
</HEAD>
<BODY>
<BASE TARGET="Main">
<MAP NAME="Rockbar">
<AREA SHAPE="RECT" COORDS="2,9 74,65" HREF="features.htm">
<AREA SHAPE="RECT" COORDS="75,9 158,65" HREF="titles.htm">
<AREA SHAPE="RECT" COORDS="159,9 237,65" HREF="meetus.htm">
```

```
<AREA SHAPE="RECT" COORDS="238,9 315,65" HREF="order.htm">
<AREA SHAPE="RECT" COORDS="316,9 395,65" HREF="ask.htm">
<AREA SHAPE="RECT" COORDS="396,9 464,65" HREF="forum.htm">
</MAP>
<DIV ALIGN="CENTER">
<IMG SRC="buttons.gif" USEMAP="Rockbar">
</DIV>
</BODY>
</HTML>
```

Listing 14.5. Content document ROCKS.HTM.

```
<html>
<head>
   <title>Rocks</title>
   <meta name="Author" content="Ned Snell">
   <meta name="GENERATOR" content="Mozilla/2.01Gold (Win32)">
</head>
<body>
<h2 align=center>The Rocks-Is-Us Totally <b><blink><font
➡COLOR="#8080C0">AWESOME</font></blink></b> Web
Site</h2>
<p><img src="gr_ban03.gif" border=0 height=15 width=595></p>
<p>Like rocks? Love rocks? Need rocks? You've come to the right place. Our
rocks are rated Number One by <a href="http://
www.sedimentary.com"><i>Sedimentary</i>
magazine</a>. Whether it's pretty quartz, sturdy shale, or marvelous mica,
we have it at rock-bottom prices.</p>
<center><p>Click any button in the top frame to rock &amp; roll at Rocks
Is Us. You can discuss rocks with other rockhounds, learn about our latest
Rocks-Media CD-ROM, ask us questions, and much more.</p></center>
</body>
</html>
```

Example 3: The "Webtop" Calculator

Document Title: The JavaScript Desktop Calculator.

Description: A browser-based calculator that can be accessed through the Web by any JavaScript-capable browser.

File: MyCalc.HTM.

Techniques Applied: JavaScript.

Figure 14.4.

The Webtop calculator.

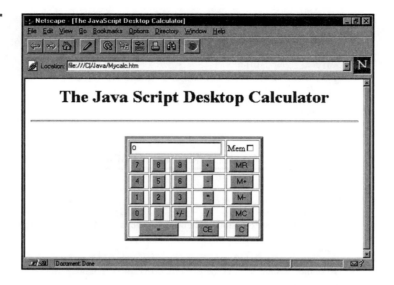

Listing 14.6. HTML document `MyCalc.HTM` (including JavaScript program in header).

```
<HTML>
<HEAD>
<TITLE>The JavaScript Desktop Calculator</TITLE>
<SCRIPT LANGUAGE="LiveScript">
<!-- the contents of the script need to be hidden from other browsers
//These variables are the control registers for the calculator.
var register1 = 0     // The last value entered into the calculor
var register2 = 0     // Work variable when doing calculations
var operator1 = " "   // Last operator button selected
var operator2 = " "   // Last operator button selected - resets onClick
var memory1   = 0     // Value stored in memory

//This function maintains the contents of the calculator display window.
function setdisplay(form, value, opvalue ) {
   form.display.value = value ;
   form.display.focus() ;
   form.display.select() ;
   operator2 = opvalue ;
}

//This function is called whenever a number button is pushed
function numpush(input, character) {
 with input {    // all properties in the with block default to input object
   var testnum = checknum (value)
   if (testnum == false || value == null || value == "0" || operator2 != " " )
{
      value = character ;
   }
   else {
      value += character ;
   }
 }
```

```
 operator2 = " " ;
}

//This function is called when the CE (Cancel Entry) button is pushed
function cepush( form ) {
   setdisplay( form, 0 , " " ) ;
}

//This function is called when the C (Cancel) button is pushed
function cancelpush(form) {
   register1 = 0 ;
   operator1 = " " ;
   setdisplay( form, 0 , "=" ) ;
}

//This function is called by mempush() when MC (memory cancel) is pushed
function mcpush(form) {
   form.memoryon.status = false ;
   memory1 = 0 ;
}

//This function is called by the onLoad event handler to reset the calculator
function reset( form ) {
   mcpush( form ) ;
   cancelpush( form ) ;
// form.memoryon.deselect() ;
}

//This function is called when an operator button is pushed. + - * / =
function oppush(form, opvalue) {
  if ( !checknum( form.display.value ) ) {
     cepush( form ) ;
     return ;
  }
//Check to see if calculation is needed
  if ( operator1 != " " ) {
     eqpush( form ) ;
  }
  register2 = parseFloat( form.display.value ) ;
  operator1 = opvalue ;
  register1 = register2 ;
  setdisplay( form, register1, opvalue ) ;
}

//This button is called by oppush() when an equals calculation is required
function eqpush(form) {
   if ( !checknum( form.display.value ) ) {
      cepush( form ) ;
      return ;
   }
   register2 = parseFloat( form.display.value ) ;
   if ( operator1 == "/" && register2 == 0 )  {
      alert("Divide by zero not permitted") ;
      cancelpush( form ) ;
      return ;
   }
```

continued

Listing 14.6. continued

```
// Perform calculations based on last operator set.
   if (operator1 == " ") {
      register1 = register2 ;
   }
   if (operator1 == "+") {
      register1 += register2 ;
   }
   if (operator1 == "-") {
      register1 -= register2 ;
   }
   if (operator1 == "*") {
      register1 *= register2 ;
   }
   if (operator1 == "/") {
      register1 /= register2 ;
   }
   setdisplay( form, register1 , " " ) ;
}

//This function is called when the +/- button is pushed
function signpush(input) {
   if (input.value.substring(0, 1) == "-") {
      input.value = input.value.substring(1, input.value.length)
   }
   else {
      input.value = "-" + input.value
   }
}

//This function is called when a memory button is pushed
function mempush(form, opvalue) {
   register2 = parseFloat( form.display.value ) ;
   if ( opvalue == "MC" ) {
      mcpush( form ) ;
   }
   if ( opvalue == "M+" ) {
      memory1 += register2 ;
   }
   if ( opvalue == "M-" ) {
      memory1 -= register2 ;
   }
   if ( opvalue == "MR" && memory1 != 0 ) {
      register2 = memory1 ;
   }
// Turn the memory checkbox on or off by setting its status
   if ( memory1 != 0 ) {
      form.memoryon.status = true ;
   }
   else {
      form.memoryon.status = false ;
   }
   setdisplay( form, register2 , opvalue ) ;
 }

//This function is used to check that form.display.value is a number
function checknum(str) {
   for (var i = 0; i < str.length; i++) {
      var ch = str.substring(i, i + 1)
      if ( ( ch < "0" ¦¦ ch > "9" ) && ch !="." && ch != "-" ) {
```

```
                  alert("Please enter numbers only.") ;
                  return false ;
              }
      }
      return true ;
}
// done hiding from browsers -->
</SCRIPT>
</HEAD>
<BODY>
<H1 ALIGN=CENTER>The Java Script Desktop Calculator</H1>
<HR>
<FORM METHOD="POST" onLoad=reset( this )>  <!--  reset when form is loaded -->
<DIV ALIGN=CENTER >
<TABLE BORDER="5">

<!--  ROW 1     -->
<TR>
 <TD ALIGN="RIGHT" COLSPAN=4>
  <INPUT NAME="display" VALUE="0" ALIGN="RIGHT"> </TD>
 <TD ALIGN="CENTER" >
  Mem<INPUT TYPE="checkbox" NAME="memoryon" SIZE=3> </TD>
</TR>

<!--  ROW 2     -->
<TR ALIGN=CENTER>
 <TD><INPUT TYPE="button" VALUE=" 7 "
  onClick="numpush(this.form.display, '7')"> </TD>
 <TD><INPUT TYPE="button" VALUE=" 8 "
  onClick="numpush(this.form.display, '8')"> </TD>
 <TD><INPUT TYPE="button" VALUE=" 9 "
  onClick="numpush(this.form.display, '9')"> </TD>
 <TD><INPUT TYPE="button" VALUE=" + "
  onClick="oppush(this.form, '+')"> </TD>
 <TD><INPUT TYPE="button" VALUE=" MR "
  onClick="mempush(this.form, 'MR')"> </TD>
</TR>

<!--  ROW 3     -->
<TR ALIGN=CENTER>
 <TD><INPUT TYPE="button" VALUE=" 4 "
  onClick="numpush(this.form.display, '4')"> </TD>
 <TD><INPUT TYPE="button" VALUE=" 5 "
  onClick="numpush(this.form.display, '5')"> </TD>
 <TD><INPUT TYPE="button" VALUE=" 6 "
  onClick="numpush(this.form.display, '6')"> </TD>
 <TD><INPUT TYPE="button" VALUE=" - "
  onClick="oppush(this.form,'-')"> </TD>
 <TD><INPUT TYPE="button" VALUE=" M+ "
  onClick="mempush(this.form, 'M+')"> </TD>
</TR>

<!--  ROW 4     -->
<TR ALIGN=CENTER>
 <TD><INPUT TYPE="button" VALUE=" 1 "
  onClick="numpush(this.form.display, '1')"> </TD>
 <TD><INPUT TYPE="button" VALUE=" 2 "
  onClick="numpush(this.form.display, '2')"> </TD>
```

continued

Listing 14.6. continued

```
<TD><INPUT TYPE="button" VALUE=" 3 "
 onClick="numpush(this.form.display, '3')"> </TD>
<TD><INPUT TYPE="button" VALUE=" * "
 onClick="oppush(this.form, '*')"> </TD>
<TD><INPUT TYPE="button" VALUE=" M- "
 onClick="mempush(this.form, 'M-')"> </TD>
</TR>

<!-- ROW 5    -->
<TR ALIGN=CENTER>
 <TD><INPUT TYPE="button" VALUE=" 0 "
 onClick="numpush(this.form.display, '0')"> </TD>
 <TD><INPUT TYPE="button" VALUE=" . "
 onClick="numpush(this.form.display, '.')"> </TD>
 <TD><INPUT TYPE="button" VALUE="+/-"
 onClick="signpush(this.form.display, '+-')"> </TD>
 <TD><INPUT TYPE="button" VALUE=" / "
 onClick="oppush(this.form, '/')"> </TD>
 <TD><INPUT TYPE="button" VALUE=" MC "
 onClick="mempush( this.form, 'MC' )"> </TD>
</TR>

<!-- ROW 6    -->
<TR ALIGN=CENTER>
 <TD COLSPAN=3><INPUT TYPE="button" VALUE="      =      "
  onClick="oppush(this.form, '=')"> </TD>
 <!-- COLSPAN -->
 <!-- COLSPAN -->
 <TD><INPUT TYPE="button" VALUE=" CE "
 onClick="cepush(this.form)"> </TD>
 <TD><INPUT TYPE="button" VALUE=" C "
 onClick="cancelpush(this.form)"> </TD>
</TR>
</TABLE>
</FORM>
</BODY>
</HTML>
```

PART

IV

Going Online, and Going Forward

FIFTEEN

Publishing Web Documents

You didn't become a Web author just to share your accomplishments with your canary. Of course, you want to get your work onto a Web server so it may be visited, loved, and lauded by those burgeoning Web masses.

Gold is a big help with publishing. By setting up a few defaults and smartly organizing your files, you'll wind up with the ability to publish your documents (and then update them later) with a few quick clicks.

However, publishing means more than sliding your files onto a server. Unless you put the word out about your document's Web presence, what good is it? You've got to publish—and then *publicize* (or else perish!).

About Servers

At this point in the workshop, you probably already know where you intend to publish your page. But in case you haven't decided, here are your options for finding a server:

> *At work or school.* Your employer or school might have a Web server on which you might be permitted store your document. Certainly, if your document is strictly work-related (or school-related), you're most likely to gain

In this chapter, you

- ❏ Learn what you need to know about your server before publishing
- ❏ Check and prepare your documents files for uploading to the server
- ❏ Configure Gold to make publishing quick and easy
- ❏ Upload your files via Gold's "One-Button Publishing," an easy activity that nevertheless requires one button, a few clicks and maybe some typing
- ❏ Publicize your page so the world knows where to find it

Tasks in this chapter:

- ❏ One-Button Publishing

permission to publish it on the server for free. However, note that free access to corporate and university servers is diminishing rapidly as demand grows and as organizations look for ways to earn money from their Internet connections. Also, many university systems, as well as some corporate systems are overtaxed, and might have outdated server hardware or inadequate connection speeds. Using a slow or unreliable system provides poor service to your visitors; forking over a few dollars a month for space on a fast commercial server might be a better choice in the long run than using free space on a poor server.

From commercial Internet service providers or their online service counterparts. Currently, these providers offer the best balance of service and cost for most new Web publishers. Many commercial providers include a modest amount of server space free with each Internet account and also might offer a wide range of space and pricing options. Although it might be convenient and cost-effective to lease Web space from the same company that provides your Internet account, there's no reason not to lease your space elsewhere. A good account provider might be a lousy Web space provider, offering high prices and/or poor service. In other words, shop around.

Build your own. If your Web page requires extra-tight security (for online sales) or makes extensive use of CGI scripts (especially for forms), an in-house Web server is your answer. Building your own Web server is a more practical solution—even for relatively small companies—than ever before, thanks to lower-priced server computers (especially Pentium-based PCs), cheaper, simpler server software (primarily from Netscape and Microsoft), and the wide availability of high-speed data lines (such as ISDN or T1).

However, a Web server is not cheap. The hardware and software for a decent server might cost about $5,000, but the 24-hour, high-speed dedicated Internet connection that a Web server demands might cost four times that much—every month. More important, while effectively administering a Web server is getting easier all the time, the job still demands a more-or-less full time expert. All of these requirements are well within the means of most companies with over 100 employees, or smaller companies whose line of business makes Web service a high priority. For other small companies, however, leasing space is a far more sensible option.

Before choosing a provider for Web space, visit that company's Web page a few times at different hours. If the server slowly sends pages at certain hours or seems to be unavailable from time to time, look for a better-equipped provider.

To learn more about setting up your own Web server, see *Web Site Construction Kit for Windows 95*, or *Web Site Construction Kit for Windows NT*, both from Sams.net Publishing.

Right before publishing, it's a good idea to test your document thoroughly, even if you've tested it previously. See Chapter 16 "Testing and Maintaining Web Documents".

Preparing to Publish

Publishing a page is a lot like painting a house: Doing the job is easy, but doing it right requires careful preparation. Before publishing, you need to take some time to properly prepare Gold's publishing features and your document files. Doing this first can prevent problems later, and make publishing a breeze.

Communicating with Your Server Supplier

The most important prelude to publishing is finding out about the requirements and limitations of the server to which you'll publish. Specifically, you'll need to know the following:

Unless you have your own server directory, do not name any page INDEX.HTM(L). Although this name is recommended for your top page (see Chapter 3), if the directory already contains a file called INDEX.HTM, the server will reject yours—or overwrite the other!

If you alter any filenames or directory locations before publishing, be sure to check and adjust any links or other internal references (<FRAME SRC>, <IMG SRC>, and so on) to the files, as well.

❏ *The communications protocol required for uploading your files.* Many servers allow you to use the Web protocol (HTTP) for uploading files, whereas some require that files be uploaded via FTP.

❏ *The complete location (full URL) where your files will be stored.* You'll need to know the complete URL of the directory in which your files will be stored, including the server name, path to your directory, and the name of your directory. Ideally, you'll have your own separate directory for all your files. Having your own directory prevents conflicts that might arise if any file on the system (a page, image, or other file) uses the same filename as one of your files.

❏ *The rules or restrictions for filenames on the server.* As you learned in Chapter 3, different server platforms have different rules for filenames. For example, DOS servers do not permit filenames longer than eight characters, or file extensions of more than three characters. Ideally, you'll find out such restrictions before you create and name your files. But if you composed your document without first finding out about the server, you should check for naming restrictions and change any filenames as needed.

❏ *The amount disk space you're allowed.* If you're publishing your page on a corporate or university computer system, you may be required to keep the total disk space occupied by all of your files (including HTML files, images, external media, and scripts) below a certain minimum. If you're leasing space from a commercial Internet provider, your monthly fee is typically determined by the amount of space your files occupy. Therefore, it's important to know the size of your entire fileset. An easy way to find this out is to open Windows 95 Explorer, highlight all of the files in your document, and then read the total size of the selected files in the status bar at the bottom of the Explorer window. (See Figure 15.1.) Note that this works only if all your files are in the same directory; if some files, such as your image files or scripts, reside in separate directories, you'll need to find the number of bytes taken up in each directory used by your document and then add the directory totals together in order to find your document total.

❏ *Where you store your scripts.* If you use CGI scripts (see Chapter 12, "Creating Interactive Forms and Image Maps"), or server-side JavaScript scripts (see Chapter 13, "Using JavaScript"), you must first make sure your server supplier supports the type of script you have written. Then you must find out the specific procedures for uploading your scripts, which might be different from uploading the rest of your document. For example, CGI scripts are usually stored in a directory called CGI.BIN; uploading files to CGI.BIN might require a special password or other security procedure.

Figure 15.1.
Determining the total size of your document, shown at the bottom of the Explorer window.

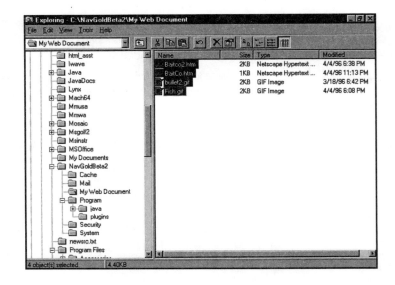

❏ *Your username and password*. Your server supplier should give you a username and password for uploading your files to the server. If your supplier does not require a password, find another supplier; your documents will not be secure on this server.

Files Checklist

If you have used relative (rather than absolute) links for local resources (other pages of your document, inline images, and so on), Gold can make sure the links still work properly on the server. See the Task section titled "One-Button Publishing" later in this chapter.

Once you know everything you need to know about the server, check (and recheck) your files and all links between files. Make sure that the links have been adjusted for any files you may have moved or renamed in the course of composing your document or preparing it for publishing.

Remember that the "links" you must check include not just the links that bind your pages together, but also the paths and filenames for the following:

❏ Inline images (see Chapter 6, "Working with Graphics")

❏ Links to external media (see Chapter 7, "Embedding Multimedia")

❏ <FRAME SRC> tags, which indicate the names and locations of the contents files that fill in frames (see Chapter 11, "Making Frames")

❏ Links to scripts

Ideally, all of the files for a document should be in the same directory on your PC, and that directory should contain nothing but the files for that one document. This scenario streamlines One-Button Publishing, as you'll discover later in this chapter.

Also, make absolutely sure that the filenames of all external media use the appropriate filename extension for the media type. (See Chapter 8.) The filename extensions are used by browsers to determine which helper application or plug-in to use to play or display the file. (If you find that you have to correct a filename extension, don't forget to go back and change the link!)

Setting Publishing Preferences

By setting up the Publish tab of the Editor Preferences dialog, you achieve two terrific things:

❏ You configure Gold for One-Button Publishing, which not only makes publishing more convenient but also makes it easy to update your document later.

❏ Using checkboxes, you set two options that help keep your files together and links accurate, to prevent the most common foul-ups that occur when copying documents to or from a server.

Follow these steps to set up the Publish tab:

1. From either the Browser or the Editor (it matters not which), choose **O**ptions | **E**ditor Preferences | **P**ublish. The Publish tab appears, as shown in Figure 15.2.

Figure 15.2.
Setting Editor Preferences.

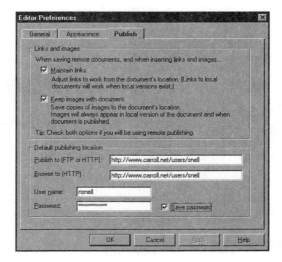

The checkmarks in the Publish tab work in two directions: They keep your files together and your links accurate when you upload to the server, and they do the same with documents, such as templates, you download from the Web to the Editor. (See Chapter 3.)

2. Under Links and images, make sure both checkboxes are checked. The first checkmark instructs Gold to automatically make all links among files in the same directory relative rather than absolute pathnames. (See Chapter 5,

"Linking Everywhere, Anywhere.") This ensures that the links will still work on the server, as long as you've uploaded all of the files and they still share the same directory.

The second checkmark automatically copies any inline image files of a document along with the document whenever an HTML file is uploaded to the server (with One-Button Publishing) or downloaded from the Web.

NOTE: Regardless of the settings in the Publish tab, it's a good practice to set up all links in your document, except those to remote resources (other URLs), as relative pathnames. (See Chapter 5.) The Publish settings might bail you out if you goof in this respect, but that doesn't mean that you shouldn't take care with pathnames.

Also note that the checkmarks in the Publish tab only work for image files stored in the same directory as the HTML file or as links to files in the same directory. If you have files stored in a separate location and the links or image tags are invalidated when the document is moved to the server, Gold is not going to save you. Therefore, check your links carefully.

3. Fill in all of the fields under Default publishing location by following these steps:

❑ In **P**ublish to, enter the location to which files will be uploaded when you use One-Button Publishing. This will probably be the same URL entered in the **B**rowse to field but might be a different location if your server provider requires that files be uploaded via FTP.

❑ In **B**rowse to, enter the Web URL that will be the document's address on the Web after it's uploaded.

❑ In User **n**ame, enter the user name your server supplier provided you for uploading your pages.

❑ In **P**assword, enter the password your server supplier provided you for uploading your pages. Note that the password does not appear as you type it, for security.

❑ Click OK.

If your PC is secure, check the checkbox next to Save password so you can upload your pages at any time, without entering a password. If you leave this box unchecked, the password must be entered every time you upload.

One-Button Publishing

If you have set up your publishing preferences and prepared your files, publishing your document is a snap. No, it's not really *One-Button Publishing*; that's the kind of thing

One-Button Publishing uploads files from a single directory only. If some of your document files are in a separate directory, you must repeat the One-Button Publishing procedure for each directory containing files in the document.

software marketing people like to call a *slogan*, whereas others just call it a *lie*. Nevertheless, publishing through Gold is quite painless.

To publish your document, follow these steps:

1. In the Editor, open the document or any page of the document (for multipage documents).

2. Click the Publish button on the toolbar or choose **F**ile I **Pu**blish. A dialog similar to the one shown in Figure 15.3 appears. The open file in the Editor is listed at the top of the window next to Publish.

Figure 15.3.
One-Button Publishing.

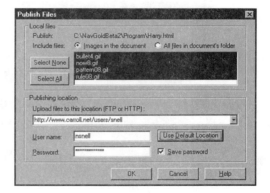

3. By default, the radio button next to **I**mages in the document is checked, and all inline images for the open file are listed in the Local files box. If the single HTML file and the images listed are all the files for your document, you're all set in the Local files box; you can skip to step 4.

   If your document contains multiple HTML files, links to external media files, frames, or anything other than just one HTML file and its inline images, you must select all the files for your document in the Local file box.

   First, display all files in the document's directory by clicking All **f**iles. When the list appears, all of the files are selected. If the directory contains nothing but the files for the one document, you're all set—move on to step 4. If not, you can click any filename to deselect it. If many files in the list are not part of your document, click Select **N**one to deselect all the files and then click the name of each file in the document until all the document's files are selected.

If you publish a document to the Default location, you can browse that document any time by choosing Go I Default Publish Location in the Browser.

4. If the entries you made in the Publish tab of the Editor Preferences dialog (see the section titled "Setting Publishing Preferences" earlier in this chapter) correctly identify the location to publish to (as well as the user name and password for uploading there), click Use Default Location to fill in the

Publishing location information. Otherwise, enter the correct upload address, **U**ser name, and **P**assword.

5. Click OK. All the selected files will be uploaded to the specified address.

> # NOTE:
> If you use One-Button Publishing to upload to an FTP address, Gold automatically transfers all of the files in FTP's binary transfer mode. The HTML files, which are text files, could be transferred via FTP's ASCII mode, but image files and many types of external media files might be corrupted by ASCII transfers. Binary mode transfers ensure that all files—text and otherwise—show up at the server ready to use.

Announcing Your Page

After your page is on the server, it doesn't do you much good if nobody knows it's there. The following sections contain tips for putting the word out.

Listing Your Page in Web Directories

First and foremost, you must get your site into the proper category listings of the major Web directories. Each has its own form and rules for entering and describing your site.

For example, to enter your site in the category listings for Yahoo, perhaps the most popular directory, you access Yahoo at

`http://www.yahoo.com`

When adding the URL of a business site to directories, do searches to find out how your competitors are listed. Then, be sure your document is associated with the same categories or keywords. If anyone finds your competitors, they find you, too.

Then, from Yahoo's top page, choose Add URL. A list of instructions appears. Following the instructions, you select a category in which you want your site listed and then scroll down to the form shown in Figure 15.4. In this form, you can enter your document's title, its URL, whether it uses Java applets or virtual worlds (VRML), and any additional categories in which you want it listed.

In contrast, Excite—one of the newer and hotter spider-based directories—allows you to *suggest* your site. (See Figure 15.5.) Like all spiders, Excite crawls around the Web cataloging its contents, and would eventually catalog your site. But by suggesting your site, you'll get it listed more quickly.

Excite can be found at

`http://www.excite.com`

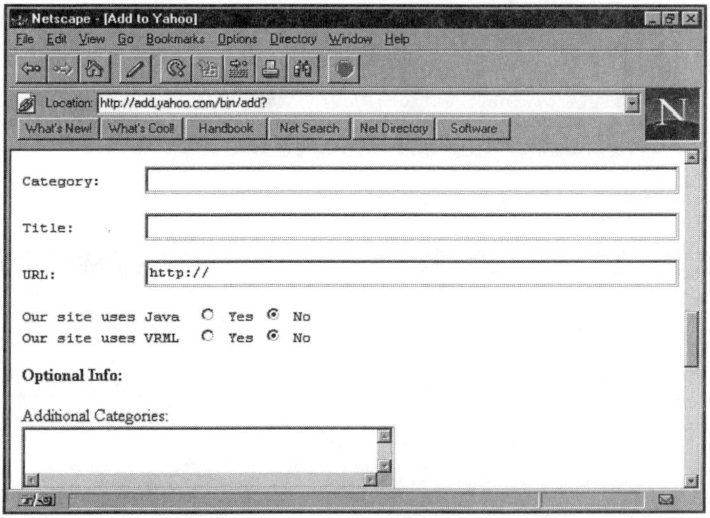

Figure 15.4.

Adding your site to the Yahoo directory.

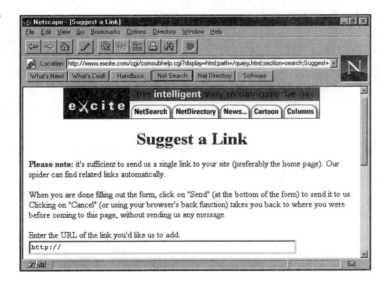

Figure 15.5.

Suggesting your site to Excite.

To make sure your page is located and properly cataloged by Web spiders, be sure to carefully and thoughtfully phrase the page's title, description, and keywords in the Document Properties section. Refer to Chapter 3.

There are many more directories and spiders on the Web, of course. You can always find the most popular ones by clicking the Search button in the Browser to reach Netscape's all-in-one search page. Select each directory, one at a time, from the text listings at the bottom of Netscape's search page to reach the directory or spider's home page. Instructions, a button, or some other indication of how to add a site usually appear on the home page.

Recently, some commercial services have emerged that offer (for a fee) to list your site with many of the most popular directories and spiders, all in one quick step. If you care more about saving time than saving money, check out The PostMaster (see Figure 15.6) at

`http://www.netcreations.com/postmaster/`

or Submit It! (see Figure 15.7) at

`http://www.submit-it.com/`

Figure 15.6.
The PostMaster.

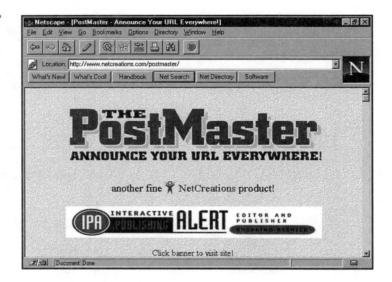

Figure 15.7.
Submit It!.

Publicizing Your Page off the Web

Don't forget that not all ways to publicize you Web page are on the Web (or even online). Be sure to list your Web site

- ❏ In your e-mail signature
- ❏ On your business cards
- ❏ On personal or company stationery
- ❏ In company advertising and marketing collateral

Workshop Wrap-Up

Publishing is a simple activity (and relatively foolproof) as long as you've taken care in the preparation of your page. Simple mistakes, like putting files for the same document in different directories, are the kinds of things that most often cause publishing problems. If you are careful with your filenames and locations, obey your server's rules, and configure Gold correctly, you'll find publishing one of the more satisfying aspects of authoring—the reward for a job well done.

Next Steps

Now...

To learn how to test and maintain your page after publishing, see Chapter 16, "Testing and Maintaining Web Documents."

Q&A

Q: I want one of those cool little counters on my page that tells me how many visitors I've had. How do I get one?

A: Counters require a special script as well as access to server logs. Typically, your Web provider will add one for you for free if you have a business account, or for a small fee if you have a personal account.

SIXTEEN

Testing and Maintaining Web Documents

The goofy thing about programming is that one tiny change can completely screw up an otherwise perfect program. That's why it's important that you carefully test your Web document not only after composing it, and not only after publishing it, but after each time you change it—and even when you don't change it. If you don't test your document thoroughly, you may be creating all sorts of problems for your visitors—which is not why you built your page.

Testing the Mechanics of Your Document

Okay, you know your document operates in the browser side of Gold without a hitch. So that means the underlying HTML code is all kosher, right?

Not necessarily. Browsers differ in the extent to which they ignore or forgive minor errors in HTML coding. If you make a small mistake in syntax, the page might look fine in one browser, show minor problems in another, and show still bigger problems in a third.

More importantly, HTML files can sometimes get slightly scrambled when moving from a PC to a server. That's because different computing platforms recognize text characters in the same way, but may have slightly different ways of representing blank spaces or carriage returns. The whole reason browsers ignore carriage returns and blank spaces in your HTML files (except in text using the Formatted property; see Chapter 4, "Composing, Editing, and Formatting Text") is so that changes to carriage returns and spaces caused by transferring a file between different computer systems won't cause problems. Still, the small changes that an intersystem transfer causes may create problems—problems you won't be aware of until the document is online and thoroughly tested.

The next few sections show you how to thoroughly test your document after it's online so that you can make sure your visitors have precisely the experience you want them to have.

Validating Your HTML Code

A good safeguard against minor HTML infractions is to check your document with an HTML validator. An HTML validator checks to see if your document follows the precise rules of HTML.

A good choice for validating your HTML is the WebTech Software HTML Validation Service, which is available at

`http://www.webtechs.com/html-val-svc/`

Figure 16.1 shows the service. Observe in the figure that a checkbox appears for Strict. Checking this box instructs the service to apply strict rules in determining your HTML compliance, which means it will report as errors stuff that really won't hurt your document, but that is not in strict compliance (for example, the use of outdated HTML tags). Unchecking Strict instructs the service to report only the coding errors that may have some effect on the performance of the document.

Next to the Strict checkbox are five radio buttons. Check one of these buttons to choose the level at which you want the code checked:

- ❏ Level 2 checks your code for compliance with HTML 2. Any coding errors, plus any code based on Netscape extensions that are not already part of the proposed HTML 3, will be reported as errors.
- ❏ Level 3 checks your code for compliance with the Netscape extensions and HTML 3. Any coding errors, plus any code based on Netscape extensions that are not already part of the proposed HTML 3, will be reported as errors.
- ❏ Mozilla checks your code for compliance with the Netscape extensions and HTML 3. Any coding errors will be reported.
- ❏ SoftQuad checks your code for compliance with extensions added by SoftQuad for the HoTMetaLPRO browser.

❏ Microsoft IE checks your code for compliance with Microsoft's Internet Explorer extensions, which support inline video, scrolling banners, and other enhancements.

Figure 16.1.
WebTech's software validation service.

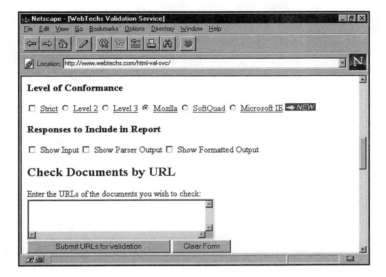

Which level should you test at? If you've used the Editor to create your page, you've almost certainly used Netscape extensions, since many of the best formatting capabilities in the Editor employ extensions. Choosing Mozilla will restrict the service's complaints to mistakes and prevent it from calling your extension-based formatting an error.

If you use the WebTech service to evaluate your document's viability in older browsers, you'll also want to view your document in such browsers, paying special attention to the aspects of the document WebTech identified as trouble spots.

On the other hand, if you're concerned about your document's viability among browsers outside the Netscape fold, testing at Level 2 or Level 3 will provide you with a report of potential trouble spots for users of HTML 2 or nonextension-supporting browsers.

Once you've selected your level, you can enter the URL of your published document and turn WebTech loose on it. The service produces a report showing any errors it encountered. You can then decide whether and how to edit your HTML code to resolve any errors you consider significant.

Testing Browser Variability

After checking out your code validity and making any corrections, you'll want to view your document (online, if possible) through a variety of browsers, just to see if any serious problems arise when using browsers other than Gold's browser or Navigator 3.0 (which is identical to Gold's browser). If you discover any problems in a particular browser environment, you must decide whether to adjust your document to eliminate the problem (which may involve compromising some of your formatting or other fancy features) or to sacrifice the performance of your document for one segment of the audience in order to preserve its performance for another.

The predominance of Navigator, coupled with the appeal of the extensions, is why so many pages tell their visitors that "This page is best viewed with Netscape Navigator." It's another way to say, "We'd rather compromise the display for non-Netscape users than live without the extensions."

Which browsers you test in depends largely on how much of the Web universe you want to appeal to. Nobody knows for sure how many people on the Web use a particular browser. At this writing, however, estimates say that at least 80 percent (some estimates say 90 percent) of Web denizens use some form of Netscape Navigator. But of those users, many still use older versions of Netscape Navigator—especially the popular version 1.2 (see Figure 16.2)—and may not have upgraded to version 2.0 or 3.0. The only really significant difference between the display of Navigator 2.0/3.0 and Navigator 1.2 is support for frames and JavaScript—2.0 and 3.0 do both, 1.2 does neither. Even if you don't use frames or JavaScript, it's a good idea to check out your page through a copy of Navigator 1.2 which, at this writing, is still available for download from Netscape (in a Windows 3.1, 16-bit version that runs fine on Windows 95).

Once you've tested for the Netscape world, there remains only 10 to 20 percent of Web users whose view of your document you don't know. Of those, a very high percentage probably use one of the many flavors of NCSA Mosaic. (See Figure 16.3.) Unfortunately, Mosaic is available in a staggering array of versions from different sources, and each version is different. But if you view your document through the current version of NCSA Mosaic, you'll know how your document appears to a significant chunk of the non-Netscape world—probably at least half of it.

You can find the download addresses for various shareware and freeware browsers in Chapter 17, "Developing Your Authoring Skills."

What else? Well, the up-and-comer lately is Microsoft's Internet Explorer (which is actually a flavor of Mosaic, or more a distant cousin). It supports pretty much the same extension set as Netscape 1.2. Since Explorer is free, it's easy to acquire and test in. But a fairly small portion of the Web uses Explorer now, and Explorer's display of your document will be virtually identical to that of Netscape 1.2. It's a good idea to test in one or the other, but it's not really necessary to test in both.

Finally, there are two more browser types to test in:

❏ Older, graphical browsers that don't support Netscape extensions, such as Cello (see Figure 16.4)

❏ Text-only browsers, such as Lynx (see Figure 16.5)

While such browsers are on their way out, you'll need to test in them and adjust your document as needed if you really want it to behave properly in any environment. However, you must accept that doing so inevitable forces you to restrict your document to the most minimal formatting. If you're really concerned about reaching everyone, supply your document in two versions: a fancy, extension-rich version and a very plain HTML 2–based version—and offer either from a universally visible top page (no frames, please!).

Figure 16.2.

A document in Gold's browser window (which is the same as in Navigator 2).

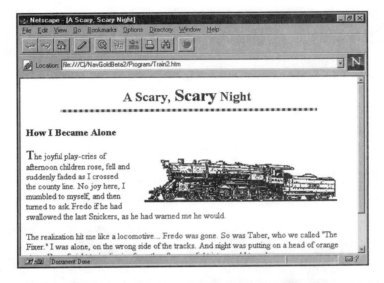

Figure 16.3.

The same document shown in Figure 16.2, through Mosaic.

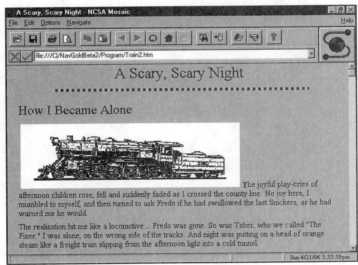

Figure 16.4.

The same document shown in Figure 16.2, through Cello.

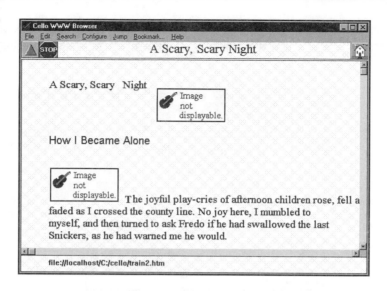

Figure 16.5.

The same document shown in Figure 16.2, through Lynx.

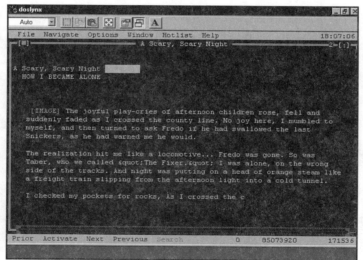

Testing Link Validity

Finally, it's important to test (and retest) all of the links in your document. Once you've verified the links among your own files—between your pages and to images and external media—you needn't recheck them unless you change a file. But if your document contains links to remote resources—other people's Web pages or any file other than those you control on the server—you'll need to check these links often, because the files they point to may have moved or their names may have changed.

Evaluating Your Document's Ergonomics

Ideally, this testing should be done before you publish, since your changes in response to the evaluation may be extensive. But by testing online, you can evaluate the real online experience, including such factors as response time and the perfor-mance of remote links.

The preceding sections in this chapter have explained only how to check your document's technical integrity. But what about its fuzzy qualities—its look, its feel, its *mise-en-scène*? And what about its interaction with visitors? Can they find what they came for? Do they see the parts of your message you want them to see? Do they naturally follow paths through your document to certain items, or are they frustrated by a lot of blind alleys and backtracking?

The best way to answer these questions would be to gather some friends (ideally friends who don't already know too much about your page or its subject) and/or cooperative strangers, and watch them browse your document (no coaching!). Watch what they choose to click on and what they skip. Note any time they move down a path and fail to find what they expected or hoped to find. And of course, listen to their comments.

Another way to evaluate usability is to consult the server logs. Server logs keep track of how many people visit your document, which of your files people visit most, and the order in which people tend to view your files. To learn more about analyzing the server logs, talk to your server administrator.

Finally, remember always to use a signature with your e-mail address. That way, people can send you comments and constructive criticism.

Updating Your Document

Updating your document is publishing redux:

❑ Publish your files as described in Chapter 15, "Publishing Web Documents." The new files automatically overwrite the old.

❑ Test, test, and test some more. (When finished, test again.)

When selecting files in the Publish Files dialog (see Figure 16.6), you need only select the files you have changed since the last time you published. If your document is complex, however, and if you have changed many files, you may find it's just as easy to republish the entire document, just to be sure you haven't overlooked a file that has changed. For example, people often remember to upload new pages that have been added to a document, but forget to upload new versions of old pages that now contain links to the new page.

When adding new pages to an existing document, carefully re-evaluate the structure and usability of the document. Over time, as pages and links are added, a previously well-structured document can begin to lose its structural integrity, branching off in illogical, patched-together ways.

Any time you add a page, re-evaluate the entire document's structure from the top. You may find a structurally consistent way to integrate new material. But eventually, after a number of changes and additions, it becomes time to start over, from the top, and reorganize all of the content back into a cohesive whole.

Figure 16.6.
Selecting files to update in the Publish Files dialog.

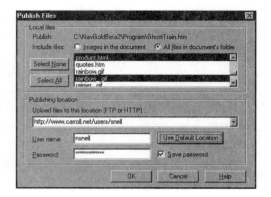

Workshop Wrap-Up

Testing is like changing diapers: It's not difficult to do, but it's an activity that invites procrastination. The longer you let the situation fester, the stinkier it gets—until the user cries out.

You don't want your visitors getting a nasty case of Web rash, do you? Your obligation to properly test your pages, and to retest them regularly, is as great as your desire to produce a good page in the first place.

Next Steps

Now...

Move on to Chapter 17, to learn how to move ahead as a Web author.

Q&A

Q: What if the HTML standard changes? Will my document suddenly not work in browsers that conform to a new standard or support new extensions?

A: Updates to HTML are *backward-compatible*; in other words, when HTML changes, new tags and attributes are added, as are new ways to do old things. But older approaches and tags still work, indefinitely.

SEVENTEEN

Developing Your Authoring Skills

This is it…*la chapitre finale*. And guess what? I tell you nothing here that immediately adds to your authoring skillset. (I know…it's a cheap trick. It's like when they forced you to show up for the last day of high school and then let you goof off all day anyway.)

What you do get in this chapter is a graduation speech, or rather, a send-off with a purpose. If you've hit most or all of this workshop, you've built a pretty solid foundation as an author. But there's always more to learn, always that one new trick that can make a good Web page into a great one. You now possess all the prereq-uisites needed to understand any advanced authoring information you may find in other books or on the Web.

So in this last hurrah, you'll find tips for developing your new skills, as well as resources for doing your post-grad work on Netscape, HTML, JavaScript, and much more.

How to Grow as a Web Author

What can you do next? How will you advance to the next level? And more important, how can you keep a keen edge on the skills you've already mastered? Here are a few important habits you can adopt to prosper and grow.

Observe

When on the Web, don't just browse. Think about the pages you visit. Study them carefully, not at a technical level, but at an aesthetic one. If a page impresses you, why? Is it the images, the layout, the writing, the colors, or some combination of these factors? Bookmark sites that impress you, and visit them often. Make a mental catalog of what grabs your interest (or loses it) as a browser. Odds are, many other people respond the same way.

Dissect

When a page really impresses you, save it in the Editor (click the Edit button while browsing the page) and then study it there. What types of image files were used, and what properties are applied to them? What is the flow of text elements and properties on the page? What special techniques show up in the HTML code if you view the source file (**E**dit I View Document **S**ource)?

In a multipage document, how much information is on a page? How many pages are there, and in what way are they interlinked?

Stay Current

Stay up on new developments, particularly in the areas of HTML 3 and JavaScript. The best way to do this is to visit Netscape's home page regularly and read any announcements posted there. You'll want to check out many of the other resources described later in this chapter.

For Further Reading

Here are some Sams titles that make excellent advanced reading following this workshop:

> *HTML & CGI Unleashed* (by John December and Mark Ginsburg)
>
> *Teach Yourself Java in 21 Days* (by Laura Lemay)
>
> *Teach Yourself Web Publishing with HTML in 14 Days, Professional Reference Edition* (by Laura Lemay)

A Directory of Author Resources Online

The following sections list URLs for Web pages that contain resources, reference material, or other information you may want to consult or exploit.

General Information on Navigator and Navigator Gold

Netscape Home
Linkname: Netscape Home Internet:Languages:Java
`http://home.netscape.com/`

Netscape Gold Rush Tool Chest
Linkname: Netscape Gold Rush Tool Chest
`http://home.netscape.com/assist/net_sites/starter/samples/index.html`

Off-the-Net Insider Newsletter
Linkname: Insider Newsletter
`http://home.netscape.com/assist/net_sites/off_the_net.html`

Netscape Page Starter Site
Linkname: Page Starter
`http://home.netscape.com/assist/net_sites/starter/index.html`

Templates

Cyberspace Portal
Linkname: Cyberspace Portal
`http://www.infomediacom.com/preview.htm`

Netscape Templates
Linkname: Templates
`http://home.netscape.com/assist/net_sites/starter/samples/templates/index.html`

WWW Homepage Starter Kit
Linkname: WWW Homepage Starter Kit
`http://www.isisnet.com/mlindsay/kitrex3.html`

JavaScript and Java

Netscape Information about JavaScript
Linkname: JavaScript
`http://home.netscape.com/comprod/products/navigator/version_2.0/script/index.html`

The Sun Microsystems Java Home Page
Linkname: Java: Programming for the Internet
`http://java.sun.com/`

A Java Applet Directory
Linkname: Gamelan
`http://www.gamelan.com/`

Yahoo Java Directory
Linkname: Yahoo–Computers and Internet:Languages:Java
`http://www.yahoo.com/Computers_and_Internet/Languages/Java/`

Netscape Information about Java

Linkname: Java Applets

`http://home.netscape.com/comprod/products/navigator/version_2.0/`
`java_applets/index.html`

Clip Art, Backgrounds, Etc.

Yahoo's Clip Art Directory

Linkname: Yahoo–Computers and Internet:Multimedia:Pictures:Clip Art

`http://www.yahoo.com/Computers_and_Internet/Multimedia/Pictures/Clip_Art/`

Index to Multimedia Information Sources

Linkname: Multimedia Information

`http://viswiz.gmd.de/MultimediaInfo/`

Internet Explorer Multimedia Gallery

Linkname: Internet Explorer Multimedia Gallery

`http://www.microsoft.com/ie/author/mmgallry/`

Netscape Page Starter Site

Linkname: Page Starter

`http://home.netscape.com/assist/net_sites/starter/index.html`

Free Graphics

Linkname: Free Graphics

`http://www.jgpublish.com/free.htm`

Clever Net

Linkname: `www4.clever.net/graphics/clip_art/clipart.html`

`http://www4.clever.net/graphics/clip_art/clipart.html`

Specifications for HTML, HTTP, and URLs

The HTML Level 2 Specification

Linkname: HTML Specification Review Materials

`http://www.w3.org/hypertext/WWW/MarkUp/html-spec/index.html`

The HTML+ 3.0 Draft Specification

Linkname: HTML+ (Hypertext markup format)

`http://www.hpl.hp.co.uk/people/dsr/html/CoverPage.html`

The HTTP Specification

Linkname: HTTP: A protocol for networked information

`http://info.cern.ch/hypertext/WWW/Protocols/HTTP/HTTP2.html`

Netscape's Extensions to HTML 2.0

Linkname: Extensions to HTML

`http://home.netscape.com/assist/net_sites/html_extensions.html`

Netscape's Extensions to HTML 3.0

Linkname: Extensions to HTML

`http://home.netscape.com/assist/net_sites/html_extensions_3.html`

Mosaic Tables

Linkname: HTML Tables in NCSA Mosaic

`http://www.ncsa.uiuc.edu/SDG/Software/XMosaic/table-spec.html`

Pointers to URL, URN, and URI Information and Specifications

Linkname: UR* and The Names and Addresses of WWW objects

`http://www.w3.org/hypertext/WWW/Addressing/Addressing.html`

Collections of General HTML and WWW Development Information

Yahoo's WWW Section

Linkname: Computers: World Wide Web

`http://www.yahoo.com/Computers/World_Wide_Web/`

The Virtual Library

Linkname: The Web Developer's Virtual Library

`http://WWW.Stars.com/`

The HTML FAQ

`http://www.umcc.umich.edu/~ec/www/html_faq.html`

The Developer's JumpStation

Linkname: OneWorld/SingNet WWW & HTML Developer's JumpStation

`http://oneworld.wa.com/htmldev/devpage/dev-page.html`

The Repository

Linkname: Subjective Electronic Information Repository

`http://cbl.leeds.ac.uk/nikos/doc/repository.html`

The Home of the WWW Consortium

Linkname: The World Wide Web Organization

`http://www.w3.org/`

Netscape's HTML Assistance Pages

Linkname: Creating Net Sites

`http://home.mcom.com/assist/net_sites/index.html`

The Spider's Web Pages on the Web

Linkname: (BOBAWORLD) World Wide Web

`http://gagme.wwa.com/~boba/web.html`

The HTML Writer's Guild

Linkname: The HTML Writer's Guide Website

`http://www.mindspring.com/guild/`

Web Directories

ALIWEB, A Great Web Index

Linkname: ALIWEB

`http://web.nexor.co.uk/public/aliweb/aliweb.html`

An Index of Indexes

Linkname: Web Indexes

http://www.biotech.washington.edu/WebCrawler/WebIndexes.html

Galaxy

Linkname: TradeWave Galaxy

http://www.einet.net/galaxy.html

Point

Linkname: Point Communications Corporation

http://www.pointcom.com/

W3 Virtual Library

Linkname: The World Wide Web Virtual Library: Subject Catalogue

http://www.w3.org/hypertext/DataSources/bySubject/Overview.html

Yahoo (My Favorite Index)

Linkname: Yahoo: A Guide to WWW

http://www.yahoo.com/

Web Search Tools

CUSI

Linkname: CUSI (Configurable Unified Search Interface)

http://Web.nexor.co.uk/susi/cusi.html

excite

Linkname: excite Netsearch

http://www.excite.com/

InfoSeek

Linkname: InfoSeek Net Search

http://www2.infoseek.com

Lycos

Linkname: The Lycos Home Page: Hunting WWW Information

http://www.lycos.com/

WebCrawler

Linkname: The WebCrawler

http://webcrawler.cs.washington.edu/WebCrawler/

Browsers

A General List

Linkname: WWW Client Software products

http://www.w3.org/hypertext/WWW/Clients.html

Netscape (Windows, Windows 95, Mac, X)

Linkname: Download Netscape Software

http://home.netscape.com/comprod/mirror/index.html

Microsoft Internet Explorer 2.0 (Windows 95)

Linkname: Download Microsoft Internet Explorer

http://www.msn.com/ie/ie.htm

NCSA Mosaic (X, Windows, Mac)

Linkname: NCSA Mosaic Home Page

`http://www.ncsa.uiuc.edu/SDG/Software/Mosaic/NCSAMosaicHome.html`

Lynx (UNIX and DOS)

Linkname: About Lynx

`http://www.cc.ukans.edu/about_lynx/`

WinWeb (Windows)

Linkname: EINet WinWeb

`http://www.einet.net/EINet/WinWeb/WinWebHome.html`

NetCruiser

LinkName: NetCruiser HomePort

`http://www.netcom.com/netcom/cruiser.html`

Web Explorer (OS/2 Warp)

`ftp://ftp.ibm.net/pub/WebExplorer/`

Cello (Windows)

Linkname: FAQ FOR CELLO (PART 1)

`http://www.law.cornell.edu/cello/cellofaq.html`

Tools for Images

Some Good Information about Transparent GIFs

Linkname: Transparent Background Images

`http://melmac.harris-atd.com/transparent_images.html`

giftrans

Linkname: source for giftrans

`ftp://ftp.rz.uni-karlsruhe.de/pub/net/www/tools/giftrans.c`

LView Pro for Windows 95 (at the OAK Simtel Mirror)

`ftp://oak.oakland.edu/SimTel/win3/graphics/lviewp1c.zip`

GIFTool (UNIX)

`http://www.homepages.com/tools/`

Sound and Video

RealAudio Home Page

Linkname: RealAudio

`http://www.realaudio.com/`

Underworld Sound Links

Linkname: Underworld Sound

`http://www.nd.edu/StudentLinks/jkeating/links/sound.html`

Index to Multimedia Information Sources

Linkname: Multimedia Information

`http://viswiz.gmd.de/MultimediaInfo/`

Internet Explorer Multimedia Gallery

Linkname: Internet Explorer Multimedia Gallery

`http://www.microsoft.com/ie/author/mmgallry/`

MPEG Archive

Linkname: MPEG Archive

http://www.powerweb.de/mpeg

WAVany (Windows Sound Converter)

ftp://oak.oakland.edu/SimTel/win3/sound/wvany10.zip

WHAM (Windows Sound Converter)

ftp://gatekeeper.dec.com/pub/micro/msdos/win3/sounds/wham133.zip

QFlat (Windows QuickTime "Flattener")

ftp://venice.tcp.com/pub/anime-manga/software/viewers/qtflat.zip

XingCD (AVI to MPEG Converter)

Send mail to xing@xingtech.com or call (805)473-0145

SmartCap (Windows QuickTime and AVI Converter)

ftp://ftp.intel.com/pub/IAL/Indeo_video/smartc.exe

The MPEG FAQ

Linkname: MPEG Moving Picture Expert Group FAQ

http://www.crs4.it/~luigi/MPEG/mpegfaq.html

Information on Making MPEG Movies

Linkname: How to make MPEG movies

http://www.arc.umn.edu/GVL/Software/mpeg.html

Servers

CERN HTTPD

Linkname: CERN Server User Guide

http://www.w3.org/httpd_3.0/

NCSA HTTPD

Linkname: NCSA httpd Overview

http://hoohoo.ncsa.uiuc.edu/docs/Overview.html

NCSA HTTPD for Windows

Linkname: NCSA httpd for Windows

http://www.city.net/win-httpd/

MacHTTP

Linkname: MacHTTP Info

http://www.biap.com/

Web Providers

An Index from HyperNews

Linkname: Leasing a Server

http://union.ncsa.uiuc.edu/HyperNews/get/www/leasing.html

Gateway Scripts and the Common Gateway Interface (CGI)

Yahoo's CGI List

Linkname: Yahoo–Computers and Internet:Internet:World Wide Web:CGI - Common Gateway Interface

```
http://www.yahoo.com/Computers_and_Internet/Internet/World_Wide_Web/
CGI_Common_Gateway_Interface/The_original_NCSA_CGI_documentation
```

Linkname: The Common Gateway Interface
```
http://hoohoo.ncsa.uiuc.edu/cgi/
```

The Specs for CGI

Linkname: The Common Gateway Interface Specification
```
http://hoohoo.ncsa.uiuc.edu/cgi/interface.html
```

Information about CGI in CERN HTTPD

Linkname: CGI/1.1 script support of the CERN Server
```
http://www.w3.org/hypertext/WWW/Daemon/User/CGI/Overview.html
```

A Library of C Programs to Help with CGI Development

Linkname: EIT's CGI Library
```
http://wsk.eit.com/wsk/dist/doc/libcgi/libcgi.html
```

An Index to HTML-related Programs Written in Perl

Linkname: Index of Perl/HTML archives
```
http://www.seas.upenn.edu/~mengwong/perlhtml.html
```

An Archive of CGI Programs at NCSA

Linkname: CGI sample scripts
```
ftp://ftp.ncsa.uiuc.edu/Web/httpd/Unix/ncsa_httpd/cgi
```

Un-CGI, a Program to Decode Form Input

Linkname: Un-CGI Version 1.2
```
http://www.hyperion.com/~koreth/uncgi.html
```

Forms and Image Maps

The Original NCSA Forms Documentation

Linkname: The Common Gateway Interface: FORMS
```
http://hoohoo.ncsa.uiuc.edu/cgi/forms.html
```

Mosaic Form Support Documentation

Linkname: Mosaic for X Version 2.0 Fill-Out Form Support
```
http://www.ncsa.uiuc.edu/SDG/Software/Mosaic/Docs/fill-out-forms/
overview.html
```

Image Maps in CERN HTTPD

Linkname: Clickable image support in CERN Server
```
http://www.w3.org/hypertext/WWW/Daemon/User/CGI/HTImageDoc.html
```

Image Maps in NCSA

Linkname: Graphical Information Map Tutorial

`http://wintermute.ncsa.uiuc.edu:8080/map-tutorial/image-maps.html`

Some Perl Scripts to Manage Forms

Linkname: CGI Form Handling in Perl

`http://www.bio.cam.ac.uk/web/form.html`

Mapedit: A Tool for Windows and X11 for Creating Image Map Map Files

Linkname: mapedit 1.1.2

`http://sunsite.unc.edu/boutell/mapedit/mapedit.html`

HTML Editors and Converters

A List of Converters and Editors, Updated Regularly

Linkname: Tools for WWW Providers

`http://www.w3.org/hypertext/WWW/Tools/`

A Better List of Converters

Linkname: Computers:World Wide Web:HTML Converters

`http://www.yahoo.com/Computers/World_Wide_Web/HTML_Converters/`

A Great List of Editors

Linkname: Computers:World Wide Web:HTML Editors

`http://www.yahoo.com/Computers/World_Wide_Web/HTML_Editors/`

Other

Tim Berners-Lee's Style Guide

Linkname: Style Guide for Online Hypertext

`http://www.w3.org/hypertext/WWW/Provider/Style/Overview.html`

The Yale HyperText Style Guide

Linkname: Yale C/AIM WWW Style Manual

`http://info.med.yale.edu/caim/StyleManual_Top.HTML`

Some Good Information on Registering and Publicizing Your Web Page

Linkname: A guide to publishing on the World Wide Web

`http://www.cl.cam.ac.uk/users/gdr11/publish.html`

Workshop Wrap-Up

That's all folks. Thanks for attending Laura Lemay's Web Workshop. Here's hoping you have a productive, enjoyable authoring experience.

Come back to this book for a refresher anytime. We're always open.

PART

V

Appendixes

AInstalling and Updating Netscape Navigator Gold

❑ Downloading Navigator Gold through a Web Browser

❑ Downloading Navigator Gold via an FTP Client

❑ To Install Navigator Gold

❑ Configuring the Browser

This appendix describes how to locate and install new versions of Netscape Navigator. Although it is possible to go directly to Netscape's FTP servers and download the file for Netscape Gold (as explained later in this chapter), this appendix recommends beginning at Netscape's home page and working down to the download from there.

Why start at the home page?

❑ On its home page, Netscape publishes announcements regarding new versions, beta versions, patches, plug-ins, and many other related issues. It's important that you see and read any announcements regarding Gold before downloading it.

❑ With each new version, the filename to download will change, and perhaps also the location. If you follow Netscape's menus to acquire the software (as described next), you'll always get the latest version. If you seek out a specific file to download, you might be getting an old version—if you get anything at all.

The only reason to go directly to the FTP servers without first going through Netscape's pages is if you do not already have a Web browser through which to navigate Netscape's Web site. In that case, follow the FTP instructions that appear later in this appendix.

NOTE: To install the fully licensed version of Netscape Navigator 3 that's included on the CD-ROM with this Deluxe Edition, consult the CD-ROM installation instructions on the page facing the book's inside back cover.

Downloading Navigator Gold through a Web Browser

To download Netscape Navigator Gold through a Web browser:

1. Access Netscape's home page at

   `http://home.netscape.com`

   If you are using Netscape, you might see the home page in its frames version. Otherwise, you'll see the no-frames version. Either way, read any important news about Gold or related products and then scroll down to Welcome to Netscape, as shown in Figure A.1 (as seen through Microsoft's Internet Explorer).

Figure A.1.
The bottom of Netscape's home page, as seen through Internet Explorer.

2. Choose Netscape Products. From the next page that appears, choose Navigator Gold from the NAVIGATOR column. A screen like Figure A.2 appears.

Figure A.2.

Reading about Navigator Gold.

3. Read through the information about Gold. Somewhere on this page, you'll find a link offering to Download Netscape Navigator Gold. Click it. The top of the download page appears.

4. Read through the download page and then choose NETSCAPE NAVIGATOR at the bottom of the page, as shown in Figure A.3.

Figure A.3.

Choosing to download Navigator.

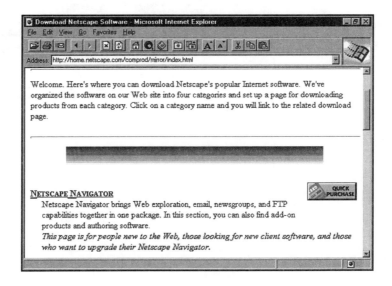

5. In the form that appears (see Figure A.4), make the selections as shown. (For Language and Location, you may choose whatever suits you.) This form ensures that you are offered the correct version for downloading. Click the button labeled Click to Display Download Sites.

Figure A.4.
Completing the form.

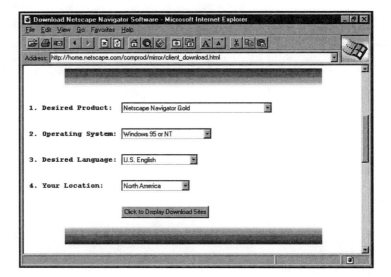

6. When done with the form, click the button labeled Click to Display Download Sites. A list appears like the one shown in Figure A.5. This list contains all the servers where the current version of Gold is stored.

Figure A.5.
Choosing a server.

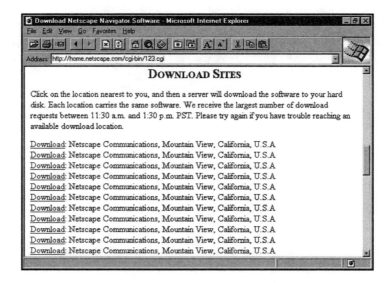

7. Click any of the Download buttons. If the server you select is not too busy, the download begins. (Complete the download according to the procedure for your browser.) A single, large .EXE file will be downloaded. This file contains the entire Gold program in a compressed format.

If the server you select is too busy, you'll receive a message to that effect. Try another Download link in the list shown in Figure A.5. At peak hours, you might need to try many servers to get through to one. If all the servers seem busy (or you get tired of trying), try again at a different hour.

Downloading Navigator Gold via an FTP Client

If you don't already have a Web browser, use your FTP client to download Gold via anonymous FTP. The Netscape mirror FTP servers (on which the latest versions of Netscape software are always stored) are

```
ftp2.netscape.com
ftp3.netscape.com
ftp4.netscape.com
ftp5.netscape.com
ftp6.netscape.com
ftp7.netscape.com
ftp8.netscape.com
ftp9.netscape.com
ftp10.netscape.com
ftp11.netscape.com
ftp12.netscape.com
ftp20.netscape.com
```

Once you're connected to the FTP server, locating the latest version of Gold may take a little exploring. Here's how to find it:

❏ The name of the directory in which Gold resides begins with a version number (2.0, 3.0, and so on) and gold; for example,

`/3.0gold/`

❏ To be sure you download the right version, look for a large .EXE file beginning with n32gold.

Finally, when you locate the file, be sure to download the file in Binary mode.

To Install Navigator Gold

Regardless of which method you use to download, you wind up with a single, very large .EXE file. This file is a self-extracting archive. (No unZIP software is required.)

To install Netscape Navigator Gold:

1. Double-click the file icon for the downloaded Gold file. A message appears while the InstallShield Wizard sets up. After a few moments, a Wizard appears like the one in Figure A.6.

Figure A.6.

Starting the Install Wizard.

It doesn't matter what directory the file is in when you start. During the installation, you'll have the chance to choose where to copy the decompressed files. You can begin the installation process wherever the file winds up after you download it.

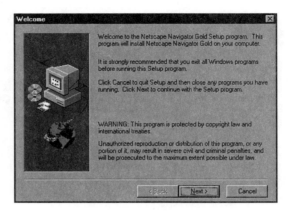

2. Click **N**ext. A screen appears, reporting the default directory into which Gold will be installed. (See Figure A.7.) If the selected directory is OK, click **N**ext. Otherwise, click **B**rowse and then choose a directory. If you enter a new directory after clicking **B**rowse, the Wizard creates the new directory for you.

Figure A.7.

Confirming the directory.

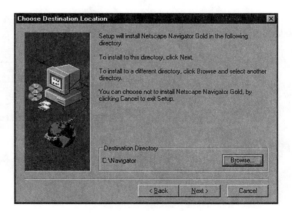

3. After you confirm the install directory, the Wizard decompresses the files and stores them in the chosen directory. A progress display appears while the files are being decompressed, as shown in Figure A.8.

Figure A.8.
Decompressing files.

4. After all of the files have been decompressed, the Wizard displays the message shown in Figure A.9.

Figure A.9.
A chance to visit Netscape.

Note that, except for registering Gold and configuring the Browser as described in the next section, the installation really is complete already. You might click **N**o at the dialog shown in Figure A.9 and get on with your work.

If you click **Y**es, the Wizard opens the Gold Browser, initiates Windows 95's Auto-Dial feature to connect to the Internet (if you do not use Auto-Dial, you'll have to initiate your Internet connection) and opens the page shown in Figure A.10. Through links on this page, you may register your copy of Gold and read helpful information from Netscape about how to configure Gold.

Figure A.10.

Netscape's setup page for Navigator (and Gold).

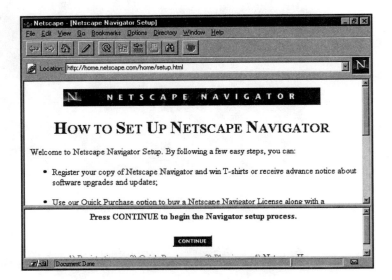

Configuring the Browser

All of the configuration required in the Editor side of Gold is explained within the chapters of this book. But you do need to do a little configuring of the Browser after installation, in order to use it fully.

All of the Browser's Preferences tabs are optional. But before you start working with the Browser, it's a good idea to set up your Mail and News preferences (see Figure A.11) by choosing **O**ptions I **M**ail and News Preferences. Then fill in the Servers and Identity tabs to set up your e-mail and newsgroup access.

Figure A.11.

Configuring mail and news access in the Browser.

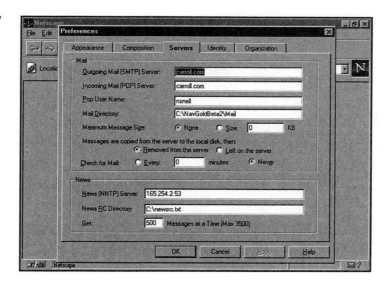

Summary of HTML Commands

This appendix is a reference to the HTML tags (and color values) you can use in your documents, according to the HTML 2.0 specification. In addition, tags defined in both the HTML 3.0 and Netscape Navigator 2.0/3.0 specifications are listed. Tags supported by HTML 3.0 and Navigator 2.0/3.0 are listed as (HTML 3.0), whereas tags that are currently only available in Navigator 2.0/3.0 are listed as (NHTML). There are also a couple of tags listed that Navigator 2.0/3.0 does not yet support; these are listed as (HTML 3.0 only).

HTML Tags

This section lists and explains all of the HTML tags that you may want to use in documents you create with Gold or in an external HTML editor such as HotDog.

To learn the general methods for adding these tags to a document, see Chapter 9, "Editing HTML Source Code."

To learn more about the specific applications of these tags, see Chapters 10 through 14.

Comments

`<!--...-->`

Any text enclosed within a comment tag is completely ignored by the Web browser. This includes tags, elements, and entities.

`<!DOCTYPE HTML PUBLIC "-//Netscape Comm. Corp.//DTD HTML//EN">`

Used with HTML document validation systems such as Halsoft at `http://www.halsoft.com/html-val-svc/` to indicate the level of HTML support included in a document. If included in a document, this tag must be placed on the very first line, before the <HTML> tag.

`<!DOCTYPE HTML PUBLIC "-//Netscape Comm. Corp. Strict//DTD HTML//EN">`

Used to indicate a more strict set of compliance tests for validation systems such as Halsoft. For more information, visit the Halsoft site listed previously. This site contains both the document validation system and a range of files covering *document type definitions* (DTD) and HTML standards.

Structure Tags

`<HTML>...</HTML>`

Encloses the entire HTML document.

Can Include: <HEAD> <BODY> <FRAMESET>

`<HEAD>...</HEAD>`

Encloses the head of the HTML document.

Can Include: <TITLE> <ISINDEX> <BASE> <NEXTID> <LINK> <META> <SCRIPT>

Allowed Inside: <HTML>

`<BODY>...</BODY>`

Encloses the body (text and tags) of the HTML document.

Attributes:

BACKGROUND="..."	(HTML 3.0) The name or URL for an image to tile on the page background.
BGCOLOR="..."	(NHTML) The color of the page background.
TEXT="..."	(NHTML) The color of the page's text.
LINK="..."	(NHTML) The color of unfollowed links.
ALINK="..."	(NHTML) The color of activated links.
VLINK="..."	(NHTML) The color of followed links.

Can Include: <H1> <H2> <H3> <H4> <H5> <H6> <P> <OL> <UL> <DIR> <MENU> <DL> <PRE> <BLOCKQUOTE> <FORM> <ISINDEX> <HR> <ADDRESS> <TABLE> <SCRIPT> <APPLET> <EMBED>

Allowed Inside: <HTML>

Tags That Can Be Included Inside the <HEAD> Block

<TITLE>...</TITLE>

Indicates the title of the document.

Allowed Inside: <HEAD>

<BASE>

Defines base values for the current document.

Attributes:

HREF="..."	Override the base URL of the current document.
TARGET="..."	Define a default target window for all links in the current document.

Allowed Inside: <HEAD>

<ISINDEX>

Indicates that the document is a gateway script that allows searches.

Attributes:

PROMPT="..."	(HTML 3.0) The prompt for the search field.

Allowed Inside: <BLOCKQUOTE> <BODY> <DD> <FORM> <HEAD> <LI> <TABLE>

\<LINK\>

Indicates the relationship between the document and some other document. Generally used only by HTML-generating tools.

Attributes:

HREF="..."	The URL of the referenced HTML document.
REL="..."	The forward relationship.
REV="..."	A reverse relationship, usually the mailto address of the document's author.
URN="..."	Universal resource number.
TITLE="..."	The link's title.
METHODS="..."	Supported public methods of the object.

Allowed Inside: \<HEAD\>

\<META\>

Used to simulate HTTP response header messages in a HTML document.

Attributes:

HTTP-EQUIV="..."	HTTP response header name.
CONTENT="..."	Value assigned to the response header.
NAME="..."	Meta information name.

Allowed Inside: \<HEAD\>

\<NEXTID\>

Indicates the next document after this one (as might be defined by a tool to manage HTML documents in series).

Attributes:

N="..."

Allowed Inside: \<HEAD\>

Headings

All heading tags have the following characteristics:

Attributes:

ALIGN="CENTER"	(HTML 3.0) Centers the heading.
ALIGN="LEFT"	(HTML 3.0) Left justifies the heading.

`ALIGN="RIGHT"`   (HTML 3.0) Right justifies the heading.

`ALIGN="JUSTIFY"`   (HTML 3.0 only) Block justifies the heading where possible.

Can Include: <A> <IMG>
 <BIG> <B> <BLINK> <I> <SMALL> <SUB> <SUP> <TT> <CITE> <CODE> <DFN> <EM> <KBD> <SAMP> <STRONG> <VAR>

Allowed Inside: <BLOCKQUOTE> <BODY> <FORM>

<H1>...</H1>

A first-level heading.

<H2>...</H2>

A second-level heading.

<H3>...</H3>

A third-level heading.

<H4>...</H4>

A fourth-level heading.

<H5>...</H5>

A fifth-level heading.

<H6>...</H6>

A sixth-level heading.

Paragraphs

<P>...</P>

A plain paragraph. The closing tag (`</P>`) is optional.

`ALIGN=CENTER`   (HTML 3.0) Centers the paragraph.

`ALIGN=LEFT`   (HTML 3.0) Left justifies the paragraph.

`ALIGN=RIGHT`   (HTML 3.0) Right justifies the paragraph.

`ALIGN=JUSTIFY`   (HTML 3.0 only) Block justifies the paragraph where possible.

Can Include `<A>` `<IMG>` `<BR>` `<BIG>` `<B>` `<BLINK>` `<I>` `<SMALL>` `<SUB>` `<SUP>` `<TT>` `<CITE>` `<CODE>` `<DFN>` `<EM>` `<KBD>` `<SAMP>` `<STRONG>` `<VAR>`

Allowed Inside: `<BLOCKQUOTE>` `<BODY>` `<DD>` `<FORM>` `<LI>` `<TABLE>`

`<DIV>...</DIV>`

Declare a block of text, but unlike the `<P>` tag, the `<DIV>` tag does not add a trailing double-line space.

`ALIGN=CENTER`	(HTML 3.0) Centers the text defined by the division.
`ALIGN=LEFT`	(HTML 3.0) Left justifies the text defined by the division.
`ALIGN=RIGHT`	(HTML 3.0) Right justifies the text defined by the division.
`ALIGN=JUSTIFY`	(HTML 3.0 only) Block justifies the text defined by the division where possible.

Can Include: `<A>` `<IMG>` `<BR>` `<BIG>` `<B>` `<BLINK>` `<I>` `<SMALL>` `<SUB>` `<SUP>` `<TT>` `<CITE>` `<CODE>` `<DFN>` `<EM>` `<KBD>` `<SAMP>` `<STRONG>` `<VAR>` `<TABLE>`

Allowed Inside: `<BLOCKQUOTE>` `<BODY>` `<DD>` `<FORM>` `<LI>` `<TABLE>`

Links

`<A>...</A>`

With the HREF attribute, creates a hyperlink to another document or anchor; with the NAME attribute, creates an anchor that can be linked to.

Attributes:

`HREF="..."`	The URL pointed to by a link.
`TARGET="..."`	The target window for the new document.
`NAME="..."`	The anchor name for a reference anchor.

Can Include: `<IMG>` `<BR>` `<BIG>` `<B>` `<BLINK>` `<I>` `<SMALL>` `<SUB>` `<SUP>` `<TT>` `<CITE>` `<CODE>` `<DFN>` `<EM>` `<KBD>` `<SAMP>` `<STRONG>` `<VAR>` `<TABLE>`

Allowed Inside: `<ADDRESS>` `<BIG>` `<B>` `<BLINK>` `<I>` `<SMALL>` `<SUB>` `<SUP>` `<TT>` `<CITE>` `<CODE>` `<DFN>` `<EM>` `<KBD>` `<SAMP>` `<STRONG>` `<VAR>` `<BLOCKQUOTE>` `<DD>` `<FORM>` `<LI>` `<TABLE>`

Lists

<OL>...</OL>

An ordered (numbered) list.

Attributes:

TYPE="..."   (NHTML) The type of numerals to label the list with.
Possible values are A, a, I, i, and 1.

START="..."   (NHTML) The value to start this list with.

Can Include: <LI>

Allowed Inside: <BLOCKQUOTE> <BODY> <DD> <FORM> <LI> <TABLE>

<UL>...</UL>

An unordered (bulleted) list.

Attributes:

TYPE="..."   (NHTML) the bullet dingbat to use to mark list items.
Possible values are DISC, CIRCLE, and SQUARE.

Can Include: <LI>

Allowed Inside: <BLOCKQUOTE> <BODY> <DD> <FORM> <LI> <TABLE>

<MENU>...</MENU>

A menu list of items. (Note: Removed from the HTML 3.0 specification.)

Can Include: <LI>

Allowed Inside: <BLOCKQUOTE> <BODY> <DD> <FORM> <LI> <TABLE>

<DIR>...</DIR>

A directory listing; items are generally smaller than 20 characters. (Note: No longer supported in the HTML 3.0 specification.)

Can Include: <LI>

Allowed Inside: <BLOCKQUOTE> <BODY> <DD> <FORM> <LI> <TABLE>

<LI>

A list item for use with <OL>, <UL>, <MENU>, or <DIR>

Attributes:

TYPE="..."   (NHTML) The type of bullet or number to label an item with. Possible values are DISC, CIRCLE, SQUARE, A, a, I, i, and 1.

VALUE="..."   (NHTML) The numeric value this list item should have (affects this item and all below it in <OL> lists).

Can Include: <A> <IMG>
 <BIG> <B> <BLINK> <I> <SMALL> <SUB> <SUP> <TT> <CITE> <CODE> <DFN> <EM> <KBD> <SAMP> <STRONG> <VAR> <P> <DIV> <OL> <UL> <DIR> <MENU> <DL> <PRE> <BLOCKQUOTE>

Allowed Inside: <DIR> <MENU> <OL> <UL>

<DL>...</DL>

A definition or glossary list. The COMPACT attribute specifies a format that takes less whitespace to present.

Attributes: COMPACT

Can Include: <DT> <DD>

Allowed Inside: <BLOCKQUOTE> <BODY> <DD> <FORM> <LI> <TABLE>

<DT>

A definition term, as part of a definition list.

Can Include: <A> <IMG>
 <BIG> <B> <BLINK> <I> <SMALL> <SUB> <SUP> <TT> <CITE> <CODE> <DFN> <EM> <KBD> <SAMP> <STRONG> <VAR>

Allowed Inside: <DL>

<DD>

The corresponding definition to a definition term, as part of a definition list.

Can Include: <A> <IMG>
 <BIG> <B> <BLINK> <I> <SMALL> <SUB> <SUP> <TT> <CITE> <CODE> <DFN> <EM> <KBD> <SAMP> <STRONG> <VAR> <P> <OL> <UL> <DIR> <MENU> <DL> <PRE> <BLOCKQUOTE> <FORM> <ISINDEX> <TABLE>

Allowed Inside: <DL>

Character Formatting

All the character formatting tags have these features:

Can Include: <A> <IMG>
 <BIG> <B> <BLINK> <I> <SMALL> <SUB> <SUP> <TT> <CITE> <CODE> <DFN> <EM> <KBD> <SAMP> <STRONG> <VAR>

Allowed Inside: <A> <ADDRESS> <BIG> <B> <BLINK> <I> <SMALL> <SUB> <SUP> <TT> <CITE> <CODE> <DFN> <EM> <KBD> <SAMP> <STRONG> <VAR> <DD> <DT> <H1> <H2> <H3> <H4> <H5> <H6> <LI> <P> <PRE> <TABLE>

<BIG>...</BIG>

Big text: Text uses larger font than standard text.

<B>...</B>

Bold: Bold text.

<BLINK>...</BLINK>

Blinking: Blinking text.

<I>...</I>

Italic: Italic text.

<SMALL>...</SMALL>

Small Text: Text uses smaller font than standard text.

_{...}

Subscript: Text is subscripted.

^{...}

Superscript: Text is superscripted.

<TT>...</TT>

Typewriter: Text uses monospaced typewriter font.

<CITE>...</CITE>

Citation: For quotes and references.

<CODE>...</CODE>

Program code: For computer program source code.

<DFN>...</DFN>

Defined: For word definitions.

<EM>...</EM>

Emphasis: When italic emphasis is required.

<KBD>...</KBD>

Keyboard: When showing text that users need to type in.

<SAMP>...</SAMP>

Sample: For examples.

<STRONG>...</STRONG>

Strong: When bold text is required.

<VAR>...</VAR>

Variable: For names of program variables.

Other Text Layout Elements

The following tags create standard page elements that resist categorization because they are not exactly text elements (although they may format text), but not exactly images or links, either. Call 'em *miscellaneous*.

<HR>

A horizontal rule line.

Attributes:

SIZE="..."	(NHTML) The thickness of the rule, in pixels.
WIDTH="..."	(NHTML) The width of the rule, in pixels.
ALIGN="..."	(NHTML) How the rule line will be aligned on the page. Possible values are LEFT, RIGHT, and CENTER.

NOSHADE="..."   (NHTML) Causes the rule line to be drawn as a solid color with no shading.

Allowed Inside: <BLOCKQUOTE> <BODY> <FORM> <PRE> <TABLE>

A line break.

Attributes:

CLEAR="..."   (HTML 3.0) causes the text to stop flowing around any images. Possible values are RIGHT, LEFT, and ALL.

Allowed Inside: <A> <ADDRESS> <BIG> <B> <BLINK> <I> <SMALL> <SUB> <SUP> <TT> <CITE> <CODE> <DFN> <EM> <KBD> <SAMP> <STRONG> <VAR> <DD> <DT> <H1> <H2> <H3> <H4> <H5> <H6> <LI> <P> <PRE> <TABLE>

<NOBR>...</NOBR> (NHTML)

Causes the enclosed text not to wrap at the edge of the page.

Allowed Inside: <A> <ADDRESS> <BIG> <B> <BLINK> <I> <SMALL> <SUB> <SUP> <TT> <CITE> <CODE> <DFN> <EM> <KBD> <SAMP> <STRONG> <VAR> <DD> <DT> <H1> <H2> <H3> <H4> <H5> <H6> <LI> <P> <PRE> <TABLE>

<WBR> (NHTML)

Wrap the text at this point only if necessary.

Allowed Inside: <A> <ADDRESS> <BIG> <B> <BLINK> <I> <SMALL> <SUB> <SUP> <TT> <CITE> <CODE> <DFN> <EM> <KBD> <SAMP> <STRONG> <VAR> <DD> <DT> <H1> <H2> <H3> <H4> <H5> <H6> <LI> <P> <PRE> <TABLE>

<BLOCKQUOTE>... </BLOCKQUOTE>

Used for long quotes or citations.

Can Include: <BLOCKQUOTE> <IMG> <H1> <H2> <H3> <H4> <H5> <H6> <P> <OL> <UL> <DIR> <MENU> <DL> <PRE> <FORM> <ISINDEX> <HR> <ADDRESS> <TABLE>

Allowed Inside: <BLOCKQUOTE> <BODY> <DD> <FORM> <LI> <TABLE>

<CENTER>...</CENTER>

All the content enclosed within these tags is centered. This tag is being phased out in favor of <P ALIGN=CENTER> and <DIV ALIGN=CENTER>.

Can Include: `<A>` `<IMG>` `<ADDRESS>` `<BIG>` `<B>` `<BLINK>` `<I>` `<SMALL>` `<SUB>` `<SUP>` `<TT>` `<CITE>` `<CODE>` `<DFN>` `<EM>` `<KBD>` `<SAMP>` `<STRONG>` `<VAR>` `<DD>` `<DT>` `<H1>` `<H2>` `<H3>` `<H4>` `<H5>` `<H6>` `<LI>` `<P>` `<PRE>` `<TABLE>`

Allowed Inside: `<BLOCKQUOTE>` `<BODY>` `<DD>` `<FORM>` `<LI>` `<TABLE>`

`<ADDRESS>...</ADDRESS>`

Used for signatures or general information about a document's author.

Can Include: `<A>` `<IMG>` `<BIG>` `<B>` `<BLINK>` `<I>` `<SMALL>` `<SUB>` `<SUP>` `<TT>` `<CITE>` `<CODE>` `<DFN>` `<EM>` `<KBD>` `<SAMP>` `<STRONG>` `<VAR>` `<DD>` `<DT>` `<H1>` `<H2>` `<H3>` `<H4>` `<H5>` `<H6>` `<LI>` `<P>` `<PRE>` `<TABLE>`

Allowed Inside: `<BLOCKQUOTE>` `<BODY>` `<FORM>`

Font Sizes (NHTML)

`<FONT>...</FONT>`

Changes the size or color of the font for the enclosed text.

Attributes:

`SIZE="..."`	The size of the font, from 1 to 7. Default is 3. Can also be specified as a value relative to the current size, for example, +2.
`COLOR="..."`	The color of the font. See the section titled "Colors by Name and Hex Value" later in this appendix.

Can Include: `<A>` `<IMG>` `<BIG>` `<B>` `<BLINK>` `<I>` `<SMALL>` `<SUB>` `<SUP>` `<TT>` `<CITE>` `<CODE>` `<DFN>` `<EM>` `<KBD>` `<SAMP>` `<STRONG>` `<VAR>` `<DD>` `<DT>` `<LI>` `<P>` `<PRE>` `<TABLE>`

Allowed Inside: `<A>` `<ADDRESS>` `<BIG>` `<B>` `<BLINK>` `<I>` `<SMALL>` `<SUB>` `<SUP>` `<TT>` `<CITE>` `<CODE>` `<DFN>` `<EM>` `<KBD>` `<SAMP>` `<STRONG>` `<VAR>` `<DD>` `<DT>` `<H1>` `<H2>` `<H3>` `<H4>` `<H5>` `<H6>` `<LI>` `<P>` `<PRE>` `<TABLE>`

`<BASEFONT>`

Sets the default size of the font for the current page.

Attributes:

`SIZE="..."`	The default size of the font, from 1 to 7. Default is 3.

Allowed Inside: `<A>` `<ADDRESS>` `<BIG>` `<B>` `<BLINK>` `<I>` `<SMALL>` `<SUB>` `<SUP>` `<TT>` `<CITE>` `<CODE>` `<DFN>` `<EM>` `<KBD>` `<SAMP>` `<STRONG>` `<VAR>` `<DD>` `<DT>` `<LI>` `<P>` `<PRE>` `<TABLE>`

Images

`<IMG>`

Insert an inline image into the document.

Attributes:

ISMAP	This image is a clickable image map.
SRC="..."	The URL of the image.
ALT="..."	A text string that will be displayed in browsers that cannot support images.
ALIGN="..."	Determines the alignment of the given image. If LEFT or RIGHT (HTML 3.0, NHTML), the image is aligned to the left or right column, and all following text flows beside that image. All other values such as TOP, MIDDLE, BOTTOM, or (NHTML) TEXTTOP, ABSMIDDLE, BASELINE, and ABSBOTTOM, determine the vertical alignment of this image with other items in the same line.
VSPACE="..."	The space between the image and the text above or below it.
HSPACE="..."	The space between the image and the text to its left or right.
WIDTH="..."	(HTML 3.0) The width, in pixels, of the image. If WIDTH is not the actual width, the image is scaled to fit.
HEIGHT="..."	(HTML 3.0) The width, in pixels, of the image. If HEIGHT is not the actual height, the image is scaled to fit.
BORDER="..."	(NHTML) Draws a border of the specified value in pixels to be drawn around the image. In the case of images that are also links, BORDER changes the size of the default link border.
LOWSRC="..."	(NHTML) The path or URL of an image that will be loaded first, before the image specified in SRC. The value of LOWSRC is usually a smaller or lower-resolution version of the actual image.
USEMAP="..."	(NHTML) Used to associate an image with a client-side image map specified by `<MAP NAME=mapname>`.

Allowed Inside: `<A>` `<ADDRESS>` `<BIG>` `<B>` `<BLINK>` `<I>` `<SMALL>` `<SUB>` `<SUP>` `<TT>` `<CITE>` `<CODE>` `<DFN>` `<EM>` `<KBD>` `<SAMP>` `<STRONG>` `<VAR>` `<DD>` `<DT>` `<H1>` `<H2>` `<H3>` `<H4>` `<H5>` `<H6>` `<LI>` `<P>` `<PRE>` `<TABLE>`

\<MAP>...\</MAP>

Define a map for a client side image map.

Attributes:

    NAME="..."   Used to define the map's name.

Can Include: \<AREA>

Allowed Inside: \<BODY>

\<AREA>...\</AREA>

Define a clickable region for a client side image map.

Attributes:

    TYPE="..."   Used to indicating the type of region bounded by the \<AREA> tag. Possible values are RECT, POLY, and CIRCLE.

    COORDS="..."   This attribute describes the points bounding the region described by the \<AREA> tag.

    HREF="..."   The URL to load when the region bounded by the \<AREA> tag is clicked on.

Allowed Inside: \<MAP>

Forms

\<FORM>...\</FORM>

Indicates a form.

Attributes:

    ACTION="..."   The URL of the script to process this form input.

    METHOD="..."   How the form input will be sent to the gateway on the server side. Possible values are GET and POST.

    ENCTYPE="..."   Only values currently supported are application/x-www-form-urlencoded and multipart/form-data (NHTML).

    TARGET="..."   (NHTML) Target window for response following form submission.

Can Include: \<H1> \<H2> \<H3> \<H4> \<H5> \<H6> \<P> \<OL> \<UL> \<DIR> \<MENU> \<DL> \<PRE> \<BLOCKQUOTE> \<ISINDEX> \<HR> \<ADDRESS> \<INPUT> \<SELECT> \<TEXTAREA> \<TABLE>

Allowed Inside: \<BLOCKQUOTE> \<BODY> \<DD> \<LI>

\<INPUT>

An input widget for a form.

Attributes:

TYPE="..."	The type for this input widget. Possible values are CHECKBOX, FILE (NHTML), HIDDEN, PASSWORD, RADIO, RESET, SUBMIT, TEXT, or IMAGE (HTML 3.0 only).
NAME="..."	The name of this item, as passed to the gateway script as part of a name/value pair.
VALUE="..."	For a text or hidden widget, the default value; for a checkbox or radio button, the value to be submitted with the form; for Reset or Submit buttons, the label for the button itself.
SRC="..."	The source file for an image.
CHECKED	For check boxes and radio buttons, indicates that the widget is checked.
SIZE="..."	The size, in characters, of a text widget.
MAXLENGTH="..."	The maximum number of characters that can be entered into a text widget.
ALIGN="..."	For images in forms, determines how the text and image will align (same as with the \<IMG> tag).

Allowed Inside: \<FORM>

\<TEXTAREA>...\</TEXTAREA>

Indicates a multiline text entry widget.

Attributes:

NAME="..."	The name to be passed to the gateway script as part of the name/value pair.
ROWS="..."	The number of rows this text area displays.
COLS="..."	The number of columns (characters) this text area displays.
WRAP="OFF"	Wrapping doesn't happen. Lines are sent exactly as typed.
WRAP="VIRTUAL"	The display word wraps, but long lines are sent as one line without new lines.
WRAP="PHYSICAL"	The display word wraps, and the text is transmitted at all wrap points.

Allowed inside: <FORM>

<SELECT>...</SELECT>

Creates a menu or scrolling list of possible items.

Attributes:

NAME="..."	The name that is passed to the gateway script as part of the name/value pair.
SIZE="..."	The number of elements to display. If SIZE is indicated, the selection becomes a scrolling list. If no SIZE is given, the selection is a pop-up menu.
MULTIPLE	Allows multiple selections from the list.

Can Include: <OPTION>

Allowed Inside: <FORM>

<OPTION>

Indicates a possible item within a <SELECT> widget.

Attributes:

SELECTED	With this attribute included, the <OPTION> will be selected by default in the list.
VALUE="..."	The value to submit if this <OPTION> is selected when the form is submitted.

Allowed Inside: <SELECT>

Tables (HTML 3.0)

The following tags are used to create tables. To learn more about applying these tags, see Chapter 10, "Building Tables."

<TABLE>...</TABLE>

Creates a table, which can contain a caption (<CAPTION>) and any number of rows (<TR>).

Attributes:

BORDER="..."	Indicates whether the table should be drawn with or without a border. In Netscape, BORDER can also have a value indicating the width of the border.

CELLSPACING="..." (NHTML) The amount of space between the cells in the table.

CELLPADDING="..." (NHTML) The amount of space between the edges of the cell and its contents.

WIDTH="..." (NHTML) The width of the table on the page, in either exact pixel values or as a percentage of page width.

ALIGN="..." Determines the alignment of the given table. If LEFT or RIGHT (HTML 3.0, NHTML), the image is aligned to the left or right column, and all following text flows beside that image. If CENTER appears as the value for ALIGN=, then the table is aligned with the center of the page (HTML 3.0 only).

BGCOLOR="..." (NHTML) The background color of the cells in the table (Navigator 3.0 only).

Can Include: <CAPTION> <TR>

Allowed Inside: <BLOCKQUOTE> <BODY> <DD> <LI> <TABLE>

<CAPTION>...</CAPTION>

The caption for the table.

Attributes:

ALIGN="..." The position of the caption. Possible values are TOP and BOTTOM.

<TR>...</TR>

Defines a table row, containing headings and data (<TR> and <TH> tags).

Attributes:

ALIGN="..." The horizontal alignment of the contents of the cells within this row. Possible values are LEFT, RIGHT, and CENTER.

VALIGN="..." The vertical alignment of the contents of the cells within this row. Possible values are TOP, MIDDLE, BOTTOM, and BASELINE (NHTML).

BGCOLOR="..." (NHTML) The background color of the cells in the row (Navigator 3.0 only).

Can Include: <TH> TD>

Allowed Inside: <TABLE>

`<TH>...</TH>`

Defines a table heading cell.

Attributes:

`ALIGN="..."`	The horizontal alignment of the contents of the cell. Possible values are LEFT, RIGHT, and CENTER.
`VALIGN="..."`	The vertical alignment of the contents of the cell. Possible values are TOP, MIDDLE, BOTTOM, and BASELINE (NHTML).
`ROWSPAN="..."`	The number of rows this cell will span.
`COLSPAN="..."`	The number of columns this cell will span.
`NOWRAP`	Do not automatically wrap the contents of this cell.
`WIDTH="..."`	(NHTML) The width of this column of cells, in exact pixel values or as a percentage of the table width.
`BGCOLOR="..."`	(NHTML) The background color of the heading cell (Navigator 3.0 only).

Can Include: `<H1> <H2> <H3> <H4> <H5> <H6> <P> <OL> <UL> <DIR> <MENU> <DL> <PRE> <BLOCKQUOTE> <FORM> <ISINDEX> <HR> <ADDRESS> <TABLE>`

Allowed Inside: `<TR>`

`<TD>...</TD>`

Defines a table data cell.

Attributes:

`ALIGN="..."`	The horizontal alignment of the contents of the cell. Possible values are LEFT, RIGHT, and CENTER.
`VALIGN="..."`	The vertical alignment of the contents of the cell. Possible values are TOP, MIDDLE, BOTTOM, and BASELINE (NHTML).
`ROWSPAN="..."`	The number of rows this cell will span.
`COLSPAN="..."`	The number of columns this cell will span.
`NOWRAP`	Do not automatically wrap the contents of this cell.
`WIDTH="..."`	(NHTML) The width of this column of cells, in exact pixel values or as a percentage of the table width.
`BGCOLOR="..."`	(NHTML) The background color of the cell (Navigator 3.0 only).

Can Include: <H1> <H2> <H3> <H4> <H5> <H6> <P> <OL> <UL> <DIR> <MENU> <DL> <PRE> <BLOCKQUOTE> <FORM> <ISINDEX> <HR> <ADDRESS>

Allowed Inside: <TR>

Frame Tags

The following tags are used to create frame-based documents. To learn more about applying these tags, see Chapter 11, "Making Frames."

<FRAMESET>...</FRAMESET> (NHTML)

Encloses a frameset definition in an HTML document.

Attributes:

COLS="..."	(NHTML) Defines the number of frame columns and their width in a frameset.
ROWS="..."	(NHTML) Defines the number of frame rows and their height in a frameset.

Can Include: <FRAME> <NOFRAMES>

Allowed Inside: <HTML>

<FRAME> (NHTML)

Used to define the contents of a frame within a frameset.

Attributes:

SRC="..."	The URL of the document to be displayed inside the frame.
MARGINWIDTH="..."	The size in pixels of the margin on each side of a frame.
MARGINHEIGHT="..."	The size in pixels of the margin above and below the contents of a frame.
SCROLLING="..."	Enable or disable the display of scroll bars for a frame. Values are YES, NO, and AUTO.
NORESIZE	Don't allow the user to resize frames.

Allowed Inside: <FRAMESET>

<NOFRAMES>...</NOFRAMES> (NHTML)

Used to define a block of text that will be displayed by Web browsers that don't support frames.

Allowed Inside: <FRAMESET>

Can Include: <A> <IMG> <ADDRESS> <BIG> <B> <BLINK> <I> <SMALL> <SUB> <SUP> <TT> <CITE> <CODE> <DFN> <EM> <KBD> <SAMP> <STRONG> <VAR> <DD> <DT> <H1> <H2> <H3> <H4> <H5> <H6> <LI> <P> <PRE> <TABLE>

Programming Tags

The following tags are used to embed program code in a document. To learn more about applying these tags, see Chapter 13, "Using JavaScript."

<SCRIPT>...</SCRIPT>

Encloses a JavaScript or LiveScript program definition and related functions.

Attributes:

LANGUAGE="..."	Either JavaScript or LiveScript.
SRC="..."	The URL of a JavaScript program stored in a separate file.

Allowed Inside: <HEAD> <BODY>

<APPLET>...</APPLET> (NHTML)

Used to incorporate a Java applet into a Web page.

Attributes:

CODE="..."	The name of the Java class to be included.
CODEBASE="..."	The URL of the directory where the Java class is stored if it is not located in the same directory as the HTML document.
WIDTH="..."	The width in pixels of the area taken up by the applet.
HEIGHT="..."	The height in pixels of the area taken up by the applet.

Can Include: <PARAM>

Allowed Inside: <BODY>

<PARAM> (NHTML)

Used to define values (or parameter) to be passed to the Java applet.

Attributes:

NAME="..."	The name of the parameter to be passed to the Java class.
VALUE="..."	The value of the parameter.

Allowed Inside: <APPLET>

<EMBED> (NHTML)

Use to embed files supported by plug-ins. Netscape calls such files *live objects*.

Attributes:

SRC="..."	A URL that describes the location and file name to be handled by a plug-in. The file extension specified in this attribute determines which plug-in module is loaded.
WIDTH="..."	The width in pixels of the area taken up by the live object.
HEIGHT="..."	The height in pixels of the area taken up by the live object.
Plug-in specific	Each individual plug-in defines its own list of attributes. Refer to the appropriate documentation for additional information.

Allowed Inside: <BODY> <TABLE>

<NOEMBED>...</NOEMBED> (NHTML)

Used to define a block of text that will be displayed by Web browsers that don't support plug-ins.

Allowed Inside: <BODY>

Can Include: <A> <IMG> <ADDRESS> <BIG> <B> <BLINK> <I> <SMALL> <SUB> <SUP> <TT> <CITE> <CODE> <DFN> <EM> <KBD> <SAMP> <STRONG> <VAR> <DD> <DT> <H1> <H2> <H3> <H4> <H5> <H6> <LI> <P> <PRE> <TABLE>

Colors by Name and HEX Value

Table B.1 contains a list of all the color names recognized by Navigator 2.0/3.0 and also includes their corresponding HEX Triplet values. These values are entered into the HTML code of a document automatically when you choose custom text colors (see Chapter 4, "Composing, Editing and Formatting Text"), background colors (see Chapter 6, "Working with Graphics," or table cell colors (see Chapter 10, "Building Tables"). Chapter 10 also shows how to code the HTML for table cell background colors manually; if you do so, you'll need one of these hex values to specify the color.

To see all these colors correctly, you will need to have a 256-color or better video card and the appropriate video drivers installed. Also, depending on the operating system and computer platform you are running, some colors may not appear exactly as you expect them to.

Table B.1 Color values and HEX triplet equivalents.

Color Name	HEX Triplet
ALICEBLUE	#A0CE00
ANTIQUEWHITE	#FAEBD7
AQUA	#00FFFF
AQUAMARINE	#7FFFD4
AZURE	#F0FFFF
BEIGE	#F5F5DC
BISQUE	#FFE4C4
BLACK	#000000
BLANCHEDALMOND	#FFEBCD
BLUE	#0000FF
BLUEVIOLET	#8A2BE2
BROWN	#A52A2A
BURLYWOOD	#DEB887
CADETBLUE	#5F9EA0
CHARTREUSE	#7FFF00
CHOCOLATE	#D2691E
CORAL	#FF7F50
CORNFLOWERBLUE	#6495ED
CORNSILK	#FFF8DC
CRIMSON	#DC143C

Color Name	HEX Triplet
CYAN	#00FFFF
DARKBLUE	#00008B
DARKCYAN	#008B8B
DARKGOLDENROD	#B8860B
DARKGRAY	#A9A9A9
DARKGREEN	#006400
DARKKHAKI	#BDB76B
DARKMAGENTA	#8B008B
DARKOLIVEGREEN	#556B2F
DARKORANGE	#FF8C00
DARKORCHID	#9932CC
DARKRED	#8B0000
DARKSALMON	#E9967A
DARKSEAGREEN	#8FBC8F
DARKSLATEBLUE	#483D8B
DARKSLATEGRAY	#2F4F4F
DARKTURQUOISE	#00CED1
DARKVIOLET	#9400D3
DEEPPINK	#FF1493
DEEPSKYBLUE	#00BFFF
DIMGRAY	#696969
DODGERBLUE	#1E90FF
FIREBRICK	#B22222
FLORALWHITE	#FFFAF0
FORESTGREEN	#228B22
FUCHSIA	#FF00FF
GAINSBORO	#DCDCDC
GHOSTWHITE	#F8F8FF
GOLD	#FFD700
GOLDENROD	#DAA520
GRAY	#808080

continued

Table B.1 continued

Color Name	HEX Triplet
GREEN	#008000
GREENYELLOW	#ADFF2F
HONEYDEW	#F0FFF0
HOTPINK	#FF69B4
INDIANRED	#CD5C5C
INDIGO	#4B0082
IVORY	#FFFFF0
KHAKI	#F0E68C
LAVENDER	#E6E6FA
LAVENDERBLUSH	#FFF0F5
LEMONCHIFFON	#FFFACD
LIGHTBLUE	#ADD8E6
LIGHTCORAL	#F08080
LIGHTCYAN	#E0FFFF
LIGHTGOLDENRODYELLOW	#FAFAD2
LIGHTGREEN	#90EE90
LIGHTGREY	#D3D3D3
LIGHTPINK	#FFB6C1
LIGHTSALMON	#FFA07A
LIGHTSEAGREEN	#20B2AA
LIGHTSKYBLUE	#87CEFA
LIGHTSLATEGRAY	#778899
LIGHTSTEELBLUE	#B0C4DE
LIGHTYELLOW	#FFFFE0
LIME	#00FF00
LIMEGREEN	#32CD32
LINEN	#FAF0E6
MAGENTA	#FF00FF
MAROON	#800000
MEDIUMAQUAMARINE	#66CDAA
MEDIUMBLUE	#0000CD

Color Name	HEX Triplet
MEDIUMORCHID	#BA55D3
MEDIUMPURPLE	#9370DB
MEDIUMSEAGREEN	#3CB371
MEDIUMSLATEBLUE	#7B68EE
MEDIUMSPRINGGREEN	#00FA9A
MEDIUMTURQUOISE	#48D1CC
MEDIUMVIOLETRED	#C71585
MIDNIGHTBLUE	#191970
MINTCREAM	#F5FFFA
MISTYROSE	#FFE4E1
NAVAJOWHITE	#FFDEAD
NAVY	#000080
OLDLACE	#FDF5E6
OLIVE	#808000
OLIVEDRAB	#6B8E23
ORANGE	#FFA500
ORANGERED	#FF4500
ORCHID	#DA70D6
PALEGOLDENROD	#EEE8AA
PALEGREEN	#98FB98
PALETURQUOISE	#AFEEEE
PALEVIOLETRED	#DB7093
PAPAYAWHIP	#FFEFD5
PEACHPUFF	#FFDAB9
PERU	#CD853F
PINK	#FFC0CB
PLUM	#DDA0DD
POWDERBLUE	#B0E0E6
PURPLE	#800080
RED	#FF0000
ROSYBROWN	#BC8F8F

continued

Table B.1 continued

Color Name	HEX Triplet
ROYALBLUE	#4169E1
SADDLEBROWN	#8B4513
SALMON	#FA8072
SANDYBROWN	#F4A460
SEAGREEN	#2E8B57
SEASHELL	#FFF5EE
SIENNA	#A0522D
SILVER	#C0C0C0
SKYBLUE	#87CEEB
SLATEBLUE	#6A5ACD
SLATEGRAY	#708090
SNOW	#FFFAFA
SPRINGGREEN	#00FF7F
STEELBLUE	#4682B4
TAN	#D2B48C
TEAL	#008080
THISTLE	#D8BFD8
TOMATO	#FF6347
TURQUOISE	#40E0D0
VIOLET	#EE82EE
WHEAT	#F5DEB3
WHITE	#FFFFFF
WHITESMOKE	#F5F5F5
YELLOW	#FFFF00
YELLOWGREEN	#9ACD32

C
What's on the CD?

This appendix briefly describes the valuable shareware, freeware, and demo programs and files included on the CD-ROM bundled with this book. In addition to all of the files and programs described, you'll also find on the CD-ROM the complete text of this book, in HTML format (you can view it with any Web browser).

To help you explore and install the CD-ROM, a directory to the CD-ROM is included, also in an HTML file. For more information, install the CD-ROM as described in its accompanying instructions, then open the directory in the Gold Browser.

While viewing the HTML directory to the CD-ROM, you can selectively learn how to install any programs that interest you.

ACDSee

ACDSee is a fast, easy-to-use image viewer for JPEG, GIF, BMP, PCX, and TGA files. You can use ACDSee as a viewer with Netscape, or to view and test images when adding them to your Web page. ACDSee features full-color image previews, panning, slide shows, drag-and-drop support, and more.

For more about viewing images, see Chapter 6, "Working with Graphics."

Adobe Acrobat Reader

This viewer enables you to view documents distributed on the Web in Adobe Acrobat (.PDF) format.

FrameGang

FrameGang is an easy-to-use program for generating HTML frame definition documents, the documents that break a Web page into multiple independent windows, each with its own URL. Using graphical tools, such as the ability to drag frame borders, you can easily customize frame documents while FrameGang automatically adjusts the HTML code for you.

For more about frames, see Chapter 11, "Making Frames."

GIF Graphics

The CD contains a collection of GIF images for spicing up your Web page. Included are background textures, horizontal bars, bullets, and icons. To learn more about using such images in your Web pages, see Chapter 6, "Working with Graphics."

GoldWave

GoldWave is a utility for recording, playing, and converting sound files. You can use GoldWave to create or convert sound files to be linked to your page as external media, or you can test your sound files by using GoldWave as a helper application.

For more about external media, see Chapter 7, "Embedding Multimedia."

Graphics Workshop

Graphics Workshop is a general-purpose utility for displaying, editing, and converting image files. You may use Graphics Workshop to prepare files for inclusion in your Web page.

For more about image files, see Chapter 6, "Working with Graphics."

HotDog

HotDog is an advanced HTML source editor. It enables you to compose and edit Web pages, and to conveniently preview them in your own browser (such as Navigator Gold). It also includes easy-to-use dialogs that let you code advanced page elements, such as tables or forms, through a simple Windows dialog.

For more about HTML source editing, see Chapter 9, "Editing HTML Source Code."

HTML Assistant

HTML Assistant is a full-featured, freeware HTML editor for composing pages to be published on the World Wide Web. It features a rich assortment of toolbar functions to simplify the application of HTML tags to create Web documents that include text formatting, graphics, links, and more.

For more about HTML source editing, see Chapter 9, "Editing HTML Source Code."

JPEG Backgrounds

The CD contains a collection of JPEG images for use as backgrounds.

To learn more about JPEG images and about using tiled images as backgrounds in your Web pages, see Chapter 6, "Working with Graphics."

MapEdit

MapEdit automatically generates the code for image maps when you select an image file and then identify regions with your mouse. MapEdit can phrase its code for two popular Web server types, or for client-based image maps.

To learn more about imagemaps, see Chapter 12, "Creating Interactive Forms and Image Maps."

Microsoft Internet Assistants for Word, Excel, and PowerPoint

Microsoft Internet Assistants are add-ins to Microsoft's Office application suite: Word 95, Excel 95, and PowerPoint 95. Each Internet Assistant transforms its application into a complete Web composition and HTML source editing tool. The add-ins enable you to easily convert Word, Excel, or PowerPoint documents into HTML documents for display on the Web, and to edit the HTML tags directly.

For more about Internet Assistants and HTML source editing, see Chapter 9, "Editing HTML Source Code."

MPEGplay 32, an MPEG Movie Player

MPEGplay 32 is a fast, easy-to-use Windows 95 MPEG movie player that you can use as a helper application in Netscape, or to test your own MPEG files before featuring them in your Web document.

For more about working with movies, see Chapter 7, "Embedding Multimedia."

PaintShop Pro

PaintShop Pro is a sophisticated image drawing, painting, editing, and conversion tool. You can use it to create new images for inclusion in your Web document, or to convert, edit, or prepare images you've acquired from other sources.

For more about image files, see Chapter 6, "Working with Graphics."

VidVUE

VidVUE is a versatile multimedia player, capable of playing many different animation, video, and audio file formats and displaying image files. You may use it to test and organize multimedia files for your Web documents.

For more about external media, see Chapter 7, "Embedding Multimedia."

For more about image files, see Chapter 6, "Working with Graphics."

Web Hotspots

Web Hotspots is an application for Windows 3.1 and Windows 95 used to create, edit, and test image maps used in World Wide Web sites. Web Hotspots provides a simple CAD interface in which the shapes, links, and other characteristics of an image map can be visually defined.

To learn more about image maps, see Chapter 12, "Creating Interactive Forms and Image Maps."

WinZip

WinZip is a Windows compression/decompression utility that allows you to conveniently decompress ZIP files and other compressed formats commonly downloaded from the Internet. When you install WinZip in a Windows 95 environment, it automatically updates the File Types registry so that when you open any ZIP file, WinZip opens automatically to decompress the file and extract any separate files within the ZIP archive.

GLOSSARY

applet A small program or application, particularly one written in Java.

browse To wander around a portion of the Internet, screen by screen, looking for items of interest. Also known as *surfing,* or *cruising.*

browser An Internet **client** that helps users browse.

CGI Common gateway interface, a facility for using **scripts** in Web pages.

client A software tool for using a particular type of Internet resource. A client interacts with a **server**, on which the resource is located. Browsers are clients.

close tag An HTML **tag** required at the end of a block of code beginning with certain tags. Close tags begin with </.

compression The process of making a computer file smaller so that it can be copied more quickly between computers. Compressed files, sometimes called *ZIP files*, must be decompressed on the receiving computer before they can be used.

cyberspace A broad expression used to describe the activity, communication, and culture happening on the Internet and other computer networks.

dial-up IP account An Internet account, accessed through a modem and telephone line, that offers complete access to the Internet through **TCP/IP** communications. It differs from a shell account in that a shell account does not employ TCP/IP on the user's PC, and might not offer complete Internet access or offer the user the

ability to use the client software of his or her choosing. Dial-up IP accounts come in two types: **PPP** and **SLIP**.

dial-up IP connection A method that allows a computer lacking a **direct connection** to access the Internet through another computer that *is* directly connected to the Internet. Even though the connection is established with a modem, the dial-up user runs TCP/IP for a true Internet connection.

direct connection A permanent, 24-hour link between a computer and the Internet. A computer with a direct connection can use the Internet at any time.

DNS Domain Name System, a method of translating IP addresses into word-based addresses that are easier to remember and work with.

domain The address of a computer on the Internet. A user's Internet address is made up of a username and a domain name.

e-mail Short for electronic mail, a system that enables a person to compose a message on a computer and transmit that message through a computer network, such as the Internet, to another computer user.

e-mail address The word-based Internet address of a user, typically made up of a username, an @ sign, and a domain name (*user@domain*). E-mail addresses are translated from the numeric IP addresses by the domain name system (**DNS**).

Explorer See **Internet Explorer**.

extension See **Netscape extension**.

FAQ file   Short for Frequently Asked Questions file, a computer file containing the answers to frequently asked questions about a particular Internet resource.

flame   Hostile messages, often sent through **e-mail** or posted in **newsgroups**, from Internet users in reaction to breaches of **netiquette**.

form   A part of a Web page in which users can type entries or make selections that are passed on for processing by a **script**.

frame definition document   An HTML document whose purpose is to define the **frames** in a frame-based document, and to identify the content files to go in each frame.

frames   Discrete sections of a Web page that have been divided into frames by a **frame definition document**.

freeware   Software available to anyone, free of charge; unlike **shareware**, which requires payment.

FTP   Short for File Transfer Protocol, the basic method for copying a file from one computer to another through the Internet.

GIF   A form of image file, using the file extension .GIF, commonly used for inline images in Web pages.

Gopher   A system of **menus** layered on top of existing resources that makes locating information and using services easier.

Gopherspace   A metaphor for all the directories and other items accessible through Gopher menus. Taken together, these resources can be imagined as an online environment, or *space*, accessible through Gopher menus.

HTML   Hypertext Markup Language, the document formatting language used to create pages on the **World Wide Web**.

HTTP   Hypertext Transfer Protocol, the standard protocol used for communications between servers and clients on the **World Wide Web**.

hypermedia and **hypertext**   Methods for allowing users to jump spontaneously among onscreen documents and other **resources** by selecting highlighted keywords that appear on each screen. Hypermedia and hypertext appear most often on the **World Wide Web**.

image map   A block of code that assigns different URLs to different areas of an **inline image**.

inline image   An image that appears within the layout of a Web page.

Internet   A large, loosely organized **internetwork** connecting universities, research institutions, governments, businesses, and other organizations so that they can exchange messages and share information.

Internet Explorer   A **browser** for the **World Wide Web**, created by Microsoft and available in the Microsoft Plus! add-in package and on the **Microsoft Network**. Can be confused with Explorer, which is the basic file/folder management system in Windows 95.

internetwork   A set of **networks** and individual computers connected so that they can communicate and share information. The Internet is a very large internetwork.

IP address   The number-based Internet address of a user or computer, made up of four sets of numbers separated by periods; for example, `192.480.77.69`. In practice, Internet users more often encounter word-based addresses (`nsnell@carroll.com`), which are translated from the numerical IP addresses by the domain name system (**DNS**).

IRC   Short for Internet Relay Chat, an Internet tool that allows two or more Internet users to participate in a live conversation through typing messages.

JavaScript A programming language for creating **scripts** that add functions to Web pages.

menu A list of choices on a computer screen. A user selects one choice to perform an action with a software program. Menus figure prominently in Windows and in the Internet resource **Gopher**.

Microsoft Network (MSN) A new online information service whose access software is built into Windows 95. MSN can provide access to some Internet resources.

MIME Multipurpose Internet Mail Extensions, a standard that allows graphics and multimedia information to be included in Internet documents such as e-mail messages.

Mosaic A **browser** for the **World Wide Web**.

multimedia A description for systems capable of displaying or playing text, pictures, sound, video, and animation.

multitasking and **multithreading** Two advanced techniques supplied by Windows 95 and 32-bit applications that allow multiple applications to run together more quickly, smoothly, and reliably.

netiquette The code of proper conduct (etiquette) on the **Internet** (the Net).

Netscape Short for Netscape Communications, a software company that developed and markets a popular Word Wide Web **browser** called Navigator. Some people casually refer to Navigator as Netscape.

Netscape extension Nonstandard enhancements to **HTML** that can add features to Web pages. The features can be viewed only through browsers that support the extensions.

network A set of computers interconnected so that they can communicate and share information. Connected networks together form an **internetwork**.

newsgroup An Internet resource through which people post and read messages related to a specific topic.

password A secret code, known only to the user, that allows the user to access a computer that is protected by a security system.

PPP Point-to-Point Protocol, a communications protocol that enables a **dial-up IP connection**.

provider A general reference to an Internet access provider, a company that has its own, dedicated access to the Internet and can therefore sell **dial-up IP account**s to Internet users.

script An external program opened by a link in a Web page to perform some special function.

scripting The activity of writing a **script**.

search engine A program that provides a way to search for specific information.

server A networked computer that *serves* a particular type of information to users or performs a particular function. Users run **client** software to access servers controlling certain types of resources (e-mail, newsgroups, and so on). **Dial-up IP accounts** are provided through Internet servers with **direct connections** to the Internet.

shareware Software programs that users are permitted to acquire and evaluate for free. Shareware is different from **freeware** in that, if a person likes the shareware program and plans to use it on a regular basis, he or she is expected to send a fee to the programmer.

shortcut A feature of Windows 95 that allows you to place an icon anywhere in Windows, even on the desktop, that you can click to open a file or program.

shorthand A system of letter abbreviations used to efficiently express certain ideas in e-mail messages, newsgroup postings and Internet Relay Chat sessions. Examples are IMO (in my opinion) and BTW (by the way).

sign on   The act of accessing a computer system by typing a required **username** (or user ID) and **password**. Also described by other terms, including sign in, log on (or logon), and log in (or login).

SLIP   Serial Line Internet Protocol, a communications protocol that enables a **dial-up IP connection**.

spider   A program that searches methodically through a portion of the Internet to build a database that can be searched by a **search engine**.

surfing   Another term for **browsing**.

tag   A code in **HTML**.

TCP/IP   Transmission Control Protocol/Internet Protocol, the fundamental internetworking protocol that makes the Internet work.

Telnet   A facility for accessing other computers on the Internet and for using the resources that are there.

UNIX   A computer operating system widely used by Web **servers**.

URL   Short for Universal Resource Locator, a method of standardizing the addresses of different types of Internet resources so that they can all be accessed easily from within a Web browser.

username   Used with a **password** to gain access to a computer. A dial-up IP user typically has a username and password for dialing the access provider's Internet server.

Usenet   A loose affiliation of sites that together control the majority of Internet **newsgroups**.

Wizard   Automated routines, used throughout Windows 95, for conveniently performing a step-by-step procedure, such as setting up Windows 95 or configuring it for the Internet.

World Wide Web (WWW or Web)   A set of Internet computers and services that provides an easy-to-use system for finding information and moving among resources. WWW services feature **hypertext**, **hypermedia**, and **multimedia** information, which can be explored through **browsers** such as **Mosaic**.

worm   A program that searches methodically through a portion of the Internet to build a database that can be searched by a **search engine**.

INDEX

Symbols

" (double quote mark), filenames in frames, 205
– (minus sign), JavaScript subtraction operator, 242
– – (double minus sign), JavaScript decrement operator, 242
!= (JavaScript not equal comparison operator), 244
% (percent), JavaScript operator, 242
  (non-breaking space), 189
* (asterisk), JavaScript multiplication operator, 242
* (asterisks), frame rows, 199
+ (plus sign), JavaScript addition operator, 242
++ (double plus sign), JavaScript increment operator, 242
.. (double period) in pathnames, 94
/ (slash), JavaScript division operator, 242
< (less than), JavaScript comparison operator, 244
<= (less than or equal to), JavaScript comparison operator, 244
<> (carats)
    HTML tags, 162
    template descriptions, 53
= (equal sign)
    in attributes, 199
    JavaScript variables, 241
== (double equal sign), JavaScript comparison operator, 244
> (greater than), JavaScript comparison operator, 244
>= (greater than or equal to), JavaScript comparison operator, 244

A

<A> tag, 92, 328
absolute pathnames, 95
ACDSee, 349
<ADDRESS> tag, 334
Address paragraph property, 65
Adobe Acrobat, 139
Adobe Acrobat Reader, 350
Adobe PostScript, 139
advertising Web pages, 289
aligning
    inline images, 120-121
    tables, 185
    text, 77-78, 333
        HTML tables, 187-188
ALIWEB, A Great Web Index (Web page), 305
anonymous FTP server, linking to, 96
<APPLET> tag, 342
applets, 353
An Archive of CGI Programs at NCSA (Web page), 309
<AREA> tag, 336
ASCII text, 139
assigning
    functions to events (JavaScript), 240-241
    properties, 70-72
assignment operators (JavaScript), 243
asterisk (*)
    frame rows, 199
    JavaScript multiplication operator, 242
attributes, 72-73
    SRC, 234
    SUBMIT, 214
    TARGET, 205
AU files, 138
audio, 138-139
    GoldWave utility, 350
    resources, 307-308
AutoDial, disabling, 42
AVI files, 137

B

<B> tag, 165, 331
backgrounds
    inline images, 127-130
    Page Wizard, 28
BaitCo, Inc. Home Page, 151-153
<BASE> tag, 325
<BASE TARGET> tag, 205
<BASEFONT> tag, 334
A Better List of Converters (Web page), 310
<BIG> tag, 331
billboards, 14
<BLINK> tag, 331
Blinking style, 80
Block Quote style, 73
<BLOCKQUOTE> tag, 333
.BMP files, 114
    converting for multimedia use, 137
<BODY> tag, 164, 324
Bookmarks folder, copying links, 99
Bookmarks menu commands, Go to Bookmarks, 100
borders
    inline images, 123
    tables, 181-182

 tag, 333
Browser
    editing pages, 40-41
    Editor
        Document Properties dialog, 45-48
        Edit button, 42
        General Editor Preferences, 48-49
        opening, 42
        HTML files, opening, 43-44
        saving pages, 44-45
        templates, 52-56
        toolbars, 49-51
    HTML source code, viewing, 165
    Location box, 99
    Page Wizard, starting, 20-22
    previewing pages, 44, 82-83

Teach Yourself JavaScript in a Week

— Arman Danesh

Teach Yourself JavaScript in a Week is the easiest way to learn how to create interactive
Web pages with JavaScript, Netscape's Java-like scripting language. It is intended for nonprogrammers, and will be equally of value to users on the Macintosh, Windows, and Unix
platforms. Teaches how to design and create attention-grabbing Web pages with
JavaScript, and shows how to add interactivity to Web pages.

$39.99 USA/$56.95 CAN   *User Level: Intermediate-Advanced*
ISBN: 1-57521-073-8   *450 pages*

Web Publishing Unleashed

— Stanek, et al.

Includes sections on how to organize and plan your information, design pages, and
become familar with hypertext and hypermedia. Choose from a range of applications and
technologies, including Java, SGML, VRML, and the newest HTML and Netscape
extensions. The CD-ROM contains software, templates, and examples to help you
become a successful Web publisher.

Price: $45.00 USA/$63.95 CAN   User Level: Casual-Expert
ISBN: 1-57521-051-7   1,000 pages

Creating Web Applets with Java

David Gulbransen and Kendrick Rawlings

Creating Web Applets with Java is the easiest way to learn how to integrate existing Java
applets into your Web pages. This book is designed for the non-programmer who wants
to use or customize preprogrammed Java applets with a minimal amount of trouble. It
teaches the easiest way to incorporate the power of Java in a Web page, and covers the
basics of Java applet programming. Find out how to use and customize preprogammed
Java applets. Includes a CD-ROM full of useful applets.

$39.99 USA/$56.95 CAN   *User Level: Casual-Accomplished*
ISBN: 1-57521-070-3   *350 pages*

Java Unleashed

Various

Java Unleashed is the ultimate guide to the year's hottest new Internet technologies, the
Java language and the HotJava browser from Sun Microsystems. *Java Unleashed* is a
complete programmer's reference and a guide to the hundreds of exciting ways Java is
being used to add interactivity to the World Wide Web. It describes how to use Java to
add interactivity to Web presentations, and shows how Java and HotJava are being used
across the Internet. Includes a helpful and informative CD-ROM.

$49.99 USA/$70.95 CAN   *User Level: Casual-Expert*
ISBN: 1-57521-049-5   *1,000 pages*

Teach Yourself Netscape Web Publishing in a Week

— *Wes Tatters*

Teach Yourself Netscape Web Publishing in a Week is the easiest way to learn how to produce attention-getting, well-designed Web pages using the features provided by Netscape Navigator. Intended for both the novice and the expert, this book provides a solid grounding in HTML and Web publishing principles, while providing special focus on the possibilities presented by the Netscape environment. Learn to design and create attention-grabbing Web pages for the Netscape environment while exploring new Netscape development features such as frames, plug-ins, Java applets, and JavaScript!

Price: $39.99 USA/ $56.95 CAN   User Level: Beginner-Inter
ISBN: 1-57521-068-1   450 pages

Teach Yourself CGI Programming with Perl in a Week

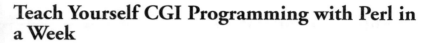

— *Eric Herrmann*

This book is a step-by-step tutorial of how to create, use, and maintain Common Gateway Interfaces (CGI). It describes effective ways of using CGI as an integral part of Web development, and adds interactivity and flexibility to the information that can be provided through your Web site. Includes Perl 4.0 and 5.0, CGI libraries, and other applications to create databases, dynamic interactivity, and other enticing page effects.

Price: $39.99 USA/$56.99 CAN   User Level: Inter-Advanced
ISBN: 1-57521-009-6   500 pages

Teach Yourself Java in 21 Days

— *Laura Lemay and Charles Perkins*

The complete tutorial guide to the most exciting technology to hit the Internet in years—Java! A detailed guide to developing applications with the hot new Java language from Sun Microsystems, *Teach Yourself Java in 21 Days* shows readers how to program using Java and develop applications (applets) using the Java language. With coverage of Java implementation in Netscape Navigator and Hot Java, along with the Java Development Kit, including the compiler and debugger for Java, *Teach Yourself Java* is a must-have!

Price: $39.99 USA/$56.99 CAN   User Level: Inter-Advanced
ISBN: 1-57521-030-4   600 pages

Presenting Java

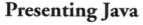

— *John December*

Presenting Java gives you a first look at how Java is transforming static Web pages into living, interactive applications. Java opens up a world of possibilities previously unavailable on the Web. You'll find out how Java is being used to create animations, computer simulations, interactive games, teaching tools, spreadsheets, and a variety of other applications. Whether you're a new user, project planner, or developer, *Presenting Java* provides an efficient, quick introduction to the basic concepts and technical details that make Java the hottest new Web technology of the year!

Price: $25.00 USA/$35.95 CAN   User Level: All Levels
ISBN: 1-57521-039-8   207 pages

Netscape 2 Unleashed

— Dick Oliver, et al.

This book provides a complete, detailed, and fully fleshed-out overview of Netscape products. Through case studies and examples of how individuals, businesses, and institutions are using the Netscape products for Web development, *Netscape Unleashed* gives a full description of the evolution of Netscape from its inception to today and its cutting-edge developments with Netscape Gold, LiveWire, Netscape Navigator 2.0, Java and JavaScript, Macromedia, VRML, plug-ins, Adobe Acrobat, HTML 3.0 and beyond, security, and Intranet systems.

Price: $49.99 USA/$70.95 CAN   User Level: All Levels
ISBN: 1-57521-007-X   Pages: 800 pages

The Internet Unleashed 1996

— Barron, Ellsworth, Savetz, et al.

The Internet Unleashed 1996 is the complete reference to get new users up and running on the Internet while providing the consummate reference manual for the experienced user. *The Internet Unleashed 1996* provides the reader with an encyclopedia of information on how to take advantage of all the Net has to offer for business, education, research, and government. The companion CD-ROM contains over 100 tools and applications. The only book that includes the experience of over 40 of the world's top Internet experts, this new edition is updated with expanded coverage of Web publishing, Internet business, Internet multimedia and virtual reality, Internet security, Java, and more!

Price: $49.99 USA/$70.95 CAN   User Level: All Levels
ISBN: 1-57521-041-X   1,456 pages

The World Wide Web Unleashed 1996

— December and Randall

The World Wide Web Unleashed 1996 is designed to be the only book a reader will need to experience the wonders and resources of the Web. The companion CD-ROM contains over 100 tools and applications to make the most of your time on the Internet. This book shows readers how to explore the Web's amazing world of electronic art museums, online magazines, virtual malls, and video music libraries, while giving readers complete coverage of Web page design, creation, and maintenance, plus coverage of new Web technologies such as Java, VRML, CGI, and multimedia!

Price: $49.99 USA/$70.95 CAN   User Level: All Levels
ISBN: 1-57521-040-1   1,440 pages

Teach Yourself Web Publishing with HTML in 14 Days, Premier Edition

— Laura Lemay

This book teaches everything about publishing on the Web. In addition to its exhaustive coverage of HTML, it also gives readers hands-on practice with more complicated subjects such as CGI, tables, forms, multimedia programming, testing, maintenance, and much more. CD-ROM is Mac- and PC-compatible and includes a variety of applications that help readers create Web pages using graphics and templates.

Price: $39.99 USA/$56.95 CAN   User Level: All Levels
ISBN: 1-57521-014-2   804 pages

Teach Yourself Web Publishing with HTML 3.0 in a Week, Second Edition

— Laura Lemay

Ideal for those people who are interested in the Internet and the World Wide Web—the Internet's hottest topic! This updated and revised edition teaches readers how to use HTML (Hypertext Markup Language) version 3.0 to create Web pages that can be viewed by nearly 30 million users. This book explores the process of creating and maintaining Web presentations, including setting up tools and converters for verifying and testing pages. The new edition highlights the new features of HTML, such as tables and Netscape and Microsoft Explorer extensions and provides the latest information on working with images, sound files, and video, and teaches advanced HTML techniques and tricks in a clear, step-by-step manner with many practical examples of HTML pages.

Price: $29.99 USA/$42.95 CAN   User Level: Beginner-Inter
ISBN: 1-57521-064-9   518 pages

Web Page Construction Kit (Software)

Create your own exciting World Wide Web pages with the software and expert guidance in this kit! This kit includes HTML Assistant Pro Lite, the acclaimed point-and-click Web page editor. Simply highlight text in HTML Assistant Pro Lite and click the appropriate button to add headlines, graphics, special formatting, links, and so on. No programming skills are needed! Using your favorite Web browser, you can test your work quickly and easily without leaving the editor. A unique catalog feature allows you to keep track of interesting Web sites and easily add their HTML links to your pages. Assistant's user-defined toolkit also allows you to add new HTML formatting styles as they are defined. Includes the #1 best-selling Internet book, *Teach Yourself Web Publishing with HTML 3.0 in a Week, Second Edition,* and a library of professionally designed Web page templates, graphics, buttons, bullets, lines, and icons to rev up your new pages!

PC Computing magazine says, "If you're looking for the easiest route to Web publishing, HTML Assistant is your best choice."

Price: $39.95 US/$55.95 CAN   User Level: Beginner-Inter
ISBN: 1-57521-000-2   518 pages

HTML & CGI Unleashed

— John December and Marc Ginsburg

Targeted to professional developers who have a basic understanding of programming and need a detailed guide, this book provides a complete, detailed reference to developing Web information systems. It covers the full range of languages—HTML, CGI, Perl C, editing and conversion programs, and more—and how to create commercial-grade Web Applications. This book is perfect for the developer who will be designing, creating, and maintaining a Web presence for a company or large institution.

Price: $49.99 USA/$70.95 CAN   User Level: Inter-Advanced
ISBN: 0-672-30745-6   830 pages

Web Site Construction Kit for Windows NT

— Christopher Brown and Scott Zimmerman

Web Site Construction Kit for Windows NT has everything you need to set up, develop, and maintain a Web site with Windows NT—including the server on the CD-ROM! It teaches the ins and outs of planning, installing, configuring, and administering a Windows NT–based Web site for an organization, and it includes detailed instructions on how to use the software on the CD-ROM to develop the Web site's content—HTML pages, CGI scripts, image maps, and so forth.

Price: $49.99 USA/$70.95 CAN   User Level: All Levels
ISBN: 1-57521-047-9   430 pages

Add to Your Sams.net Library Today
with the Best Books for Internet Technologies

ISBN	Quantity	Description of Item	Unit Cost	Total Cost
1-57521-039-8		Presenting Java	$25.00	
1-57521-030-4		Teach Yourself Java in 21 Days	$39.99	
1-57521-049-5		Java Unleashed	$49.99	
1-57521-007-x		Netscape 2 Unleashed	$49.99	
0-672-30745-6		HTML and CGI Unleashed	$49.99	
1-57521-018-5		Web Site Administrator's Survival Guide	$49.99	
1-57521-009-6		Teach Yourself CGI Programming with Perl in a Week	$39.99	
0-672-30735-9		Teach Yourself the Internet in a Week, Second Edition	$25.00	
1-57521-004-5		Teach Yourself Netscape 2 Web Publishing in a Week	$35.00	
1-57521-004-5		The Internet Business Guide, Second Edition	$25.00	
0-672-30718-9		Navigating the Internet, Third Edition	$25.00	
1-57521-005-3		Teach Yourself More Web Publishing with HTML in a Week	$29.99	
1-57521-072-x		Web Site Construction Kit for Windows 95	$49.99	
1-57521-047-9		Web Site Construction Kit for Windows NT	$49.99	
		Shipping and Handling: See information below.		
		TOTAL		

Shipping and Handling: $4.00 for the first book, and $1.75 for each additional book. If you need to have it NOW, we can ship product to you in 24 hours for an additional charge of approximately $18.00, and you will receive your item overnight or in two days. Overseas shipping and handling adds $2.00. Prices subject to change. Call between 9:00 a.m. and 5:00 p.m. EST for availability and pricing information on latest editions.

201 W. 103rd Street, Indianapolis, Indiana 46290

1-800-428-5331 — Orders   1-800-835-3202 — FAX   1-800-858-7674 — Customer Service

Book ISBN 1-57521-128-9

A · V I A C O M   S E R V I C · E

The Information SuperLibrary™

Bookstore

Search

What's New

Reference

Software

Newsletter

Company Overviews

Yellow Pages

Internet Starter Kit

HTML Workshop

Win a Free T-Shirt!

Macmillan Computer Publishing

Site Map

Talk to Us

CHECK OUT THE BOOKS IN THIS LIBRARY.

You'll find thousands of shareware files and over 1600 computer books designed for both technowizards and technophobes. You can browse through 700 sample chapters, get the latest news on the Net, and find just about anything using our

We're open 24-hours a day, 365 days a year.

You don't need a card.

We don't charge fines.

And you can be as **LOUD** as you want.

CD-ROM
What's on the CD?

Installing the CD-ROM

The companion CD-ROM contains Netscape Navigator™ Gold 3 for Windows 3.1, Windows 95, Windows NT, and Macintosh, plus many of the shareware programs mentioned in the book and all of the source code and files for the examples in the book.

To install the CD-ROM, please locate the section below which corresponds to your system and follow the instructions.

Windows 95/NT 4 Installation Instructions

1. Insert the CD-ROM into your CD-ROM drive.

2. From the Windows 95 desktop, double-click on the My Computer icon.

3. Double-click on the icon representing your CD-ROM drive.

4. Double-click on the icon titled setup.exe to run the CD-ROM installation program.

Windows 3.1/NT 3.51 Installation Instructions

1. Insert the CD-ROM into your CD-ROM drive.
2. From File Manager or Program Manager, choose Run from the File menu.
3. Type `<drive>\setup` and press Enter, where `<drive>` corresponds to the drive letter of your CD-ROM. For example, if your CD-ROM is drive D:, type `D:\SETUP` and press Enter.

Follow the on-screen instructions.

Macintosh Installation Instructions

1. Insert the CD-ROM into your CD-ROM drive.
2. When an icon for the CD appears on your desktop, open the disc by double-clicking on its icon.
3. Double-click on the icon named Guide to the CD-ROM, and follow the directions which appear.

Technical Support from Macmillan

We can't help you with Windows, HTML problems, or software from third parties, but we can assist you if a problem arises with the CD-ROM itself:

E-mail Support: Send e-mail to `support@mcp.com`.

CompuServe: Type `GO SAMS` to reach the Macmillan Computer Publishing forum. Leave us a message, addressed to `SYSOP`. If you want the message to be private, address it to `*SYSOP`.

Telephone: (317) 581-3833

Fax: (317) 581-4773

Mail: Macmillan Computer Publishing
Attention: Support Department
201 West 103rd Street
Indianapolis, IN 46290-1093

Here's how to reach us on the Internet:

World Wide Web (The Macmillan Information SuperLibrary):
`http://www.mcp.com/samsnet`